A Tribute To Rebirth
In The Land Of Our Ancestors

# MIRACLE NATION

*Seventy Stories About The Spirit Of Israel*

# Israela Meyerstein

**Mazo Publishers**

# Miracle Nation: Seventy Stories About The Spirit Of Israel

Copyright © 2018 Israela Meyerstein

*Website:* www.miracle-nation.com
*Email:* israela.meyerstein@gmail.com

ISBN: 978-1-946124-46-3 – Soft Cover (Paper)
ISBN: 978-1-946124-48-7 – Hard Cover (Cloth)

*Published by*
Mazo Publishers
P.O. Box 10474
Jacksonville, FL 32247 USA
USA: 1-815-301-3559

*Website:* www.mazopublishers.com

*Follow News about Israela Meyerstein and Mazo Publishers*
Send your request by email to:
mazopublishers@gmail.com

Permission to include the text and pictures
in this book has been granted to the author and publisher.

**All rights reserved.**
No part of this publication may be translated, reproduced, stored in a retrieval system, or transmitted in any form or by any means, electronic, mechanical, photocopying, recording or otherwise, without prior permission from the publisher.

*Dedication*

*In honor of the miraculous State of Israel
on reaching the occasion of her 70th birthday.*

*In memory of the souls of my paternal grandparents, aunt, uncle,
and many other relatives I never met
who perished in the smokestacks of Treblinka.*

*To my husband, with whom I share so much in common,
including being second generation children of the Holocaust.*

*To my children and grandchildren
who are the future of the Jewish people.*

# CONTENTS

8 ~ Acknowledgments
9 ~ About the Author
10 ~ Foreword by Dr. David Breakstone
12 ~ Preface
18 ~ Introduction

*Part I*
*Beginnings: Jewish History As Prologue*

24 ~ *Chapter 1: The Chosen People; Chosen for What?*

26 ~ *Chapter 2: Those Wandering Jews: Secrets of Survival*

31 ~ *Chapter 3: Out of the Ashes of the Shoah: Finding a Safe Haven*
- Searching for Home ~ Joe Gosler
- Escape to Russia ~ Kathy Kacer
- Discovering the Remarkable Lives of Joseph and Rebecca Bau ~ Israela Meyerstein
- Poems from America in Memory of Family ~ Dr. George Gorin

51 ~ *Chapter 4: Israel's Birth: Miracles Do Happen*
- Song – It's a Miracle ~ Rita Glassman
- A Tale of Two Bar Mitzvahs ~ David Gamliel
- A Palestinian Jew: Dreamer, Soldier, Builder, and Philanthropist ~ Nick Dahan
- From the Pampas to the Negev: A Volunteer from Abroad ~ Israela Meyerstein
- From Russia to Redemption in the Land of our Forefathers ~ Zodek Mazo

71 ~ *Chapter 5: Ingathering of the Exiles: A Nation of Immigrants*
- Destination: Return to Zion ~ Shlomo Alima
- My Mother Rachel: Seeking Better Education for Women ~ Dr. Janette Lazarovits
- Butterflies for Freedom and Next Year in Jerusalem ~ Israela Meyerstein
- Song ~ Leaving Mother Russia ~ Cantor Robbie Solomon
- The Boy with Two Mothers ~ Israela Meyerstein
- Embroidered *Aliyah* Stories: the LEAP project ~ Nicole Rosenberg

*Part II*
*Tikkun Olam Values*

*97 ~ Chapter 6: The Earth is the Lord's: Protecting Our Environment*
- A Refreshing Water Story ~ Israela Meyerstein
- Tevel B'tzedek: Creating a More Just, Compassionate, and Beautiful World ~ Rabbi Micha Odenheimer
- A Still Small Voice Grows Stronger in the Arava Desert ~ Rabbi Michael Cohen
- Water Knows No Borders ~ Sophie Clarke

*113 ~ Chapter 7: Saving a Life Above All: Pikuach Nefesh*
- A Good Neighbor Policy to Save Lives ~ Major-General Yair Golan
- Saving Children's Hearts ~ Dr. Shaanan Meyerstein
- Henrietta Szold: Mother of Hadassah ~ Israela Meyerstein

*125 ~ Chapter 8: Justice: Creating a More Equitable and Compassionate Society*
- Leket Israel: From One Good Idea to Feeding Thousands ~ Israela Meyerstein
- Fighting for Equality, Personal Liberty, and a Just Society ~ Sharon Abraham-Weiss
- The Language of Social Change ~ Professor Julie Cwikel
- Women of the Wall: Seeking Social Justice, Gender Equality, and Religious Pluralism ~ Nechama Namal

*142 ~ Chapter 9: God loves all of His Creations: On Being Inclusive*
- I saw Elohim Today ~ Rabbi Judith Edelman-Green
- No Soldier Left Behind: Special in Uniform ~ Lt. Col. Tiran Attia
- Yad Sarah: Volunteering to Build a World of Caring ~ Adele Goldberg
- ALEH: An Inclusive Community Creating Better Lives for Individuals with Disabilities ~ Elie Klein

*159 ~ Chapter 10: Loving Thy Neighbor: Building Friendship and Cooperation*
- In the Galilee There are Stones ~ Rabbi Yoav Ende
- Rays of Light: Learning and Volunteering with Neighbors ~ Zimra Vigoda
- Israeli Jews and Arabs Stand United at the Junction ~ Lydia Aisenberg

*171 ~ Chapter 11: Compassion for the Poor, the Vulnerable, and the Stranger*
- Fat Meir's Kitchen ~ Ruti Glasner
- Refugee Clinic ~ Dr. Bernie Green
- IsraAID: Humanitarian Help for Strangers Everywhere ~ Yotam Polizer
- White Knight on Four Wheels ~ Lydia Aisenberg

*186 ~ Chapter 12: Light unto the Nations: Technology for the Good of Mankind*
- Here Comes the Sun: Harnessing Israeli Technology to Bring Energy, Water, and Light to the World ~ Genna Brand for Sivan Yaari
- ReWalk and UPnRIDE: Helping Severely Disabled People Stand Tall and Walk ~ Dr. Amit Goffer
- Enlightenment Begins at Home: Tech-Career ~ Naphtali Abraham and Tsofen ~ Sami Saadi

## Part III
### Healing The Spirit And Seeking Peace

*202 ~ Chapter 13: Healing the Spirit in Creative Ways*
- Livui Ruchani: Spiritual Care ~ Rabbi Judith Edelman-Green
- Haverut: Healing the Spirit through Creative Arts and Community ~ Rachel Fox-Ettun
- Horses That Heal: My Passion for Therapeutic Riding ~ Dr. Anita Shkedi
- TIKVOT: Restoring Hope and Lifting Spirits after Trauma ~ Simone Farbstein
- Fulfilling an Israeli Mikveh Dream ~ Rabbi Dr. Haviva Ner-David

*222 ~ Chapter 14: Seeking Peaceful Coexistence*
- Building an Oasis of Peace; Can a Song Heal? ~ Yuval Ron
- The Parents Circle – Families Forum ~ Rami Elhanan, Robi Damelin
- On the Road to a Richer Zionism: Israel through Fresh Eyes ~ Avi Meyerstein
- Imagining an Idea Whose Time has Come ~ Nick Dahan
- Netiv L'Shalom: Mosaic Path to Peace ~ Tsameret Zamir

*247 ~ Postscript*
- Letter from Kids4Peace: A Young Person's View
- Song for Peace ~ Rita Glassman
- Eli Eli ~ Anat Hoffman
- Prayer for Peace

*254 ~ Reflections: Ideas for group discussions and projects emanating from the stories*

259 ~ Notes
262 ~ Contributors
270 ~ Also by the Author

# ACKNOWLEDGMENTS

I am truly grateful to the many special people who shared with me their life stories, journeys, work accomplishments, dreams, and passions. Without them, there would not be seventy meaningful stories celebrating the Spirit of Israel. Their generous collaboration lifted my spirits and brought me even closer to the Israel I love.

The first suggestion to write the book actually came from my granddaughter, who asked if I would write another book sometime. When I actually began considering the project, immediate helpful encouragement came from Gail Lipsitz and colleagues in Israel – Dr. Julie Cwikel and Rabbi Judith Edelman-Green, along with helpful referrals from Jeff Daube, Ronnie Kleinfeldt, and Ran Goldstein.

Special thanks to friends and colleagues who took personal time to carefully review a very long manuscript, and then share feedback and suggestions. They include: Dr. David Breakstone, Dr. Paul Ruskin, Danny Siegel, Rabbi Paul Schneider, Rabbi Shmuel Herzfeld, Dr. Alex Sinclair, Dr. Neil Rubin, and Dr. Robert O. Freedman.

To Chaim Mazo, my publisher, whose professionalism, guidance, flexibility, and support, were always present and greatly appreciated.

Special thanks to my husband Michael, with whom I share a love of Israel and Jewish tradition. He has given me lifelong support and encouragement for my creative projects. I appreciated his editorial help and patience as I feverishly tried to complete the book in time for Israel's 70th birthday.

And to my sons and their wives who have inspired me by the Jewish humanistic values they practice in their lives, and my dear grandchildren, who give me pride and hope for the future.

And finally, I am grateful for Hashem's inspiration and the miraculous State of Israel, the little nation that could.

# ABOUT THE AUTHOR

Israela Meyerstein has been treating families, couples, and individuals for over forty years by helping them manage parenting and family relationships, couple issues, coping with separation, divorce, and remarriage, medical illness, fetal loss, as well as focus on spirituality and healthy personal coping.

Ms. Meyerstein received an MSW degree in 1973 from Columbia University School of Social Work, followed by a Third Year Fellowship in Social Work at the University of Texas Medical Branch in Galveston, Texas, where she was later appointed Faculty Associate in the Division of Community and Social Psychiatry of the Medical School.

Ms. Meyerstein directed a Family Therapy Training Program at Sheppard Pratt Hospital from 1986-1998. She has trained hundreds of professionals of varied disciplines, and has taught Family Therapy courses in college and graduate level programs. Ms. Meyerstein has authored over thirty published articles and chapters on couples and family therapy, spirituality, medical illness, remarriage, and therapist training.

Israela co-founded the Baltimore Jewish Healing Network in the 1990s. Together with Rabbi Gila Ruskin, she co-led Spiritual Study/Discussion groups for those struggling with medical illness. She wrote her first book, "Bridge to Healing: Finding Strength to Cope with Illness" (which was also translated into Hebrew: Gesher Lemarpeh: Meziat Koach Lehitmoded im Machalah), to help patients, family members, and professionals navigate the physical, emotional, and spiritual challenges of coping with medical illness and treatment.

# FOREWORD
## Dr. David Breakstone

As deputy chairman of the executive of The Jewish Agency for Israel, whose job is to ensure a deep and meaningful connection between Israel and the next generation of world Jewry, I have come to the conclusion that the most immediate threat that the international campaign to delegitimize Israel poses is its negative effect on our own young people. In casting Zionism as a racist and colonialist movement that has spawned an apartheid society, it has left even those of our children who grew up in strongly committed Jewish homes doubtful about the Zionist idea and confused in terms of their relationship to the State of Israel. That is a tragedy, and one that might have been avoided had we invested more in advancing an understanding that Zionism has always been, and continues to be an idealistic endeavor driven by humanistic values.

This is why *Miracle Nation* is so important. It articulates that narrative beautifully and compellingly, and would bring much solace to Theodor Herzl, founder of the movement. Already 120 years ago, he declared in the name of those assembled at the Zionist Congress that "those of us who are today prepared to hazard our lives for the cause would regret having raised a finger if we were able to create only a new social system and not a more righteous one."

The visionary of the Jewish state, who is too often mistakenly perceived as having concerned himself exclusively with seeking a political and territorial solution to the "Jewish question," also believed passionately in the mission of fashioning a Utopian society in the Land of Israel. Zionism for him was not only about ending the abnormality of the Jewish condition of homelessness and escaping the scourge of antisemitism, but also about giving birth to a nation characterized by social justice, equal opportunity, the fair distribution of resources, care for the stranger in our midst, and even environmentalism.

That is precisely the spirit that infuses this volume. *Miracle Nation* is a moving compendium of the multifarious faces of Israel that reflect and convey the essential vitality and morality of Israel's human temperament. By sharing them with us, Israela Meyerstein has succeeded in providing a timely and persuasive response to the growing perception that support of Israel requires the abandonment of one's liberal values.

It does this not by pretending that Israeli society is not flawed, but by highlighting the myriad efforts of deeply dedicated individuals

*Foreword*

profoundly committed to redressing what is wrong. It is impossible to read their stories of personal engagement in *Tikkun Olam* (repairing the world) without being inspired by the immense reservoir of social entrepreneurship that exists within the Zionist enterprise and which gives expression to its original intent of molding the Jewish state in the image of Biblical prophecy.

Clearly devoted to that ideal herself, Israela Meyerstein offers a new generation, less familiar with what lies beneath and beyond the headlines, a people to embrace and with whom to engage, a people whose inheritance is Herzl's legacy. Only two months before he died, he bequeathed to future generations an ethical will as compelling today as it was more than a century ago. "Even after we possess our land," he wrote, "Zionism will not cease to be an ideal, for Zionism includes not only the yearning for a plot of Promised Land legally acquired for our weary people, but also the yearning for moral and spiritual fulfillment." The stories in this book are of those who have enthusiastically taken up that mantle, illustrating just how strongly this ideal remains essential to the Zionist ethos.

The need for a safe haven for the Jewish people may have been a primary catalyst for bringing the Zionist movement into being, but that is not an answer resonant to young people who have never experienced anti-Semitism and who can barely fathom its dangers. Surely a personal lesson in the perils it continues to pose might be useful, but more important is that they gain an understanding of and become excited by the possibilities that Jewish statehood holds for applying Jewish values to the public domain so that, in keeping with God's promise given to Abraham, we might not only become a great nation in this land, but also so that through us "the peoples of the earth shall be blessed."

"All that you have cultivated will be worthless and your fields will again be barren, unless you also cultivate freedom of thought and expression, generosity of spirit, and love for humanity. These are the things you must cherish and nurture," wrote Herzl. His is the Zionism *Miracle Nation* seeks to reclaim and proudly proclaim to a new generation. As we celebrate 70 years of Israel's independence, it is a most welcome anthology of inspiration that at one and the same time says we have a tremendous amount to be proud of, but also much yet to do. It also provides the hope and the optimism that we've got the wherewithal to get it done.

*Dr. David Breakstone is the deputy chairman of the executive of The Jewish Agency and conceptual architect and founding director of the Herzl Museum and Educational Center in Jerusalem.*

# PREFACE

*Time:* September 1948

*Scene:*
An imagined evening in a small bedroom.
Mother and father gaze at their newborn infant girl.

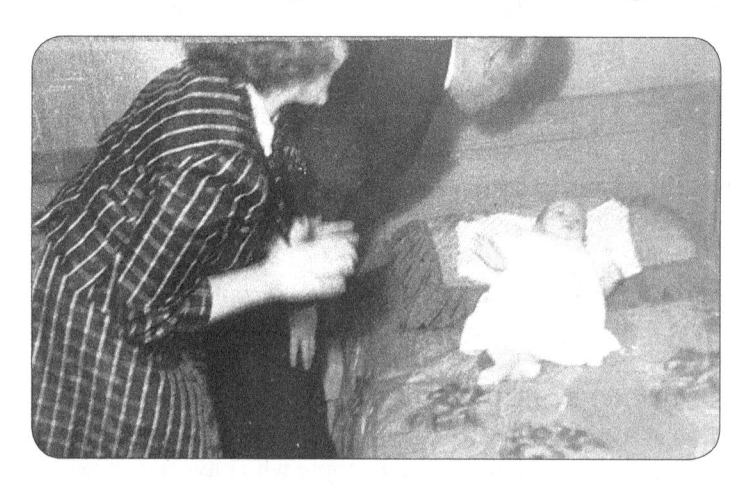

*Mother:* "I feel so grateful, watching her rest peacefully."

*Father:* "Yes, she looks so innocent. They say a fetus has all the knowledge of the world before birth, but on the way out through the birth canal, an angel pinches her above the lips and makes her forget everything. It's good that a baby is innocent ... especially about all the horrors of the world."

*Mother:* "She will give us a fresh start to rebuild our family. I am relieved that she is healthy and will pray every day for her wellbeing. When we lost our dear little Faith to illness, I thought I would never recover, but this baby gives me renewed hope."

*Father:* "Yes, even though almost two years have passed since little Faith's death, I still feel so much guilt and responsibility. I am a doctor but I couldn't save her. She was only three and a half years old. After the surgery, once the infection set in, there was no hope, and the sorrow won't go away."

*Mother:* "These past years have been so hard, especially when we

## Preface

were separated during the War while you were serving in Europe. I worried about you constantly."

*Father:* "Yes, I missed you terribly and felt so alone. After the war ended, when I learned from the Red Cross that Momma, Poppa, my younger brother, Tevl, and my beautiful sister Roska, along with other relatives, were exterminated in Treblinka, I wondered how I could recover from such devastating losses?"

*Mother:* "We must find a way to move forward ... especially for our daughter's sake, or she will always live in dark shadows. We must make a new start and leave the past behind. Let's give her a name with new meaning, to signify a new beginning."

*Father:* "There are too many dead relatives to choose from to find a name for her. She needs a name that offers hope, a name that honors our people. What about naming her after the newborn State of Israel, just a few months old? We could call her Israela."

*Mother:* "That is such an unusual, but beautiful name ... I never heard it before."

*Father:* "I suppose if she had been a boy, the name would be 'Israel,' referring to the name given to Jacob after his struggle with the angel. It is actually the name of the Jewish people, who have always struggled to survive and thrive."

*Mother:* "I hope we can provide a peaceful and happy life for our new little girl, Israela. May she always be blessed with good health and the wisdom to live up to her name."

*Mother and Father:* "Amen."

## *The Little Circling Boats*
## Israela Meyerstein

My first in-person encounter with my "namesake" Israel occurred when my father took me on a trip in 1962 to meet my Israeli family. We traveled at sea for two weeks, first on the rough Atlantic Ocean and then on the balmy Mediterranean. I woke up early the morning that my father and I were about to reach our destination of Haifa harbor. The bright sun was shining on the beautiful aquamarine water as the large ship made its way closer to shore. The undulating coastline of the land of Israel came into view, a sandy beach stretching as far as eyes could see.

My father suggested we go up on deck to witness the spectacle of reaching Haifa harbor: "There is nothing quite like arriving in Israel by boat. That's how many of the immigrants got here, often facing great difficulties on their journey."

I leaned on the deck railing to scan the scene, as the ship slowly approached the shore. Suddenly a flotilla of tiny boats came into view and began circling the big ocean liner. Each boat was filled with a few people who were waving to people on the deck above. Who were these people? "They are the early greeters," my father said, "hoping to see people who came on our ship." What an unusual way to greet visitors, I thought. That was my first reaction to Israel, this friendly little country, after whom I am named.

We waited with anticipation, watching each little boat pass our lookout point. Suddenly, my father became visibly excited. He pointed enthusiastically to a man in a distant boat below who was almost bald like my father. "Do you see that tall man in the white shirt, with dark sunglasses who is waving in our direction? That's my brother Yitzchak. I haven't seen him since 1953, when I made my first trip to the new state of Israel. In 1935, I was a medical student in Geneva, Switzerland, and I was able to obtain a student visa for Yitzchak to attend a Shomer Hatzair Soccer competition in Palestine. After the competition he returned home to Poland, and the next year he was able to bring his wife and little daughter to Palestine, where he has lived since."

My father starts shouting; "Yitzchak, Yitzchak," to catch his attention, but we were still too high above and far away to be heard. Suddenly, my father pauses, as if frozen in his tracks. He becomes quiet, his eyes filling with tears. I couldn't tell what kind ... joy? Or was it pain? Or shock? Then he explains: "Do you see the woman standing right next to Yitzchak? That must be my sister, Miriam, but her hair is all white and she looks so old. I haven't seen her since the summer of 1937, when I returned to my hometown village of Grayevo (outside Bialystok) for a family reunion. We were a close family and it was painful to say goodbye before leaving with a visa to the United States. I sensed that I would never see my elderly parents or other relatives again, as Hitler was threatening at the border."

I listened intently, trying to absorb the drama of the story as my father continued: "When Hitler invaded Poland with his Blitzkrieg in September 1939, Miriam and her husband fled by foot to Russia with their baby daughter. They lived in Siberia for several years, then made their way to Tajikistan. From the few letters that got through, I learned how difficult it was to live as Jews in communist Russia. Miriam had to smuggle in a mohel for the bris of her second child. They would hide money in bars of soap out of fear of the KGB, who routinely came to spy on them. Thankfully, in the late 1950s the Polish government allowed former Polish citizens to repatriate to Poland and from there Miriam and her family were able to get passage to Israel in 1960. She was so happy that she could finally raise her children openly as Jews."

Then my father concluded sadly, "Of course, they were the lucky ones; the rest of the family perished."

The words stung, and I felt sorry for my father's having lost so much and been separated from his remaining siblings for such a long time. I don't know if I had heard all the parts of my father's story before, but he always seemed to carry something within him that made him sad. Occasionally he would talk about the anti-Semitic dogs that chased him, encouraged by Polish neighborhood kids calling him a dirty Jew. Most of the stories about lost and murdered family members, however, remained hidden within his heart. As a child perhaps I sensed that delving into details would just cause him too much pain. Once I asked him whose pictures were on his dresser, and he told me: "mother, father, younger sister, brother." Oddly, I never realized that I didn't even know what grandparents were.

Suddenly, our deep conversation was interrupted by a meeting of eyes: Yitzchak and Miriam had located us on the deck, and everyone began waving and shouting excitedly. We still couldn't hear each other's voices, but our eyes locked. My father seemed so happy, yearning to connect and spend time with his closest surviving relatives. I knew then that this would be the start of a wonderful adventure with my newfound family and getting acquainted with my namesake, Israel.

*Preface*

## *Nikita and My Kibbutz Cousins*

On this trip we visited Uncle Yitzchak and his wife, Ruth, in their apartment in Tel Aviv. We met their daughter, Esther, her husband, and their two little children, Ori, age seven, and Rotem, age five. The family had driven all the way from their home up north in Kibbutz Menarah, which literally sat on the Lebanese border, separated by only a several-meters-wide dirt path. Esther had stayed there after Army service to help establish the kibbutz.

I learned that my little cousins lived in Children's houses with other children, like camp bunks. They went to school on the kibbutz, played on the green fields, and each day at dinner, after the parents' work, the children would go to their family's cottage for bonding time before returning to the Children's house for sleep. I learned that many a night the children had to sleep in underground bunkers for safety, due to the danger of Arab terrorists who might try to infiltrate the kibbutz from Lebanon and harm the residents. Despite the challenging conditions of life, my little cousins were bubbly with enthusiasm, friendly, and fun loving.

I tried to engage them as best I could in my broken Hebrew. I must have been a novel curiosity as the "big cousin from America." Ori and Rotem were intrigued by a small wooden mouse pin that I wore on my shirt. No bigger than an inch, with black felt ears, a thin long black tail, and rhinestone blue eyes, the mouse was popular in America among young teens. My cousins wanted to give the mouse a name and I proposed "Nikita." Having watched on television Nikita Khrushchev's provocative and frightening behavior at the United Nations, where he slammed his shoe down on the podium, threatening to bury America, I must have subconsciously been trying to shrink Nikita down to mouse size.

The name Nikita caught on famously and the little cousins began shrieking "ha-achbar Nikita" (the mouse Nikita), while running around the apartment holding him and giggling hysterically each time they introduced him to their parents. Chasing each other, they let long Hebrew phrases roll off their tongues like cascading waterfalls. When it was time to go, I decided to leave Nikita at Aunt Ruth's home, so that the cousins could play with him whenever they visited their grandparents.

Ruth's apartment was a place I would visit many times in subsequent years. My heart always beat with anticipation as I walked up the cement path leading to #5 Moshe Sharett. I looked forward to Ruth's enthusiastic declaration of my name in Hebrew along with a big embrace. A vibrant, intelligent, and strong woman, Ruth worked in a lab in Tel Aviv, was an avid reader, and talented piano player, who remained interested in politics well into her later years. I especially appreciated how she gathered extended family when I came to visit, truly modeling *hachnasat orchim* (hospitality) for her children and grandchildren. Remarkably, Ruth lived in her own apartment until she died at age 107.

Fast forward a mere fifty years ... While I had made nearly a dozen visits since 1962, in 2012 I began a practice of annual visits to Israel to do volunteer work so as to feel more connected to the land and the people. On this first annual visit, I went to see my cousin Rotem in Haifa. I decided to surprise her with a little wooden mouse to see if she might remember our experience fifty years before as children.

As we sat at her kitchen table drinking tea, I handed her a gift, with a little wooden mouse attached to the ribbon. Without skipping a beat she said: "Oh, it looks just like Nikita!" Even more startling, however, was that Rotem stood up and walked over to the ledge above her kitchen table, where she retrieved none other than fifty-year-old Nikita, looking dapper and good as new! Rotem explained that Nikita had lived with Ruth until her death, and when they cleaned out Ruth's apartment, Rotem took Nikita to live with her in Haifa. It was hard to describe the poignant intensity of the moment reuniting with my cousin and Nikita, and remembering our long connection that went back to childhood days. All we could say was "Wow!" Inside, I felt a warm sense of gratitude for being in Israel again with my family.

# INTRODUCTION

Perhaps it was determined from birth that I would have a lifelong relationship and identification with Israel, being named after the State and growing up at the same time. However, our early years couldn't have been more different. While Israel faced physical, military, economic, emotional, and spiritual challenges to survival, as a poor country absorbing thousands of refugees, survivors, and immigrants, my early years were spent in a comfortable home on the upper west side of New York City.

My childhood view of Israel was shaped by my mother, my father, and my aunt, immigrants who came from Poland in the years before World War II. For these three people, the creation of the State of Israel was a very personal, miraculous, and inspirational redemption of the Jewish people, after sustaining great losses during the Holocaust. It was a time when Israel was the little David, trying to survive and thrive against the many Goliath Arab armies seeking to destroy her. For so many Jews, Israel was the only place Jews were welcomed.

Everyone who has been to Israel remembers their very first experience. At age thirteen, I traveled around the country with my father's closest family, taking in the beautiful and diverse scenery. What I found most surprising was the way you could see the entire outline of the country from the air, since Israel is even smaller than the state of New Jersey. I was entranced by the mysteriousness of the Negev desert and the peacefulness of the Mediterranean Sea. I was awestruck by the beauty of the Galilee: its green hills and valleys with their geometric fields and fisheries. I remember it was right there on the bus, as I hummed the theme song from the movie "Exodus", that I fell in love with Israel, At that moment, as a Jew, I felt that Israel was my second home.

I have returned to visit Israel numerous times over the years: as a Masada Zionist camp counselor at Kfar Silver, as a volunteer social work intern at Hadassah Hospital while living in Israel for a year, as a tourist multiple times, a SarEl participant during the Intifada, an *Ulpan* student, and a family therapy conference attendee. When my son was studying medicine in Israel, we visited him almost every year, and when he graduated, I missed Israel and yearned to feel more a part of this amazing little country.

I believe that we live in a historically privileged time in Jewish history when Jews have their own state, and I didn't want this opportunity in my lifetime to pass me by. Since all of my children and grandchildren live in the United States, short of *Aliyah*, I hoped that frequent visits to volunteer might be a way to reconcile my attachment to my two spiritual homes and help me feel more connected to Israel.

Since 2012, I have come each year to do pro-bono teaching in social work and family therapy, as well as hands-on efforts. During my visit I collaborate with professionals, meet Israelis of various persuasions, and connect with family and friends. My husband has joined me and does pro-bono consulting with non-profit civil society organizations. Quite honestly, these visits are like a drug-free high, and have deepened my connection to the spirit and ingenuity of the people, the incredible beauty of the land, and the vibrant, life affirming culture that is uniquely Israel.

My other agenda in making these annual visits was to demonstrate to my adult children how much Israel matters to me, a love that I wanted to pass down to the next generation. Born in a different historical era, they couldn't possibly see the world through my lens, but they certainly could observe my actions. As a post-World War Two baby boomer and "second generation" after the Holocaust, I don't take Israel for granted. I remember my dread in May 1967, when Israel was surrounded by Arab neighbors calling for "Death to Israel" while the world stood by. The lightning-fast Six-Day War victory converted my existential terror into euphoric pride. At Camp Ramah that summer, the Israeli staff who came were viewed as true heroes of the Jewish people. Israel's victory created a new sense of optimism and security, and in those days, only a few voices warned of future moral and political dilemmas that would soon emerge from the occupied territories.

By contrast to me, my grown children are a generation born well after 1967, one that never experienced being barred from visiting the Kotel (Western Wall) in Jerusalem. More removed in time from the Holocaust, they are less intimidated by anti-Semitism. They have witnessed the emergence of Palestinian nationalism, and concepts of a "Chosen People" and tribal allegiance don't resonate with them as much as with earlier generations. They have an admirable commitment to social issues such as promoting justice in society, respecting minorities, and protecting the environment. When they observe things happening in Israel that don't reflect these values, they feel disappointed, although they recognize that Israel is a vibrant democratic country with many freely dissenting voices.

Initially it was emotionally difficult for me to experience their generation's critiques of Israel. I came to realize, however, that their responses came not from apathy, but from caring deeply as Jews. In fact, their views stemmed from important Jewish humanistic and ethical values that we and their schools had taught them. I appreciate that each has found a pathway to remain engaged constructively in their relationships with Israel through a lens of Jewish values. I have been inspired by their involvements, and they have taught me a more nuanced love for Israel.

I still agree with David Ben-Gurion, Israel's "founding father" and first Prime Minister, that Israel is a miracle. It is not perfect, but with all its warts, it is still miraculous. Deeply knowledgeable about the Bible, Ben-Gurion believed that Israel's purpose in the world was to exemplify Biblical values, and apply them to contemporary issues such as health, equality, and the environment. He encouraged all citizens to share responsibility for the country through service in a civilian army, and engagement in an extensive network of civil society organizations. Ben-Gurion believed that Israel should excel at home and be a "Light unto the Nations" by helping others around the world.

Israel's achievements in agricultural technologies, high-tech, medical inventions, and intellectual research are stunning. Not only does she have the greatest number of startups after Silicon Valley, but Israel has an equally impressive collection of "humanitarian" startups and pilot programs focused on improving the quality of life for people in Israel and all around the world. It is these efforts that most inspire me. Moreover, the people of Israel have an inherent spirit of hope, optimism, creativity, innovation, directness, and "chutzpah" (daring), that is balanced by family and community responsibility, and sincere caring to improve the world.

Like other developed nations, Israel has its share of challenges and contradictions. There are increasing gaps between the rich and poor, the religious and the secular, the modern Orthodox and the Haredim (ultra Orthodox). Its citizens also wrestle with the tension between universal humanistic values and Jewish thriving. While my love for Israel is unconditional, I am pained when I don't see sacred values in practice, because I believe they have been given to us for a purpose. At the same time, Israel continues to be held to a higher standard in the world, the only country whose right to exist is questioned when a mistake is made. Absent a meaningful peace in the region and growing isolation in the world, Israelis have long accepted that "ein breirah," there is no choice but to do what is necessary for survival, or in the words of Golda Meir, Israel's first and only female Prime Minister, "The Jews have a secret weapon; we have nowhere else to go."

The idea for this book came to me one morning as I was sitting in a small park in Tel Aviv, where my husband and I had stopped to rest during a long walk on route to the Rabin Center. Reflecting on the ever

## Introduction

constant anti-Israel propaganda on the one hand, along with awareness of the amazing projects that Israel has generated, I decided to write a book highlighting the many individuals and groups within Israel who are engaged in the holy work of *Tikkun Olam* (repairing the world). I wanted to display their "can do" spirit, generosity, and desire to help others that is part of the Israeli character.

Intended for the next generation of young people such as my grandchildren, and those already on college campuses who are inundated with anti-Israel messages, as well as people who have grown up inspired by Israel, I wrote this book as a labor of love in tribute to Israel's 70th birthday. To gather the seventy or so stories, I personally reached out to many remarkable people and invited them to contribute or share writing the stories. I felt honored to "meet" so many inspiring people. The process of writing the book brought me even closer to the Israel I love.

It was impossible to cover all the good that emanates from Israel, a country that has a huge voluntarism sector. As a vibrant democracy, Israel certainly embodies the statement: "Two Jews, three opinions." The points of view expressed in the stories do not necessarily represent the views of all segments of Israeli society. The stories were chosen for their connection to the various humanistic values they illustrate.

The book is divided into three parts. Part I, Beginnings: Jewish History as Prologue, examines the concept of the Chosen People, asking "chosen for what?", then explores Jewish secrets of survival over the centuries. Memoirs and poems of survivors of the Holocaust are followed by stories concerning the miraculous birth of the nation. Immigration stories of the ingathering of exiles from around the world show how Israel is a nation built on the strength and diversity of immigrants.

Part II focuses on Biblical values and *Tikkun Olam*, with stories illustrating values such as the Earth is the Lord's, Saving a life above all, Justice Thou shalt pursue, God loves all of his Creations, Loving thy neighbor, Compassion for poor and vulnerable people and the stranger, and being a Light unto the Nations.

Part III explores Healing the Spirit and Seeking Peaceful Coexistence, illustrated in beautiful healing stories and collaboration efforts between Jews and Arabs. Each chapter has questions that could be used for classroom discussion or personal reflection.

I hope you enjoy this 70th birthday celebration honoring the State of Israel. Perhaps the inspiring stories will strengthen your engagement with Israel, and even motivate you to adopt new meaningful causes

## Introduction

in your own work of repairing the world. As Israel turns seventy, the traditional age of wisdom, my birthday wish is that the values that sustained our ancestors and gave the Jewish people purpose in the world continue to shine brightly as guidelines for living in the future, so as to reflect divinity and ennoble mankind. Surely that will make the world a better place.

*Yom Huledet Sameach* and Happy Birthday Israel!

---

### *The Way It Was – May 14, 1948*

### NATION DECLARES STATE OF ISRAEL
(Yom HaMedina, Friday May 14, 1948)

*The Masada Youth of the Zionist Organization of America created a special edition in recounting news stories as they originally appeared on that momentous day of May 14, 1948, celebrating the 36th anniversary of Israel's Independence.*

# PART I

*Beginnings:
Jewish History As Prologue*

*Chapter 1*
# THE CHOSEN PEOPLE; CHOSEN FOR WHAT?

The Jewish people who founded the modern state of Israel trace their national origins back in time to around 1800 B.C.E. The book of Genesis tells the history of the covenant between God and Israel. In Genesis, Abraham became the first Jew by voluntarily proclaiming his monotheistic relationship with God.[1] As a result of listening to God's directives, Abraham is blessed and promised that he will become the father of a great nation, and his descendants will be "as numerous as the stars in Heaven and the sand upon the seashore." (Gen 22:17). God further promises: "I will assign the land you sojourn in to you and your offspring to come…" (Gen 17:8). This is when the concept of a "Chosen People" began.

Some five hundred years later God acts through Moses to defeat the great Pharaoh of Egypt, and rescues the ancient Hebrews from slavery. These events took place in preparation for the monumental event of the Exodus, whose dramatic crescendo is reached at the Red Sea, with the miraculous parting of the waters, and then preventing the Egyptians from recapturing the Hebrew slaves.

A *Midrash* (Jewish legend) tells that God going went around from nation to nation asking each if they would like to receive his holy *Torah* (Five Books of Moses) and follow all the laws and precepts in order to become a "Chosen People." God received no affirmative response until he came to the Children of Israel, who agreed by saying: "*Naahseh venishmah* – We will do and we will listen". A further *Midrash* explains that Mount Sinai was chosen as the mountain for the giving of the Law because of its beautiful quality of humility.

During the Israelites' journey in the wilderness, the people felt God's symbolic presence, guidance, protection, and sustenance each day through observing the pillars of cloud and fire, and receiving manna. It has been said that the Torah was intentionally given in the wilderness, where the people would more likely experience their vulnerability and dependence on God. The giving of the Torah in the desert, and not in Israel, also suggests that the Torah is relevant everywhere, even in the barest of lands. The people received the Ten Commandments fifty days after the Exodus from Egypt. As Moses ascended into a cloud on the mountain, nature became still, and God's voice and presence filled the world. There at Sinai the unique relationship with the nation of Israel was created, based on the people's direct knowledge and experience of God. What was the purpose of this miraculous experience?

God's expectation was that the whole nation would fulfill their destiny as "a Kingdom of priests and a Holy nation." (Exodus 19:5) Fulfilling the *mitzvot* (commandments) became the mission of the Chosen People: To live a holy life and merit inhabiting the Promised Land. Many times the people are reminded: "When you have occupied the land and settled it, take care to observe all the laws and rules that I have set before you." (Deut. 11:31-32). In giving the Torah to the children of Israel, God chose to centralize His moral experiment for mankind in the Jewish people as a kind of "pilot" or "demo" project ("Out of Zion shall go forth Torah."). God wanted man to be His partner in caring for and repairing the world by practicing Godly attributes of justice and compassion. Being "chosen," does not mean better than others, nor deserving preferential treatment. Rather it means that Israel will be held to a higher standard and cannot behave just like its neighbors. In so doing, Israel may be viewed as "a nation that dwells alone." (Num 23:9).

The Exodus was a radical event of revolutionary importance, laden with meaning and important lessons for future generations.[2] First, it insisted that while most of the world is downtrodden, human beings are meant to be free, not slaves to powerful rulers. Second, it communicated a belief in redemption and improving the world through practicing human dignity, sanctity of life, justice, equality, loving one's neighbor, and compassion for the poor and the stranger.

There were eras in early Biblical history when the Jewish people displayed moral weakness and corruption. The text recounts how God sent prophets as spiritual leaders to educate, inspire, and chastise the people. Witness Ezekiel's word of warning: "If you really amend your behavior and your actions, if you really treat one another fairly, then I shall let you stay in this place, in the country I gave forever to your ancestors of old." (Ezekiel 11:19).

To this day, Prophetic texts are read weekly in synagogues around the world. This practice is to teach contemporary Jews to stay on a righteous and moral path of spiritual growth, and to remind them that being members of a Chosen People must help shape the behavioral choices they make. The "Chosen People" must feel and act responsibly not only towards other Jews (*kol Yisrael aravim zeh lazeh*), but towards others as well ("Am I not my brother's keeper?")

Now that the Chosen People have the privilege of living in their ancestral homeland once again after 2,000 years in exile, they have the opportunity to experience healing as a people, as well as fulfill their mission of promoting Torah values of justice and compassion, not only within their own borders, but throughout the world as well.

*Chapter 2*

# THOSE WANDERING JEWS: SECRETS OF SURVIVAL

"If the statistics are right, the Jews constitute but one quarter of one percent of the human race … his contributions to the world's list of great names in literature, science, art, music, finance, medicine and abstruse learning are (also) way out of proportion to the weakness of his numbers …

The Egyptians, the Babylonians and the Persians rose, filled the planet with sound and splendor, then faded to dream-stuff and passed away; the Greeks and Romans followed and made a vast noise, and they are gone … All things are mortal but the Jew; all other forces pass, but he remains. What is the secret of his immortality?"

Mark Twain, 1899

"The Jew is the symbol of eternity … He is the one who for so long guarded the prophetic message and transmitted it to all mankind. A people such as this can never disappear. The Jew is eternal. He is the embodiment of eternity."

Leo Tolstoy

"Of all the peoples of the western world three thousand years ago, it is only the Jews who live in the same place, speak the same language, and practice the same religion."

Barbara Tuchman

"The Jewish people became a model of persistence, how one takes suffering and ennobles it."

Rabbi Yitzchak Greenberg

"Every Jew, no matter how insignificantly, is engaged in some decisive and immediate pursuit of a goal. It is the most perpetual people on the earth."

Johann Wolfgang von Goethe

How did the Jews survive as a nation during twenty centuries of exile dispersed from their land, facing persecution, economic hardship, expulsion, forced conversion, pogroms, lands closed to refugees, and then the Holocaust, in which one third of the Jewish people were killed by Hitler as the world stood by? This question was of great interest to His Holiness the Dalai Lama, who viewed the Jews as "survival experts." Concerned about his own Tibetan people in exile, he invited a visiting delegation of Jewish scholars to Dharamsala, a remote, mystical area of northern India facing the majestic Himalayan Mountains.[1] From the lively discussions with those scholars, the Dalai Lama concluded that memory is the emotional secret to Jewish survival.

## *Remembering and Telling the Story*

The Torah is filled with commandments, values, and rules to remember and teach the laws to subsequent generations. Each year as Jewish families gather to celebrate Passover, the most widely observed Jewish holiday, they are commanded to feel as if they personally came out of Egypt. The phrase "Remember that you were strangers in the land of Egypt and that God redeemed you for the purpose of being a Holy nation," is repeated 37 times in the Torah.

The *Haggadah*, read at the Passover Seder, literally means "telling," reminding Jews of their roots, traditions, and destiny. Questions, discussions, and debate are welcomed during the Seder evening, including encouraging young children to ask the Four Questions and expect answers. Those with less patience for the long service, humorously summarize the Passover (and other) holiday stories as: "They tried to kill us, we survived, let's eat."[2] The Seder always concludes with the phrase: "Next year in Jerusalem."

## *Hoping for Return to Zion*

If I forget you, O Jerusalem

Let my right hand wither.

Let my tongue cling to the roof of my mouth

If I do not remember you,

If I do not set Jerusalem

Above my highest joys.

Psalm 137:5-6

Abraham Joshua Heschel [3] describes the Jews' attachment to their land as a two thousand year love affair that gets reinforced in daily prayers and rituals. Heschel states: "When Israel was driven into exile, the pledge to return to Zion became a prayer, the prayer – a dream, the dream a passion, a duty, a dedication ... to abandon the land would be to repudiate the Bible." The message of return to Zion was reinforced throughout the exile in Prophetic messages of comfort: "There is hope for your future, says the Lord, and your children shall come back to their country." (Jeremiah 31:17).

While yearning to rebuild the Temple in Jerusalem, Jews focused on prayer and good deeds as a way of serving God, thus creating a "portable homeland" in exile. The sages realized that democratizing religious practice to encompass individual family households would help preserve Jewish culture. For example, home blessings over wine and bread became a remembrance of, and substitute for Temple rites. Holy days such as *Tisha B'Av*, (the ninth of Av) commemorating the destruction of both Temples, and even celebratory events such as a wedding, that incorporated the breaking of a glass as a ritual, remind Jews of the destroyed Temples and their incomplete happiness in exile.

## *Judaism as a Family Religion*

God's covenant was with Abraham, his family, and his descendants, down to Jacob and his twelve sons, described in a genealogy of specific names and intergenerational transmission: "Moses received the Torah at Sinai and passed it to Joshua, Joshua to the elders, the elders to the prophets, and the prophets to the men of the Great Assembly." (Pirke Avot Ch.1)

Blu Greenberg[4], an Orthodox feminist, attributes survival of the Jews to the family unit: the mother's role as creator of the household and the importance placed on children. As teacher and feeder of the young, the mother imbued lessons "with kindness on her tongue." Tradition recognizes her crucial role by having the husband recite *Ayshet Chayil* ("A Woman of Valor") every Friday evening at the start of the Sabbath meal. Despite the numerous jokes and sarcastic humor aimed at the Jewish mother, she is probably responsible for the survival and continuity of Judaism through family celebrations of holidays involving children's participation.

## *Judaism as a Civilization*

Many marvel how creating a new way of thinking and experiencing the world, radically different from other ancient religions, enabled a tribe of desert nomads to have had such a profound influence. [5] The Jews were the first civilization to have a day of rest for prayer, study, and recreation, in honor of God's resting on the seventh day after creating the world. The Sabbath introduced an understanding of time that offered man freedom of choice. So great is the gift of the Sabbath that it has been said: "More than the Jewish people have kept the Sabbath, the Sabbath has kept the Jews." (Achad Ha'am, an early Zionist thinker).

Rabbi Mordecai M. Kaplan believed the secret of survival was that Jewish rituals and traditions were invested with such universal ethical meanings. Family life was strengthened by larger community support of shared values, practices, and observances, hence the message: "Do not separate yourself from the community." (Pirke Avot).

While Jews were confined to ghettos without choice, such cloistering probably also strengthened interdependence and protected against assimilation. Community structures with local councils created a form of self-governance even while in exile.

During years of wandering the Jews remained a people with a religion, a distinct language, customs, literature, art, and ideas that interacted and evolved with their surroundings. While Hebrew was nearly extinct as a spoken language by the fourth century except in Holy books, it was revived in the late 19th century, largely by the efforts of one man, Eliezer ben Yehuda. Clearly evidence of another miracle, today there are about ten million Hebrew speakers in the world.

## *Scholarship and Books*

The Qu'ran called the Jews the "People of the Book." Ben-Gurion once said: "We have preserved the Book and the Book has preserved us." The Bible gave the Jews a history, a system of guidelines for life, and a purpose in the world. Even during times of persecution, Jews were authors of their own story. Those who returned from exile with Ezra and Nehemiah in the sixth and fifth centuries B.C.E. participated in an energetic revival in the land of Israel with a new Temple, new holiday calendar, new laws, and new scholarship. The returning Jews brought with them books written in exile. The Torah reached its final form, combining the oral literatures of Judah and Israel with contemporary scribes and wisdom literature. The books of the Maccabees and the book of Esther recorded triumphs over enemies, teaching Jews to respond by taking action and fighting against wrongdoings in order to prevail.

After the destruction of the Second Temple in Jerusalem in 70 C.E. and exile, Judaism was saved by sages who taught, interpreted, and preserved tradition. Talmudic volumes contain endless discussions about details of life through questioning, debate, even humor. According to Oz & Oz, the techniques of reading texts, such as argumentation, inventiveness, self-critique, challenging authority, and even irreverence in Jewish families can be traced to a scholarly tradition that believes in the power of words to create reality and are the ancient codes of Jewish survival.[6]

## *Purpose as a Light unto the Nations*

While Jews have a rich collective ancestral history, shared roots alone without a sense of purpose are not sufficient for survival. The late Holocaust survivor and Nobel Laureate Elie Wiesel understood that the Jewish experiences of oppression and genocide compel Jews to speak out against injustice and indifference, and to advocate for the rights and dignity of distressed people everywhere. His message was: "Remember the Holocaust; remembrance must shape our character and has the capacity to transform the future." Wiesel's persistent call to remember the Holocaust helped survivors acquire a new moral mission as important witnesses for future generations.

Wiesel also lived his message in 1985 when he challenged President Reagan to visit a Jewish memorial in Germany instead of Bitburg, a German Soldier cemetery, saying: "I belong to a people that speaks truth to power." Wiesel also urged the Dalai Lama to "learn the facts of life that the twentieth century taught us: namely that a focus on prayers and ritual alone is not sufficient; we must make our actions speak louder than words."

Israeli President Reuven Rivlin, speaking at the opening ceremony of Holocaust Remembrance Day, once said: "It was not the Holocaust or fear that kept us going through two thousand years of our exile, it was our spiritual assets, our shared creativity."

According to Rabbi Yitz Greenberg, with each dispersal Jews had to "start up" over again, thereby learning flexibility and adaptability, strengthening their conviction in their purposeful significance in the world.[7]

While Hitler tried to rid Europe of its Jews, today Jewish communities have been re-sprouting all over Europe so as to not give Hitler a posthumous victory.

*Chapter 3*

# OUT OF THE ASHES OF THE SHOAH: FINDING A SAFE HAVEN

In 1936, Chaim Weizmann, Israel's future first President, commented: "For the Jews, the world is divided into places where they cannot live and places where they cannot enter." Unable to escape, find a refuge or safe haven, Jews faced doors closed to them in many countries. Perhaps the plight of the ship, St. Louis, epitomized the world's attitude of cruel indifference to Jews in peril. Leaving Hamburg, Germany in 1939 with almost 1,000 refugees, the ship was barred from Cuba, the United States, and Canada, and was sent back to Europe, where many of them eventually perished in concentration camps. To make matters worse, bowing to Arab pressure, the British instituted the infamous White Paper, severely limiting Jewish immigration to Palestine to 15,000 per year, for a total of 75,000, a policy which continued throughout the years of the *Shoah* (the Holocaust).*

The *Shoah* capped the worst century in Jewish history – two out of three Jews of the nine million Jews living in pre-war Europe were murdered. Despite the passage of time, the staggering figure of six million Jewish victims is still hard to fathom. Each one represents a story about a human being who was a spouse, a parent, a baby, a child, a sibling, or other relative, part of a family and community fabric that was cruelly ripped apart. Many historians attribute the United Nations' subsequent support for a Jewish state as due to the unfathomable horror of the *Shoah*. In retrospect, that a state emerged just three years after the liberation of Auschwitz does sound rather miraculous. And yet, even today, despite all of the evidence and testimonials, trials and convictions of perpetrators, Holocaust denial is still being promulgated.

The stories in this chapter tell of hidden children with changed identities, frightening and daring escapes, and terrible journeys through ghettos and death camps. Poems written by my father in his later years, helped me to better understand the grief and guilt he experienced living in America and losing close family members. The stories represent only a tiny fraction of the cruel devastation wrought upon the Jewish people.

---

\* "Shoah" in Hebrew means "calamity," while "Holocaust" is an English word that means "burnt offering" or "sacrifice to God." The six million Jews were neither burnt offerings nor sacrifices to God; they were innocent human beings murdered by the Nazis in abominable ways.

*Chapter 3*

At the same time, the stories illustrate courage, ingenuity, heroism, and valor in coping with inhumanity. The stories show how kibbutzim and youth villages helped young survivors find community and begin to rebuild their lives. For so many, Israel was a refuge and homeland that accepted them with open arms and was their only option.

## *Searching for Home*
## Joseph Gosler

My mother told me that my birthdate, July 27, 1942, was just an ordinary summer day in the Netherlands, yet there were British bombers in the air, returning from their mission over Hamburg, Germany. In the Netherlands signs of the future looming ahead were everywhere: restrictions on Jewish academics, limits on where Jews could shop and work, and most sadly, the building of forced labor and transition camps in central and north-east Holland.

An ongoing German military presence was unnecessary in Holland because the large fascist organization called the NSB (National Socialist Movement) ran Holland through the SS and their Dutch supporters. This union proved to be devastating for Dutch Jews, resulting in proportionately fewer survivors in Holland than in any other European country.

I was one of the fortunate ones. At age seven months, a time when an infant can barely see beyond his mother's breast, I was plucked away by the newly formed underground and secretly brought to the Dyjkstra's, a Protestant family living in Wageningen. My name was changed to Peter Dyjkstra and I became part of their family registry. Their daughters, Anneke and Folie, each more blond and blue eyed than the other, a sharp contrast to my dark brown hair and hazel eyes, became my sisters. They were my family and world until the end of the war, when I was almost three years old. I was too young to comprehend the bombing, food rationing, tanks, trucks, and soldiers in the background.

At the end of the war my biological parents, Maurice and Henriette, came for me, but they seemed like strangers. My birth parents, like other Jews, were mired in a sea of mourning, having lost family and friends. They experienced emotional and physical pain, as well as guilt over surviving. My mother suffered a nervous breakdown and my father was cut off emotionally. I felt anxious, confused, afraid, angry, abandoned, and untrusting.

While they loved and provided for me and my sister, Marja, born after the war, they were so needy and self-absorbed that the normal bonding between a parent and child did not occur until I was well into my thirties. To me, my birth parents were strangers who took me away from "Moeder" and "Faeder." I could not adjust to them and I acted out in alarming ways, such as lighting the bathroom curtains on fire and frequently wandering off in search of my underground Dutch family.

Haunted by memories and struggling financially due to the post-war recession, my parents applied for visas to the United States when I was six years old. Unfortunately, the waiting list was at least two years long and my parents couldn't find a "host" to sponsor them, a prerequisite for immigration, so they decided to go to Israel instead.

We traveled by train from Amsterdam to Marseilles, and boarded a cargo ship bound for Haifa. Passengers, all Jewish immigrants, slept in steerage at the bottom of the ship, which was packed with families, metal beds, suitcases, and buckets. There was a long line for the one bathroom. The turbulent and frightful five day trip is etched in my mind. A storm created a horrific scene for several hours, as suitcases slid from one end to the other, spilling buckets of urine across the floor, beds rattled like chattering teeth, and babies cried incessantly, as the flickering lights created a haunting disco light show.

We arrived the following day in the port of Haifa, from the darkness and fear into daylight, with the calm, warm breezes of Haifa's harbor and the hope of Israel. The country, just one year old, invited us with open arms. In 1949 the young nation needed everything, most of all immigrants. Our family was directed to a large immigrant camp with canvas tents for shelter. Soon after we were sent to Beit HaShita, a Mapam (Marxist-Zionist) oriented kibbutz, formed in the 1930s, initially through the purchase of land from neighboring Arab villages.

Each member experienced the transition to kibbutz life differently. The separation of children from their parents was a heavenly reality for me, but it was terrible for my parents and my sister. I craved the distance and independence to roam with children my own age. For a child bewildered and resistant to his parents' attention, and still unknowingly mourning his own losses, the kibbutz was a perfect haven.

But even a haven can be less than idyllic. I was a new kid on the block who couldn't speak the language. My Hebrew tutor Beersheva, a woman with a broad smile, warm brown eyes, and a long black braid, took me under her wings and gave me the nurturing I craved. I often came late to my classes just to have more time with her. Except for Beersheva, however, I felt lonely and isolated, small and insignificant, a stranger even to myself.

I envied the other boys and wanted to be liked by them. I even resorted to stealing one boy's stamp album to be noticed, which only resulted in my being picked on more, and many fights. I wouldn't consider involving or worrying my parents (ever!) nor showing dependency. So like the Hebrew tribes who wandered in the desert for forty years until they found the righteous path, I eventually learned through trial and error how to reduce the acrimony between the *yeladim* (kids) and myself. Thereafter, I had no further problems with the boys in the kibbutz, and in fact, formed deep friendships with several of my antagonists.

The daily activities of the kibbutz routines forced me out of my isolation and became familiar and comforting. I welcomed the secure structure: getting up at six-thirty, putting on my khaki shorts and sleeveless T-shirt, and running barefoot in a single line through the kibbutz for exercise. Breakfast in the cafeteria was followed by classroom study and lunch around noon. After lunch we worked in the olive groves and vineyard, and by mid-afternoon, hot and exhausted, we napped or had quiet time. Dinner was followed by athletic games on the lawn in front of the cafeteria. Exhausted at the end of the day, I could barely stay awake until the 8 p.m. curfew and fell into a deep sleep.

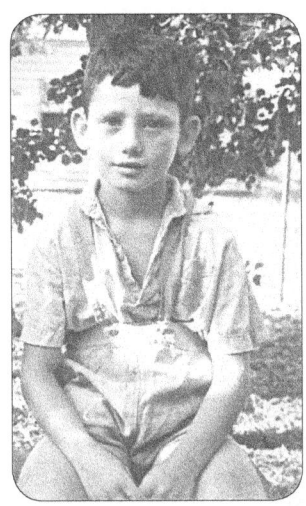

*Joe Gosler, 8 years old.*

For the first time I began to enjoy life, and felt part of a large, extended family. In the kibbutz the group is larger than the sum of the individual parts. I had friends, felt safe, welcomed my chores, and was fully engaged in my own childhood. I loved the holidays, like Purim, where my sister dressed as Queen Esther and I was a dancing Cossack. However, my favorite was Sukkot, especially building the first sukkah, made from strong wooden branches and shaped into a rectangular pattern. We wove young sapling branches horizontally in and out between every other vertical branch to create secure walls on three sides.

Roof branches with clusters of grapes and thin branches laden with green olives hung on the interior walls. On a rough, wooden table were baskets of carrots, potatoes, cabbages, leeks, and melons. The cacophony of sounds, the buzzing of bees and flies, the croaking of frogs, and the distant high pitched howls of jackals, blended with the perfume of fresh ripened fruits and vegetables. All this under a canopy of stars created a bacchanal for the senses and a place of peace and wonderment.

On weekends my friends and I explored nearby caves to find mysterious bones and other treasures. We jumped like mountain goats rushing down the hills, our callused feet barely touching the ground, zigzagging past gravelly stones, clusters of irises and poppies, tufts of grass, and an assortment of bramble bushes. We pretended to be Maccabees, fighting evil forces that might harm us. Our mighty wooden swords and home-made bows and arrows overwhelmed our imaginary enemies in our quixotic play. I felt secure in a world of *haverim* (comrades), and fantasized about joining the *No'Ar*, the quasi-military youth organization that was a bridge to the Haganah.

Had I not come to Israel, my life would have been profoundly different. The sense of fairness and community that I inhaled so deeply in Israel became part of my DNA, coming directly from my experience of life on the kibbutz. The attributes I hold dear, such as love for exploration, learning, a spirit for life and a respect for the living would not be as central to my being, if not for my years on the kibbutz.

As I grow older, I worry about whether we have learned enough from history about tolerance of the other. Just as the kibbutz for me was a place of friendship, comfort, and security, my deep wish for Israel is that through tolerance, embracing of diversity, and treating all citizens fairly with kindness, it will be the land of "milk and honey" that it was designed to be, so that we can feel as if under a sukkah of peace, as in the prayer, "*Ufros aleynu sukkat shelomecha* – Spread over us Your Sukkah of peace."

## *Escape to Russia* [1]
## Kathy Kacer

"Tell me about the time we escaped to Russia, Mama," pleaded eight-year-old Adam, as he pulled the covers up around his chin. "I want to hear it again."

Mama reached over to stroke her son's cheek. "If I tell you the story, will you go straight to sleep?"

"I promise!" Adam nearly shouted out loud, before settling back onto his pillow.

"Fine," Mama replied. "Let's see ... How does it begin?"

Adam smiled. He was waiting for that cue. "*Tate* (father) had already escaped to Lvov where he got a job as a carpenter, building wooden frames for airplanes."

"Ah, yes," Mama nodded as she settled onto the bed.

"In 1939, your father knew it would only be a matter of time before the Nazis came looking for Jews in Poland. He decided to cross the eastern border and take his chances with the Russians. When the war broke out, everything was in a state of chaos; anybody could cross the open border, so your father had no difficulty getting through."

"And then he wrote you a letter," Adam continued.

"Yes, as things got worse for Jews in Poland, a letter arrived, saying: '*Bring me Adash.*'"

"That's me," Adam interrupted. "And I was only ten months old."

Mama closed her eyes while Adam waited, knowing that this was the place in the story where Mama always drifted back in her mind. Adam was too young to remember, but his mother was his memory – his eyes and ears into the past.

A moment later, Mama opened her eyes and continued. "It took a couple of months to make the arrangements. By December, we left our home and traveled by train to a small village close to the border."

Adam always marveled at how his mother made this journey. By December 1939, German soldiers were already on the lookout for Polish Jews trying to escape. Adam's mother knew how to speak German, and besides, she could talk herself out of any situation.

"I was looking for a farmer who would help us cross the border," Mama continued. "I found someone, but at first he refused, saying, 'It's too dangerous. The snow is up to your waist and it's too difficult to travel. The Russians will shoot you, and me too, so I won't help you.'"

"I begged, I pleaded, I cried, I offered him money, but nothing worked."

## Chapter 3

"And then he looked at your boots," Adam proclaimed triumphantly.

"Adam, do you want to tell this story, or shall I?" Adam smiled and lay back in his bed, while Mama continued. "I was just about to turn away, when he glanced down and noticed my warm leather boots and said, 'Money is worthless, but your boots might be useful to me.' I couldn't believe it, but then I realized that my boots were very valuable. They could be traded for a cow! So I said to him, 'I'll give you the boots if you take me and my son across the border.'"

Finally, he said, "I'll take you one kilometer from the border, but then you're on your own. Take it or leave it."

And so I nodded, and said, "Agreed!"

Adam let out a slow breath. This was the part of the story where his heart always raced. What would have happened if the farmer refused to take them near the border? Adam knew, from his parents' stories, that millions of Polish Jews had been killed in concentration camps by the Nazis. Perhaps he and his mother would have been among them. He would not be here, listening to this story.

"Early the next morning we left for the border," Mama continued. "It was snowing so hard, we could hardly see. And the rough country road rocked the wagon from side to side. I was afraid you might bounce out of my arms, so I held you tightly with one arm, while clutching the side of the wagon with the other. It was a terrible journey lasting several hours, not knowing where we were. I had put all my trust in a strange man who promised to keep us safe.

"Finally, the wagon came to a stop and the farmer ordered me to get off. 'Keep walking in that direction and you'll get to the border,' he said. I gave him my boots, and with that, he turned the wagon around and disappeared, leaving us alone on the road. I picked up our cases and started to walk. The farmer said it was only one kilometer to the border, but it was the longest and hardest kilometer I have ever walked.

"I'll admit to you that I was scared, Adam. Here I was, a young woman with a baby who was crying in my arms. I almost wanted to just give up and sit down by the side of the road. But what kept me going was imagining your *Tate's* face and the letter that he had sent me. *'Bring me Adash,'* it said. Because your father was waiting for us, I could not let him down.

"Finally, as it was beginning to grow dark, I saw a wooden post across the road. We had made it to the border! But two Russian soldiers stood guard behind the post with their guns pointed at us!"

"We'll shoot you if you take one more step," they shouted as we approached. But instead of turning around, I shouted back, "Go ahead, shoot me!"

"At that point, nothing was going to stop me. Lucky for me I spoke some Russian. So I said, "I must get to my husband who is working in Russia."

"Don't come any further," one of the guards ordered.

"But we're Jews," I said. "We need help." They still wouldn't budge. So I took a deep breath, stood up as tall and straight as I could and said, "I'm coming closer."

"Perhaps the soldiers were impressed by my good Russian, or maybe they felt sorry for me, but finally, the soldiers lifted the wooden post and told me to follow them."

"It wasn't over yet, was it Mama?"

Adam knew that the most amazing part of the story was still to come.

Mama smiled. "The soldiers led us to their headquarters. In a large room, seated behind a desk, was a Russian Colonel. He cursed us in Russian and shouted, 'We don't need people like you here!'

"I tried every argument in the book, but nothing would budge this man. Finally, the Colonel turned to one of the sergeants and said, 'Get rid of this garbage.'"

"I thought it was the end of us. I felt hopeless as we silently followed the sergeant out of the room and back outside."

"And that's when the sergeant spoke to you," Adam said.

"Yes," Mama replied. "That was the most remarkable moment of all. Outside, the sergeant turned to me and whispered in my ear: 'On Yvray. He's a Jew.'"

"At first, I didn't know what he was talking about. 'Who?' I asked. And the Sergeant replied, 'the Colonel. He's a Jew and so am I.'"

"All that yelling had been so that no one would suspect that these two men were Jewish. I was speechless."

"Don't worry," the sergeant continued. "I'm going to help and take you to a farmer who lives close by and he will take you to your husband."

"And that's exactly what he did. He took us to the farmer who went with us to your *Tate*," Mama finished telling the story.

"And tell me again what *Tate* said as soon as he saw me," Adam begged. It was the last part, and the most important piece of all.

Mama said, "He took you in his arms, looked at me, and he said, 'Thank you for bringing me my Adash.'[2]"

"And that's why I'm here today."

Adam lay back on his pillow with a contented smile.

"That's why we're all here," said Mama.

*Chapter 3*

# *Discovering the Remarkable Lives of Joseph and Rebecca Bau*
## Israela Meyerstein

On a quiet street in Tel Aviv, I recently visited a museum whose size belies its importance. At the entrance to the Bau Museum, I was warmly greeted by Hadasa Bau and Clila Bau-Cohen, the daughters of Joseph and Rebecca Bau. They created the museum in memory of their parents, who remarkably survived ghetto and concentration camps during the *Shoah*, made subsequent *Aliyah* to Israel, and contributed in important ways to Israeli society. Over several hours the sisters shared the story of their parents' lives with sincerity, loving admiration, and even humor. The following is what I learned from them during my visit.

Joseph Bau was born in 1920 in Krakow, Poland, and from an early age he displayed artistic talent. He later studied at the University of Plastic Arts in Krakow, where he developed skill as a graphic artist and a draftsman, along with an affinity for Gothic lettering, a skill that would later save his life. When Hitler invaded Poland in 1939, Joseph's studies were interrupted, and Jews were confined to the Krakow Ghetto. There, Joseph was able to work by making maps and signs of the ghetto and concentration camps for the Nazis, who were enamored with the Gothic font. In the ghetto, Joseph simultaneously secretly forged documents and stamps for the Jewish underground to help Jews to escape. He himself never tried to escape because he wanted to help others.

In 1943 the ghetto inhabitants were moved to Plaszow Concentration camp. The sisters showed a black case filled with paints and brushes that Joseph took along with him. The case had a secret bottom compartment where Joseph hid precious family photos. Confiscated by the Nazis, the case was miraculously found later in the storage facility of industrialist Oskar Schindler, who personally returned it to Joseph at the Brinlitz concentration camp in 1945, with the hidden paintings and photos intact.

In Plaszow Joseph again survived by working as a draftsman, drawing maps and inscribing signs in Gothic lettering. He collected paper from cigarette butts discarded by the Nazis, and used them to create tiny drawings and poetry. He made a deck of playing cards depicting scenes of normal family life. He used these scenes as fortune-telling cards to raise prisoners' morale and hope for the future. He also made miniature books documenting the brutal realities of camp life to create a personal record of his experiences, which were later published in a memoir: "*Dear God, Have You Ever Been Hungry?*" Joseph used his art cathartically to deal with the trauma and stress.

*Out of the Ashes of the Shoah: Finding a Safe Haven*

One day, while on an assignment, Joseph met and flirted with Rebecca Tannenbaum, who served as a manicurist for Amon Goeth, the sadistic camp commandant. Goeth routinely tortured prisoners and shot them for sport. Goeth would hold a gun at Rebecca's elbow, and threatened to shoot her if she nicked or scratched him. Although courtship was forbidden in the camp, Joseph and Rebecca's relationship grew. Joseph traded his bread, starving himself, for a silver spoon that a jeweler made into two wedding rings.

On February 13, 1944 Joseph disguised himself as a woman in a kerchief, and snuck into his mother's barracks. There his mother performed an unofficial wedding ceremony for her son and Rebecca (a scene which is adapted and portrayed in the movie, Schindler's List). When the guards came by the women's barracks to search for men, Rebecca and her bunkmates hid Joseph under rags they used as a pillow. Miraculously he was not discovered, while those caught were beaten to death. Later, Joseph somehow managed to return to the men's barracks.

Hadasa then told the story of how Rebecca saved Joseph's life. As Plaszow was being closed and inmates were selected for Auschwitz and other camps, Rebecca called in a favor with Goeth's Jewish male secretary. She reminded him that she had saved the man's mother. Rebecca was able to get Joseph's name substituted for her own on the list of people who would work in Schindler's factory in Brinlitz, Czechoslovakia. Rebecca chose to go to Auschwitz in Joseph's place because she believed she could survive but worried that Joseph wouldn't.

In late 1944 Joseph worked with Oskar Schindler in his factory, falsifying papers so Schindler could obtain rations for the 1,000 plus workers he sheltered in his factory. Tragically, Joseph's father, mother, and younger brother were murdered in the Shoah. After the war, Joseph found Rebecca recuperating in a hospital. They reunited and got remarried in 1946. Joseph completed his studies at Krakow University, then worked drawing caricatures for Polish newspapers. In 1950 the family, with three year old Hadasa, who was the first child born to a Schindler family, arrived in Israel penniless and knowing little Hebrew. Joseph began working as a graphic artist in Tel-Aviv. He also did advertisement and illustration for the Israeli government.

Hadasa spoke fondly of Oskar Schindler, the Righteous Gentile. They told me that many survivors of Schindler's List sent money to help support Schindler after the war. Whenever Schindler visited Israel, their father organized a reunion of the Schindler families to meet him. Schindler told the girls: "I am your grandfather, because I was

*Chapter 3*

a father to your father." After Schindler died in 1974, he was buried in Israel. Survivors remembered him with gratitude by putting stones on his grave.

Joseph opened his own studio in 1960, which is now the museum. I was shown the equipment he used to build a movie theater from scratch. He used a sewing machine motor and X-ray equipment to construct a projector, and set up a dark room and copying machine. He taught himself animation techniques and became a pioneer in Israel's animated film industry, producing shorts for movies and television public service announcements. Joseph created unique Hebrew fonts for opening and closing titles of most Israeli movies from the 1950s through the 1970s, earning him the title "Israel's Walt Disney."

Hadasa and Clila pointed to the many artifacts, books, and samples of Joseph's work that adorned the studio walls. The sisters enthusiastically showed me a reproduction they had just created of Joseph's original black case and its contents. They proudly described his love of Hebrew language and wordplay, such as the title of one of his Hebrew language books called "Brit Milah." They felt his greatest talent was the humor, wit, and playfulness found in his creative work. He excelled in drawing, calligraphy, illustration, and painting, and infused his art and writing with humor, optimism, and hope. His artwork has been exhibited in museums and galleries around the world, including at the United Nations headquarters in New York. Despite his prodigious accomplishments, however, Joseph was a modest person.

The sisters saved some of the surprises about their father until the end. They told me that they often wondered why the Israeli government didn't give their father greater public recognition for his amazing contributions. It wasn't until 1998, four years before his death, that he was nominated for the prestigious Israel Prize. And it was only after his death, that Hadasa and Clila learned the reason for the low profile. Joseph Bau worked for the Mossad as their chief forger! He forged documents to help Eli Cohen penetrate the Syrian political echelon, and he forged the necessary documents to capture and extradite Adolf Eichmann.

Clearly, Hadasa and Clila deeply loved and were proud of their parents, whom they viewed as heroes, not victims. Their parents showed courage, optimism, dignity, and even humor, in circumstances intended to crush the human spirit. They coped with impossible hardships without losing their spark of humanity and love for other people. Joseph and Rebecca's wisdom and bravery led to saving the lives of many people. Viewing their wartime experiences as a series of miracles, Joseph and

Rebecca were able to see good even in the worst situation. The sisters remember their father always saying, to the effect, "that in everything bad, there is always something good emerging. Never get angry at the world."

As my visit to the Bau museum drew to a close, Hadasa and Clila thanked me for coming to learn about the amazing legacy they received from their parents. The sisters' strongest desire is to keep the museum open so they can continue to tell about the remarkable lives of their parents, Joseph and Rebecca Bau. I thanked them for their graciousness and most inspiring story. I told them I would feel privileged to write about their museum to help keep their parents' memories alive.

Please see the website: www.josephbau.com.

Chapter 3

## Poems From America
## – in Memory of Family –
## Dr. George Gorin

### Midnight Before Disaster

Taking a sad farewell of my parents
forever on this earth
on a dark July night,
on the way to the train
words to puncture tension
died within us.

Each of us sobbed inwardly
choking on a lump
thick with emotions
that refused to spill tears.

My childhood fears, which I thought
I conquered abroad
crawled out from the dark forest
that stood gaping, whispering
ominous threats and I could not
be comforted by my parents,
whose strength was sapped by a
mixture of fatigue and resignation.

*Dr. George Gorin*

As a people accustomed to curses
and threats cast upon us by the wrath
of our own God and His Prophets,
we knew our days of disaster
in the past in which we paid with blood
for having chosen to be
what we were.

The local hooligans marked our homes
with red paint
as a sad irony on what God has done
in our favor in Egypt when He wooed us
in the hope of acceptance of His law.

Here I was with an American visa
in my pocket leaving my dear ones
isolated from the world,

surrounded by an enemy
who was sharpening his knives
for slaughter the moment
the arch-enemy will cross the border.

In the stillness of the night
I could hear the restless breathing
of a community of Jews while all doors
of the world were being shut
and refugees were turned away
and chased into the arms of death.

My parents knew of my agonizing pain
and hastened the goodbyes.

I stood at the window looking
at the two prematurely aged people,
helpless as if standing at a gravesite
forced to accept the verdict of fate.

It happened suddenly: a whistle
and the train pierced the night
accompanied by smoke and sparks
while my past receded into limbo,
a place I was never to see again.

George Gorin, *Intermezzo* (p. 18, 1984)


## *My Little Sister*

When I last saw her,
my little sister
was blooming into
a pretty young lady.

Said I: "I will come
from afar to the wedding
of the most beautiful
bride."
There was no music
no bridal canopy,
nor bridal veil.
Shorn and naked

she was pushed
into the flames.

That evening
I was overseas
in company of noisy
army officers.

In the din
kept ringing
in my ears
cries of
Mazel Tov,
Mazel Tov
to the bride."

> George Gorin, *Intermezzo* (1984), p.23

## *My Uncle*

This is an epitaph
for a saint.
I inherited his humility
and disdain for things
material and the sadness
of his face.

His red beard and
flaming eyes reflected
the burning temple
during his midnight
lamentations over
Zion's downfall.

He was not of this world
from which he was taken
through the torch the Nazis
put to one thousand Jews
in the Bialystok synagogue
on Yom Kippur.
I know he died with

*Out of the Ashes of the Shoah: Finding a Safe Haven*

His last breath wheezing
The Name in fiery syllables.

>George Gorin, Echoes and Shadows, 1985 p.45

## *My Grandfather's Tombstone*
*(A Stone will cry out from a wall, Habakuk, 2, 11)*

The Germans made my birthplace
Judenrein and the scavengers
dug up the Jewish cemetery and
plowed under the bones into a pig's market place.

The monuments became cornerstones
for houses and street pavements.
My grandfather's tombstone cries out
to the world: "Here lies Faivel Moshe, 1917."

His DNA is part of my genes,
his blood flows in my veins,
my brain suckled from his fountain
and he burdened me with my fate.

Poland will never be Judenrein.
You cannot wipe off a millennium.
Kazimierz, King of Poles,
speak up from your grave.

We came as your guests while running
From persecutions everywhere.
We loved the land that we were not
allowed to own, the bright summers,
frosty winters, the big rivers,
and dense forests, we were comforted
by the conscience of the few
and we feared the hatred of the many.
It was our home and our roots were torn out.
Now the souls of the dead flutter
around your houses that were our homes
and will disturb your sleep with nightmares
about what happened to your Jewish neighbors.

>George Gorin, *Intermezzo* (1984)

## Chapter 3

*Hyakinthos\**
*(a prayer)*

Please God of Abraham, Isaac
And Jacob. I have one prayer
In my heart:

Seed the fields of Thine Earth
every spring with one million
blue and white flowers to be
called Moishelach, Shloimelach,
Saralach and Ryvkelach.

Let the souls of the perished
Jewish children shine all over
the earth in the eye of your
sun by day and as stars in the
sky by night, thereby telling
the world that we are not your
forgotten people.

Amen.

*(\*Youth loved by Apollo who killed him by accident.*
*Apollo made hyacinths grow from his blood.)*

George Gorin, *The Burning Bush* (1986), p.60.

## *El Maleh Rachamim* [3]

Merciful God, who dwells on high
Bring a final peaceful rest in the shelter of the
Divine Presence
Amidst the ranks of all the holy martyrs and the pure
Whose radiance shines brilliantly as the Heavens
To the souls of our brothers and sisters
The six million martyrs of the house of Israel in
Europe
Who were killed, slaughtered, gassed, burned,
buried alive
By their murderers, the Nazis and their
collaborators
In Auschwitz, Treblinka, Majdanek, Mauthausen,
Bergen-Belsen, Sobibor, and the many other
killing places.

We pray that their souls be uplifted.
May they rest in Paradise.
Master of mercy,
Shield them in the hiddenness of your
protective wings to all eternity.
Bind up their
souls in the bundle of life forever.

Earth, do not
cover up their blood.
God is their portion.
May they rest in peace.

And, let us say: Amen.

*Chapter 3*

"Suffering makes a people greater, and we have suffered much. We had a message to give the world, but we were overwhelmed, and the message was cut off in the middle. In time there will be millions of us-becoming stronger and stronger-and we will complete the message."

David Ben-Gurion

"I will restore my people Israel.
   They shall rebuild ruined cities and inhabit them;
   They shall plant vineyards and drink their wine;
   They shall till gardens and eat their fruits.
   And I will plant them upon their soil,
     Nevermore to be uprooted
       From the soil I have given them
        Said the Lord your God."

Amos 9:14-15

*Chapter 4*
# ISRAEL'S BIRTH: MIRACLES DO HAPPEN

"In order to be a realist, you must believe in miracles."

David Ben-Gurion

"A people does not get a country on a silver platter."

Chaim Weizmann, Israel's first president,<br>referring to Natan Alterman's famous poem

"In fact this country was founded on a silver platter, made up of six million bodies."

Israeli General Yosi Peled [1]

"Israel was not created in order to disappear. Israel will endure and flourish. It is the child of hope and the home of the brave. It can neither be broken by adversity nor demoralized by success. It carries the shield of democracy and it honors the sword of freedom."

President John F. Kennedy

"Let us stand silent in memory of our dearly beloved sons and daughters who gave their lives for the liberation of our homeland and the security of our people. They gave us all they had. They poured out their very lifeblood for the freedom of Israel, even as the living waters quench the thirst of the arid soil. Not in monuments of stones or trees shall their memories be preserved, but in the reverence and pride which will, until the end of times, fill the hearts of our people when their memory is recalled."

David Ben-Gurion

Chapter 4

## *It's A Miracle* [2]
Music and lyrics by Rita Glassman,
From the CD *"A World of Peace in Song & Prayer."*
www.RitaGlassman.com  All Rights Reserved © 2015

It's a miracle, that we're here at all
after everything changed
the world was rearranged
It's a miracle that we didn't fall
when the earth began to shake
and our hearts started to break
It's a miracle that we didn't fall
that we're here, that we're here at all.

It's a miracle, when we break the wall
the one that divides, the one that only hides
It's a miracle, when we
hear the call
to lift up our voice
When we know it is our choice
It's a miracle, when we come to see
it's no good unless, every one of us,
every one of us is free

Every morning when we rise
somewhere there's a cry
somewhere there's a fire burning
When will this story end, can you be my friend?
Can the wheels of hate stop turning?

Maybe it's today, we will find a way
to see the grace of God in everyone
And if we are afraid, maybe we can pray
and soon enough the angels they will come

It's a miracle, we can love at all
after all that we lost
in a storm our lives were tossed
It's a miracle, just to dance and sing
after every shattered hope
to still believe in dreams
It's a miracle, what we're standing for
making peace, not war

being whole, not half
being home at last
in a world that's free
in a world of peace.


Between 70 C.E. and 1948 the Holy Land was conquered and reconquered many times, although a small remnant of Jews remained in the Land all along. Rabbi Abraham Joshua Heschel remarked that never before had a nation continued to hope for a return and then been restored to its ancient homeland after a lapse of almost two thousand years. [3]

To me, the establishment of the State of Israel is the stuff of dreams and miracles, along with amazing bravery and sacrifice. Theodor Herzl (1860-1904) dreamt of a Jewish State, that he believed was the only way Jews would have safety in the modern world. Subsequent to witnessing horrible anti-Semitic pogroms in Europe, Herzl came to the First Zionist Congress in Basel in 1897, determined to "lay the foundation stone of the house which is to shelter the Jewish nation."

The conference ended with all of the delegates singing *Hatikvah*, a song of hope.

## *Hatikvah* (The Hope)
### Naphtali Herz Imber (1886), Music by Samuel Cohen.

*Kol od balevav penimah,*
  *As long as in the heart within*
*Nefesh Yehudi homiyah*
  *the Jewish soul yearns,*
*Ulefa-atei-mizrach, kadimah*
  *And toward the eastern edges, onward*
*Ayin letzion tsofiah,*
  *an eye gazes toward Zion.*
*Od lo avdah tikvateinu*
  *Our hope is not yet lost,*
*Hatikva bat shnot alpayim,*
  *The hope that is two-thousand years old,*
*Lihyot am chofshi be-artzeinu,*
  *To be a free nation in our land,*
*Eretz Tzion, v'yirushalyim.*
  *The land of Zion and Jerusalem.*

## Chapter 4

Herzl wrote *The Jewish State* (1896), as part of his campaign for Jewish political self-emancipation. His slogan was: *"Im tirzu, ain zo agadah* – If you will it, it is no dream". In the novel, *Alteneuland*, (1902), Herzl imagined a flourishing society in Palestine, with the desert in bloom and multiple religions living in harmony.

Zionism, intended to transform the existential condition of the Jews, was a romantic idea inviting European Jews from "civilized" Europe to come to the Holy Land. Although the land was a rocky, swamp ridden, malarial, desert climate with few opportunities for employment, thousands of Jews fled Eastern Europe to work, build, and sing in their ancient land.

Chaim Weizmann, a scientist who had devised a method for distilling acetone in large quantities as a solvent for enhancing explosives, had a friendship with Lord Alfred James Balfour of the British Foreign Office. The British government was very interested in the usefulness of Weizmann's work for their World War I effort. When asked by the British Cabinet what Weizmann wanted as payment, Weizmann allegedly replied: "a homeland for my people in Palestine."

While other major geopolitical factors also contributed, the Balfour Declaration on November 3, 1917, was the first public recognition by world powers of the Jews' historic link to the land of Israel and the importance of a national Jewish homeland.

> Foreign Office
> November 2, 1917
>
> Dear Lord Rothschild,
> I have much pleasure in conveying to you, on behalf of His Majesty's Government, the following declaration of sympathy with the Jewish Zionist aspiration, which have been submitted to and approved by the Cabinet.
> "His Majesty's Government view with favour the establishment in Palestine of a national home for the Jewish people, and will use their best endeavors to facilitate the achievement of this object, it being clearly understood that nothing shall be done which may prejudice the civil and religious rights of existing non-Jewish communities in Palestine, or the rights and political status enjoyed by Jews in any other country."
> I should be grateful if you would bring this declaration to the knowledge of the Zionist Federation.
> Yours sincerely,
> Arthur James Balfour

The Balfour Declaration had a tremendous impact on stimulating immigration to Palestine, as well as Arab resentment and violence, which in turn, led to the creation of the Haganah to protect Jewish settlements.

With the breakup of the Ottoman Empire after World War I, Great Britain was given a Mandate over Palestine. In 1937 the British Peale Commission recommended partitioning the land, with 20% going to the Jews and 70-75% to the Arabs. Chaim Weizmann felt that "it would be foolish not to accept it, even if it were the size of a tablecloth."

In 1947, the Exodus, dubbed "the ship that launched a nation," left Baltimore harbor with a volunteer crew to rescue thousands of displaced children from the *Shoah* in Europe and bring them to Palestine. However, the British blockaded Haifa harbor and sent them to displaced persons camps. Fortunately, an outcry about the deplorable treatment of these refugees gained worldwide sympathy just at the time of political discussions about the need for a Jewish state.

In 1947, U.N. Resolution 181 dissolved the British Mandate and created the Partition Plan, dividing Palestine into two states, one Jewish and one Arab, with Jerusalem internationalized. On November 29, 1947, the U.N. General Assembly voted to adopt the plan – 33 in favor, 13 opposed, and 10 abstentions. Even though Abba Eban later called the 1948 borders "Auschwitz borders" to describe Israel's geographic vulnerability, the Jews accepted the plan, but the Arabs rejected it.

David Ben-Gurion (1806-1973), head of the provisional government and World Zionist Organization, was a visionary leader with a genius for building a national culture. He drafted the final version of the Israeli Declaration of Independence, and the following day, May 14, 1948 (5th of Iyar in the Hebrew calendar), Ben-Gurion went to Dizengoff House in Tel Aviv, (now called Independence Hall), where he announced the establishment of the State.

When I visited Independence Hall in recent years, chills still went up and down my spine as I watched the original film of Ben-Gurion addressing the People's Council, followed by the people's reactions and dancing in the streets.

The Declaration begins with "The land of Israel was the birthplace of the Jewish people and will be open to the immigration of Jews from all countries of their dispersion." The Declaration makes a commitment to "liberty, justice, and peace," and "full social and political equality of all citizens, without distinction of race, creed, or sex." It also guarantees freedom of conscience, worship, education, and culture. Set up as a parliamentary democracy based on proportional representation, Israel was intended to be a Jewish state with a majority Jewish population,

*David Ben-Gurion declares Israel's independence in Tel Aviv, beneath a large portrait of Theodor Herzl, founder of modern Zionism, on May 14, 1948 (5 Iyar 5708).*

along with the respect for the rule of law, rights of minorities, a free press, and free elections.

The new state of Israel was recognized the same night by the United States and three days later by the USSR. Shortly thereafter, the armies of seven Arab nations prepared to invade the fledgling State and throw the Jews into the sea to finish Hitler's job. Facing annihilation, the new state was fighting for its very existence. Without the Palmach and outside help, especially from the Soviet Union, another Holocaust would have befallen the Jews at the hands of the Arabs.

The stories in this chapter focus on the momentous days during the War for Independence, a brutal war that led to much loss of life and dislocation of populations on both sides. The first story is told from the perspective of a young person painfully watching the fall of Jerusalem's Old Jewish Quarter. The exodus of Jews slowly marching with their few belongings in a line out of the city was a scene eerily resembling what happened in Europe just years before. Despite the disaster, the boy was also able to experience a Bar Mitzvah in the midst of war.

Another story describes tactics of the Haganah and Jewish underground in their fight against both the British and the Arabs.

A story about volunteers from abroad shows how Jews around the world anxiously worried about little Israel's survival. Almost five thousand people tried to help by coming to fight in the War for Independence. Others volunteered in *Youth Aliyah* villages and kibbutzim to give shelter, education, and skills to young survivors to help them rebuild their fragmented lives.

Lastly, a story written in 1948 by an immigrant reflecting on the years of building the country since the late 19th century, shows the determination and hard work of the early Zionists.

Israel came to represent victory of life over death, hope over despair. As a Jew, I feel intense pride over Israel's birth and consider Israel a poster child for Post-Traumatic Growth, a phenomenon of becoming stronger and creating a more meaningful life in the wake of staggering trauma. Just bouncing back would be resilience, but in significant ways Israel bounced back higher than ever before. The slogan "Never again" heightened survivors' determination to affirm life, to start over, and to live life to its fullest.

Chapter 4

# A Tale of Two Bar Mitzvahs
## David Gamliel

On May 14, 1948, the last British soldier left Palestine. That evening Ben-Gurion declared Israel's independence, and joy and dancing broke out in the streets. It didn't take long, however, until the tears of joy turned into tears of sorrow. The road to Jerusalem was attacked and shut down, and many Jews were killed. After that, the armies of Syria and Iraq invaded from the north to attack and destroy the fledgling Jewish state, later joined by armies of five additional Arab countries.

The situation continued to worsen in the Old City, and despite heroic efforts, on Friday morning, May 28, 1948, the Jewish Quarter fell. Climbing on the roof of a building overlooking the Old City, I could see a long line of old men, women, and children walking sadly away from their homes. Then I saw another line of younger people being sent to prison. I began shaking, worrying what would happen to our home in the Old City.

Our house sat virtually on the "green line" dividing the Arab and Jewish areas of Jerusalem. With fighting raging all around, it became too dangerous there, and we were forced to move to temporary quarters. The Arab siege led to food and water shortages, and I was the one who went out in the midst of the shooting to get the slim rations for my whole family.

At the start of Israel's War of Independence I had just turned twelve years old. I was born in Jerusalem in 1936. My parents, Avraham and Rachel Gamliel, were immigrants from Yemen, a centuries-old Jewish community. Life in Yemen wasn't easy for Jews due to the many restrictions that were imposed, based on fanatic interpretation of the Koran.

As a child, my mother heard Bible stories about going to Jerusalem "on the wings of eagles." Instead, her husband sold everything and bought a donkey for my mother and sister to ride on as they journeyed from Yemen to the Holy Land, hiding by day and walking at night. My mother was inventive and made a pacifier out of a pebble wrapped in cloth to comfort and quiet my sister during the difficult and dangerous journey.

In Jerusalem, my father sold newspapers to support the family. He became known as "king of the newspapers." One bitterly cold snowy day in the winter of 1944 he went out in scant footwear despite my mother's protests. He caught pneumonia, and due to a shortage of antibiotics, he died at age 38, leaving my mother a widow with eight children. My mother did her best to support us, selling newspapers by day and washing floors in office buildings by night. My mother was a *tzadeket* (righteous woman) who would share food with poor children. Her illiteracy did not prevent her from doing good work her whole life, until she died at age 96.

As the first boy in the family, I became the man of the house at age eight. I got up at 4:00 a.m., *davened*, and by 4:30 ran to the print shop to get the newspapers for delivery and sale on the street. From 7:00 a.m. until 5:00 p.m. I was in school, and then I ran back to sell evening newspapers. Only later could I do my schoolwork. I worked in this manner to help support my family through high school.

At age ten I secretly helped my oldest sister in the Haganah. When Israeli soldiers were injured, I ran to get dirt to cover their blood and erase the scent, so that British soldiers' dogs couldn't find them. During the siege, the Arabs had all kinds of weapons and tanks, while the Israelis had only one thousand rifles. My peers and I would run and distribute the rifles to different locations to make it look like we had more weapons than we actually had.

*David Gamliel, 8 years old, preparing his newspapers for sale.*

Little by little the situation started to improve. My mother felt that since I was already acting as a man, it was time for me to become a Bar Mitzvah. Although the usual age is 13, some say that an orphan, by virtue of greater life experience, should become Bar Mitzvah at age twelve. But who had money to buy tefillin? Certainly not us. We decided that the only option was to retrieve my dead father's tefillin from the deserted family home near the fighting.

Making our way through a network of trenches and sandbags, with sporadic gunfire around us, my mother and I reached the door of our empty house. Crouching low, mother removed her white kerchief from her head and held it aloft on a stick. As if on cue, a Jordanian sniper's bullet ricocheted off the stone wall of the house. Knowing that the sniper would take a few seconds to reload, my mother immediately reached up and shoved the house key into the lock. Again, she held her

## Chapter 4

kerchief up on the stick and was answered with another whizzing bullet. This time, she quickly turned the key and opened the front door. For the third time, she waved her kerchief on the stick, and after the third bullet we both hurled ourselves across the threshold and slammed the steel door of the house shut.

Our house was a mess because soldiers had used it as a defensive position. The rainwater barrels on the roof were riddled with bullet holes, and water had leaked into the rooms below. The little remaining furniture was scattered and overturned.

"Ima, how do we even know that the tefillin will still be here?" I asked.

"Don't you worry, son," my mother answered with a confidence born of sheer desperation. "Hashem would not let anyone but you dare to take your dead father's tefillin. The Almighty has been keeping them safe for you for this day."

Sure enough, when I reached into the back of the shelf in the dusty armoire, my father's tefillin bag was there, waiting.

We fortunately made it back without being seen by the Jordanian snipers stationed on the Old City walls who would randomly shoot mortar rounds through the thin corrugated metal barrier wall. Back in the shelter with my father's tefillin and nothing to do, I decided that it was a perfect morning for my Bar Mitzvah. The closest shul was a one-room Mughrabi synagogue down the street. I ducked outside, crouching and hugging the exterior stone walls, with my father's tefillin bag hanging from my clenched teeth, carefully making my way down the street. The whistling of an incoming mortar round was a signal to crouch in a doorway and wait. After the inevitable explosion, there would be a brief quiet period during which I crawled closer to the shul. I figured that every bomb has an address, and when it is my time, it would find me.

I pounded with my fists on the door of the shul, and old Rabbi Shlush answered, asking what I wanted.

"My mother says I need to become a Bar Mitzvah," I explained. Rabbi Shlush's face lit up.

"In that case, by all means, come right in my dear boy!"

After ushering me inside, the Rabbi called out to the street from the window of the shul: "Yitzchak! Moshe! *Bo'u* – come!"

Two older men temporarily abandoned their positions and burst through the door and voiced concern: *"Hakol beseder?* – Is everything all right?"

"Come and do a mitzvah," the Rabbi instructed. "This young boy needs to lay tefillin for the first time."

The frail Rabbi showed me how to lay tefillin according to the Yemenite tradition. My father's tefillin seemed oversized on my twelve year old arm, but the soft leather felt comforting. The hasty *shacharit* (morning) prayer was interrupted by the staccato of intermittent gunfire and the "boom" of periodic mortar rounds. Only a little farther to the east, in the ravaged Jewish Quarter, stood the Kotel (Western Wall), defiled, desolate, and unreachable. Who knew how many generations would have to pass before Jews would again be able to approach the massive, timeless stones to pour out their hearts before God?

Having finished *shacharit*, I rewound my newly inherited tefillin while Rabbi Shlush rested his hands on my head to bless me, Yitzchak and Moshe were becoming restless to return to their positions. As they were about to leave, one dug his dusty hand into his pants pocket, and with a satisfied grin on his face, he pried a sticky old candy from the pocket and tenderly tossed it at me, nicking my ear. "Mazel tov," he winked. And with that, the men left to retake their positions. That was *my* Bar Mitzvah.

Fast forward to the spring of 2014 when my grandson, Natan, celebrated his Bar Mitzvah in a large synagogue in Baltimore. Unlike me, Natan waited until age 13 because his father, my oldest son, is alive. Like me, Natan inherited a pair of tefillin from his father, but under much happier circumstances. Natan led the service, chanted Torah and Haftorah during a wonderful and spiritually uplifting service. Yet something felt incomplete, as if some unfinished business remained.

So on a Thursday morning in June in Jerusalem, the extended Gamliel clan gathered around me, their Saba David, now the family patriarch, at Azarat Yisrael, the Masorti area at the southern end of the Kotel. Righting the wrongs of history, my first grandchild Natan led the large family gathering in morning prayers and expertly chanted the Torah portion. No longer cowering in the sights of Jordanian snipers, Jews by the thousands were now flocking to the Kotel. The Jewish Quarter, destroyed not so long ago, was now beautifully rebuilt and filled with life.

Unlike the musical background of my Bar Mitzvah – bombs – the descendants of Avraham and Rachel Gamliel were loudly and joyfully celebrating together, singing and dancing under the comforting gaze of the Kotel in the eternal Holy City. While I am normally a stoic person, I wept openly with joy. Choked up and wiping happy salty tears on my tallit, I looked upward to Heaven and whispered:

"*Baruch atah Adonai, eloheinu melech haolam, shehecheyanu vekiyemanu vehigianu lazman hazeh.*"

Chapter 4

# A Palestinian Jew:
## Dreamer, Soldier, Builder, and Philanthropist
### Nick Dahan

My father, Aharon Dahan, was a "son of Tiberias", an ancient city that was the seat of the Sanhedrin following the second Temple period, one of four spiritual centers in Israel where codification of the Oral Law occurred, and the Jerusalem Talmud was compiled. Tiberias was a city of mixed religions, ethnicities, and histories, with Jews there all along. The Christians came in the 5th century, Muslims conquered it in the 7th century, and the Crusaders arrived later. The city was built up in the 14th to 18th centuries, and in 1771 Hasidic Jews from Europe came. My father's ancestors came at least two hundred years before the establishment of the State.

Aharon's father worked by leasing spaces to merchants in the marketplace. He built a modest home in Kiryat Shmuel, a Jewish settlement outside the old city. In Tiberias, Arabs and Jews, (both Ashkenazic and Sephardic) lived and worked together, speaking Arabic, Hebrew, and some Aramaic. My father was born in 1925 in a Catholic hospital, where the clerk named him Haron, in honor of the Arab Caliph, Haron el-Rashid, a courageous soldier and just leader, who promoted education. My father's given Hebrew name was Aharon, named after Moses' brother, the High Priest who sought peace and unity. I can honestly say that my father lived up to both of his names.

When Aharon was ten, a generous man paid for him to attend Talmud Torah. Aharon admired this trait of helping others to acquire education, and dreamed that someday he would be able to do the same for others.

From his father, Aharon learned the virtues of discipline, hard work, and overcoming obstacles.

From his mother, he learned generosity and the desire to help others, especially needy people.

From his family, he learned to appreciate one's portion in life, as in the proverb, "He is rich who is content with his lot."

Aharon was a dreamer and believed Herzl's words: *"Im tirzu ein zo agada* – If you will it, it is no dream." Herzl's speech, the Balfour Declaration, and the British taking Palestine as a mandate, strengthened Aaron's conviction that a Jewish homeland was a moral imperative to provide a safe haven for Jews worldwide.

In the 1920s the Arabs became increasingly resentful of Jewish immigration to Palestine, and violence against Jews erupted in 1920, 1921, and subsequent riots in Hebron, Jerusalem, Jaffa, and Haifa in

1929. In 1939 a violent mob attacked the neighborhood where Aharon's family lived, killing some of their neighbors. An Arab named Musa, who rented space from Aharon's father, saved the family from the angry mob. Overnight their world had changed. No longer feeling safe, the family relocated to Haifa, a community that was protected by the Haganah.

At age 17, Aharon joined the Haganah to patrol the beaches and guard against German submarines, as Jews developed a force to protect themselves. At age 18, Aharon learned elite truck driving skills in the British Navy. However, the British became obstacles when they strictly limited Jewish immigration to Palestine. Aharon then joined the *"Irgun Tzva-ee Leumi"* (Etzel), an underground that was more extremist than the Haganah.

Arms were desperately needed by the underground. In one episode Aharon and fifty other Irgun members disguised themselves in British military uniforms and drove to a British base in northern Israel. Presenting the necessary documents, they were admitted, and then stole all of the ammunition and weapons in dozens of trucks. Two months later, after ambushing a train carrying British weapons from Gaza to Haifa, they threatened that unless British soldiers cooperated with them, another mine would explode. Forty British soldiers scrambled to help unload ammunition for the Irgun ... even though there was no second mine.

After the U.N. General Assembly adopted the Partition Plan on November 29, 1947, the Arabs ambushed a Jewish bus near Lydda, initiating the war. The focus now shifted to a fight for survival and independence. After capturing Yahudia, Irgun and Lehi forces attacked Deir Yassin, where many Arab women and children were killed and many others fled.

Jaffa fell into Jewish hands on May 13, 1948. While Israeli Independence was declared on May 14, 1948, there was no time to celebrate, as the surrounding Arab countries invaded.

There was not yet a national army as the various undergrounds operated independently, with their own leader, power base, troops, and often conflicting politics and strategies. Along with the threat posed by fighting the Arabs, the Israelis faced an existential threat from within. Integrating all of the fighting groups into one standing army, the Israel Defense Forces, was a politically difficult task.

During the first ceasefire in the war, a dispute over an Irgun-organized shipment of weapons from Europe on a vessel called the Altalena threatened an outbreak of civil war. Menachem Begin, head of the Irgun, boarded the ship as it approached the shore where hundreds of Israeli soldiers were waiting on a Tel Aviv beach. Begin had negotiated with Ben-Gurion, commander of the Israel Defense Forces, where the ship should dock and who would get what weapons. When Begin ordered the ship to dock near the beach instead of the agreed upon location, Ben-Gurion ordered the ship destroyed and set ablaze with Begin, a would-be Prime Minister, still aboard. Some Irgun soldiers were even considering deserting the army to support him.

Begin managed to get ashore, and Aharon drove and escorted him to a radio station to address the nation. Tensions mounted as the future of a unified state was at risk. However, at the radio station, Begin showed real statesmanship, calling for unity and not war, saying: "There will be no fraternal strife while the foe is at the gate." He ordered his soldiers back to their army bases. Two days later the temporary truce with the Arabs fell apart and war resumed, but this time the Arabs faced a united people.

Aharon served in the 82nd Tank Battalion in the 8th Armored Brigade, capturing Lydda airport as a base, and then going south to fight key battles. After twenty months of fighting, the war ended in January 1949. Ben-Gurion and Chaim Weizmann began building the institutions of democracy and absorbing waves of immigrants into a state without financial resources. Reflecting on those days, my father said: "We were willing to sacrifice everything in order to have our independence. It was a historic moment and a time of immense pride as nothing was more important than accomplishing the mission of uniting the Jewish people for future generations. Everybody was on fire." Aharon felt proud to be part of the military escort protecting Chaim Weizmann when he went to Jerusalem for the inauguration.

My father served in the army for 18 years, fighting in three wars to help protect the country. He believed that the "Jews' overcoming obstacles to accomplish the seemingly impossible helped define the Israeli character: confidence in beliefs and goals, and faith in what you can do." Aharon counseled others not to be afraid to dream, reminding them that "when Herzl dreamed the State of Israel, everybody made fun of him and thought he was a nut," but look at what he accomplished.

My mother's family came from generations of "Palestinian" Sephardim, ancestors who survived the Spanish Inquisition. My maternal great grandparents were among the first sixty-six families who founded the city of Tel Aviv in 1909, recorded in an iconic photo on the sand dunes that testifies to that momentous event.

My parents moved to the United States in 1958 when I was seven years old. Through hard work my father became a successful builder and businessman. He never forgot the needy, and became a true *Baal*

*The founding families of Tel Aviv gathered together in 1909 on the beach.*

*Tzedakah*. He took philanthropy extremely seriously, emulating the generous man who helped him attend school when he was a child. My father used his wealth to foster Jewish education and identity by creating Beth Tfiloh High School in Baltimore. Together with my mother, Rachel, they created a foundation to support scholarships for Russian and Sephardic students, a Center for Sephardic Culture, a Unity Park, departments in Bar Ilan University, and hospitals in both Israel and America, fulfilling the values with which they were raised. Before he died my father generously helped launch the new Bar Ilan Medical School in Tzfat (Safed).

I have been enriched by my parents' values of family strength, dreaming, working hard, and giving back to the community. Their lives have inspired me to live up to their good names and devote my energies to working for economic prosperity, freedom, and peace for Israel and her neighbors.

*Chapter 4*

## *From The Pampas To The Negev: A Volunteer From Abroad*
In Memory of Dr. Salvador Minuchin (1921-2017)
### Israela Meyerstein

From 1971 to 1972, I was a social work intern at Hadassah Hospital in the Departments of Pediatrics and Child Psychiatry. It was there that I had the opportunity to observe Family Therapy sessions conducted by Dr. Avner Barcai, a therapist trained by Dr. Salvador (Sal) Minuchin. I was mesmerized by the sessions, and decided then to become a family therapist. I read everything I could find about family therapy, and came across a beautiful article about *"An Ecological Framework in the Treatment of a Child"* by Salvador Minuchin. At the end of the article, a footnote described Minuchin as an Argentinian Jew who came to fight in Israel's War for Independence.

I was intrigued to learn Minuchin's therapeutic perspective and touched by his commitment to Jewish survival. Looking back over the years, I am grateful that I had the opportunity to attend many of his workshops, receive supervision from him as a mentor, and develop a warm personal friendship with him and his wife, Pat, over the past

*Dr. Salvador Minuchin, 2012.*

twenty years. With his recent death, the family therapy field has lost one of its pioneers and founding fathers. Sal was a brilliant theoretician, innovative practitioner, and teacher of Structural Family Therapy, who inspired thousands of therapists around the world during his more than seventy-year career. He was especially popular in Israel, where he visited often to do family therapy workshops and trainings, while also visiting his closest family relatives.

The following is Sal's story, much of which I heard directly from him. Sal was the grandson of Lithuanian immigrants who fled Russian pogroms in the 19th century. His grandfather became a farmer in the province of Entre Rios, Argentina, on land that had been purchased by Baron de Hirsh for Jewish immigrants. Sal described his hometown of San Salvador as a Russian *shtetl* transported to Argentina. He grew up surrounded by extended family and a tightly organized Jewish community. In the midst of a larger Argentinian culture that was mostly anti-Semitic, the Jews stuck together and felt responsible for one another.

Sal was the oldest child in his family, and developed a sense of responsibility, loyalty, and leadership. He learned fairness, honesty, and justice from his father, and helpfulness from his mother. At age 20 Sal went to medical school. In the 1940s, when the Argentinian dictator Juan Peron took control of the universities, Sal joined the student revolts, and was jailed together with other students. He credits his strength to challenge authority in the pursuit of justice to this early experience. Sal completed medical school in 1946 and took a residency in Pediatrics, specializing in medical psychology.

In 1948, Sal was setting up a pediatric practice. When war broke out in Israel, he decided to join the fight for Israel's survival and independence as a nation. He sold his equipment, took brief training in emergency procedures, and joined a group of Argentinian men and women who set off for Israel. There he served as a doctor in the Fourth Regiment of the *Palmach*. Sal recounted how overwhelming it was for him to go from an office setting, to learning a new language, and carrying life and death responsibilities for the lives of young soldiers, who had come from around the world to fight. He added, however, that they all were very committed and worked together, feeling that Israel's fate was in their hands.

After the war Sal went to America in 1950 to study psychiatry. He married in 1951, and immigrated to Israel together with his wife. Sal became the co-director with Shulamit Klebanoff of residential institutions for disturbed children for *Youth Aliyah*. The Youth Villages took in Holocaust orphans from Europe, as well as young refugees from Arab countries. Sal credits this experience with giving him greater understanding of the importance of culture and context, which greatly influenced his later work with families. He came to view perplexing behaviors of traumatized children as rooted in their wartime experiences or cultural background, rather than as emotional pathology. He also observed the benefits of structure and group support in helping these children rebuild their lives.

Returning to the United States as an immigrant, Sal personally experienced the challenges of a new language. From his early years in Argentina as part of a minority, and the poverty his family experienced during the Depression, Sal developed a strong commitment to help poor people and victims of discrimination. He described them as "my Jews" and felt that "all people who suffer injustice are my brothers." Sal and his wife, Pat, a developmental psychologist, worked tirelessly to try and improve institutions that dealt with the poor, such as New York's foster care system.

To me, Sal was more than a master therapist, teacher, and friend. He was a heroic figure who used the force of his personality in the pursuit of justice and repairing the world. I believe he expressed his Jewish spirituality through *Tikkun Olam* (repairing the world). Sal's work was about the holy task of improving the world by helping the underserved in our midst with love and dignity.

## From Russia to Redemption in the Land of our Forefathers
### Zodek Mazo, 1948

The Mazos were a small family who lived in the environs of Borisov in White Russia. Rabbi Mazo, my great-grandfather, was the crown of our family. In 1788, during the lifetime of my great-grandparents, all of the Jews, like my relatives, settled in the villages belonging to the rich landowners, and would lease land, flour mills, and inns from them.

These were hard times for the Jews and the non-Jews alike. By 1850, the struggle for freedom became strong in Russia, and at the beginning of Czar Alexander II's reign, the peasants were emancipated. The Jews now faced competition for jobs, and from then on, Jews began to leave for the larger cities.

By 1881, the Zionist idea of building Palestine became strong in Russia. This was the beginning of the time of Herzl and the Lovers of Zion. Many Jews left Russia to work in the land of Palestine. Among them was my oldest brother, Nathan, who joined the colonies that were under the supervision of Baron Rothschild.

In 1894, the cruel Czar Alexander III died, and his son, Nicholas II, became Czar. Called the "bloody king," Nicholas was assassinated by the Bolshevicks in 1918. During these troubled times of revolution and war, our family realized that they had to leave Russia. After continued troubles in Bolshevik Russia, our family was able to get out in 1925 and make our way to Palestine.

We have been here for 23 years. It hasn't been easy to come with a family and get established. But we have overcome our difficulties, and we have had the privilege of living a free life here, with free immigration, and freedom to buy land. We are elated that we are in the land of our forefathers, the land where our people will be redeemed.

We have seen the building of our land with our own eyes: the great achievements in agriculture, industry, art, and the rebirth of our language. The sands have been transformed into villages and fruitful cities that number over three hundred, and are being tilled according to the most modern methods. New beautiful cities have been built, such as Tel Aviv. And all this has been the work of our own people, our *chalutzim* (pioneers) who gave their lives for the replenishing of our land. We continue to work, even though the struggle is great. We are hopeful that we will overcome all of the obstacles by hard work.

The great tragedy that overcame our people in Europe has proven that there is no place for redemption other than in the land of our

## Chapter 4

forefathers. The generation that will come after us, the youth that is born here, and the youth that will come from the remnants of the Diaspora, will strengthen and finish the beloved rebuilding of our land, and cause this prophesy to come true:

"One by one, you will gather unto the house of Israel, and instead of the thorn, shall the cypress come up, and instead of the nettle shall the myrtle tree come up. The mountains and the hills shall break forth before you singing, and all of the trees of the field shall clap their hands when G-d will return the Jews to Zion."

*Postscript:* Zodek Mazo was a cousin of Chaim Mazo, the publisher of this book. Zodek's message to the future generations to strengthen and continue the rebuilding of Israel helped to influence Chaim and his family to make *Aliyah* in 1994.

*Chapter 5*

# INGATHERING OF THE EXILES: A NATION OF IMMIGRANTS

"I will put My breath in you and you shall live again, and I will set you upon your own soil."

Ezekiel 37:14

A Song of Ascents: When Adonai returned us to Zion we were like dreamers.

Psalm 126

"I carried you on wings of eagles."

Ex. 19:4

"And I will return from captivity My people Israel; they shall rebuild the ruined cities and live in them."

Amos 9:14

When the new Israeli Knesset (parliament) convened on February 14, 1949, Israel's first President, Chaim Weizmann, announced that the aim of the Jewish state would be first and foremost to "gather in the exiles from all parts of the world." This certainly included survivors of the *Shoah*, but also the 750,000 Jews who were expelled from Muslim lands when Israel declared statehood. Because Jews had been shut out of so many countries, Israel's purpose was to be a homeland where all Jews could freely enter and immediately become citizens.

Israel definitely needed Jews to settle, build, and defend the land, and Israel's population has actually increased tenfold since the founding of the state. Relative to its size, Israel has absorbed more immigrants than any other nation, with newcomers from every continent and over one hundred countries, arriving in multiple waves of immigration. The varied ethnic traditions from which immigrants came created a rich tapestry and contributed significantly to Israel's development as a diverse, multicultural society.

Israel organized numerous missions to rescue Jews to safety from Muslim countries: Operation Magic Carpet (from Yemen, Aden, Djibouti, Eritrea, Saudi Arabia); Operations Ezra and Nehemiah (from Iraq); From Ethiopia: Operations Moses (1984-5) and Shlomo (1991); and the vast immigration of over a million Russian Jews from the Soviet Union in the 1970s and 80s. The absorption of such huge numbers of immigrants from different socioeconomic, educational, and cultural backgrounds created huge strains on housing resources and employment, with immigrants lingering in transitional housing for long periods of time. Cultural and language absorption was done creatively through *Ulpanim* – intensive language courses.

While the process of immigrant absorption was and is difficult, Israel was truly built on the power of immigrants, so it is only fitting that a new holiday was created to honor them. Called First *Aliyah* Day, it is celebrated on the seventh day of the Jewish month of Heshvan, corresponding to the Torah portion of *Lech Lecha,* in which God commanded Abraham to leave his home in Haran (Iraq) and go up or "make *Aliyah*" to the Promised Land.

The varied stories about immigration in this chapter are inspiring because of the risks involved in leaving one's home, and the sacrifices required for starting over in a new land, culture, and environment. Some Jews made *Aliyah* as a religious injunction to return to Zion, and others were motivated by Herzl's message about a Jewish state. Many came due to worsening conditions for Jews in their country of origin. Jews' lives in Muslim countries became increasingly dangerous, and many had to flee or were kicked out. Some came seeking better education and quality of life in Israel, while others wanted personal and religious freedom to express themselves as Jews. And some came from rural villages in Africa, affected by hunger, drought, and instability. And others came because they wanted to live their lives fully in their ancestral Jewish homeland.

## Destination: Return to Zion
### Shlomo Alima

"By the river of Babylon
We sit down and weep
When we remember Zion..."

Psalm 137:1-2

My family comes from generations of living in Iraq, the oldest Jewish Diaspora community in the world, and a leading center of Jewish learning, with famous academies that gave rise to the Babylonian Talmud and much scholarship. After Babylonia fell to Persia, King Cyrus gave the Jews permission to return to Judea in 537 B.C.E., and according to the Bible, 40,000 did so. Perhaps you could call them the original Zionists.

In more modern times Iraqi Jews were a prominent, highly visible, and prosperous minority in urban and commercial centers. By 1900 Jews made up 1/3 of the population of Baghdad, around 80,000 people. They built many educational institutions, hospitals, and numerous synagogues. In fact, Iraq was the second largest *Mizrachi* (eastern) community numbering 130,000.

My family story is about leaving everything behind to pursue our Jewish destiny in the historic land of Israel. Daily prayers and rituals instilled a passion in my ancestors to return to Zion. My grandfather, Salach, believed that a Jewish person should live in the Holy Land. His brother, Tzion, a Rabbi who had already set up a yeshiva in Jerusalem, encouraged him to come.

Although Salach lived a comfortable economic life as a fabrics merchant, owned two stores, and traveled on business trips to India, he was willing to sell everything and go to Jerusalem, even without any promise of material sustenance there. In the midst of winter 1925, Salach and his pregnant young wife, Chana, left Baghdad with few belongings to embark on a long and dangerous overland journey. Money from selling his stores was used to bribe people for rides on donkeys, camels, bicycles, and taxis. The more than two-month journey through Syria and Lebanon had to be done largely at night to avoid detection, which would have resulted in death. Finally they reached and crossed the border into northern Palestine.

Salach and his family settled in the Bet Yisrael neighborhood near Mea Shearim in Jerusalem, where Salach wound up doing odd jobs to support his family. Eventually he bought a tiny two-room house with

*Chapter 5*

*This picture is from the wedding of Shlomo Alima's parents.*

no running water and an outdoor bathroom. Water had to be carried in buckets from the end of the neighborhood, and there was only cold water for showers. One day when Salach was on line for free food, some people suggested he change his name in Hebrew to "Mizrachi," since he came from the east.

In that little home, Salach and Chana raised twelve children, four girls and eight boys. My mother, Shulamit was the second oldest. All the children had to work because the family was very poor. For Jews from Arab lands without a secular education, few economic opportunities existed, so they took whatever jobs were possible. My mother regretted that all she could do was clean houses, but it was needed for the economic survival of the family.

At age 18 my mother married Nuriel Alima, whose family came from Baakuba, Iraq. Nuriel was born in 1917, and in the 1930s he left his family and went to Palestine. The Mizrachi family acquired the distribution rights to the Palestine Post, and Nuriel was in charge of deliveries of the newspaper in Jerusalem. In 1947 the paper began to be called The Jerusalem Post in anticipation of statehood.

On the morning of December 31, 1947, Nuriel headed to work. Although he was warned not to enter a certain neighborhood for safety reasons, he dismissed the concerns because he felt well known in the neighborhood. Unbeknownst to him, however, the British had informed some Arabs that he was coming. When Nuriel passed the British checkpoint, the Arab National Guard stopped and searched him, let him pass, and then shot him in the back, stabbed him to death, and set fire to all of his papers. His burnt body was found a few hours later. He was only thirty years old when he died, leaving a wife, daughter, and two-year-old son ... me.

On January 1, 1948, my father was the last Jewish person to be buried in the cemetery on *Har Hazaytim* (Mount of Olives) as access to it was closed to Jews. It wasn't until July of 1967 that I was able to visit his grave to set a stone in his memory. On *Har Herzl* his name appears on a monument listing civilians who died in terrorist acts. For my mother, sister, and myself, life became very hard, so we moved into my grandparents' little house. My father was not the only casualty to war and death in my family. Within three months, my mother lost her closest brother, Meir, in the War for Independence. After that double blow, my mother was changed forever and closed up emotionally.

During the War for Independence, most of my family fought with the Lechi/Etzel. My mother's sister went to fight in the Palmach. After the war, they were sent to establish border settlements and kibbutzim to cultivate the land. Together with others, they established Kibbutz Rosh Hanikra, located coincidentally just around where my grandparents had crossed into Palestine in 1925.

Conditions for Jews in Iraq over the decades began to worsen, and in 1941, a violent "Farhud" consisting of riots, murder, destruction of homes and property was unleashed against Jews in Baghdad, perhaps signaling the beginning of the end for Iraqi Jews. After 1945 there were frequent demonstrations, discrimination, dismissals from jobs, fines, and military trials of Jews. As the decision to establish a Jewish state in Palestine approached, life became increasingly unsafe for Jews. Respected Jewish businessmen were hanged publically in October 1948. When Iraq attacked the new state of Israel in collaboration with other Arab armies, Iraqi Jews were viewed as a fifth column. When Jews could leave, their property and financial resources were seized. In 1950-51 the Israeli government organized a massive airlift out of Iraq via Iran and Cyprus that brought 130,000 Jews to Israel. The rescue, called Operation Ezra and Nehemiah, was named after the prophets who led the Jewish people from exile in Babylonia to return to Israel in the 6th century B.C.E.

Although the older generation of my family wasn't highly educated, they always worked hard and contributed to the growth of the nation. I was the first in my family to graduate high school and college. Other members of the younger generation went to university after the army,

*Chapter 5*

becoming nurses, cancer researchers, special education teachers, businessmen, and lawyers. Our family certainly followed the Biblical commandment of *"p'ru urevu* – be fruitful and multiply", as by the time my grandmother Chana died at age 100 in the year 2000, there were nearly fifty grandchildren and almost sixty great-grandchildren living all over the land, from Rosh Hanikra in the north to Eilat in the south, and from Rehovot and Hod Hasharon to Jerusalem.

When I reflect on my family I realize that we were part of one of the most climactic events of the Jewish exodus from Arab and Moslem lands. I remain awed by the courage and determination it took to leave their birthplaces, homes, and businesses in Iraq. In Palestine they lived through difficult and tragic experiences in the building of the State of Israel. Yet they were motivated and inspired by the age-old yearning to return to Zion, their homeland, as envisioned by the prophets:

"There is hope for your future, says the Lord, and your children shall come back to their country." (Jeremiah 31:15-17).

## My Mother Rachel: Seeking Better Education for Women
### Dr. Janette Lazarovits

As a child there were many times when I couldn't understand why my mother did certain things, such as not allowing us to socialize with other neighborhood children. Now as a grandmother myself, I realize that she wanted us have lives different from the culture from which she came. My mother Rachel was born in 1936 on the small island of Djerba, Tunisia, where over 80% of the Jews were Cohanim (Priestly class). Djerba was known for its silver filigree and elaborate gold-plated headdresses and necklaces, a craft handed down from generation to generation.

The Jews of Djerba trace their roots to the Babylonian exile from Judea in 586 B.C.E. Later after the destruction of the second Temple in 70 C.E. and exile, many Cohanim settled in the Jewish quarters, where they spoke Arabic, Hebrew, and later French in the bigger cities of Tunisia. They dressed like their Muslim neighbors in red felt hats, tunics, and pantaloons, but Jews wore a special black band at the bottom of the pantaloons as a sign of mourning for the destruction of the Temple.

In 1942, Tunisia was the only Arab country to be completely occupied by Hitler, whose work was easier because the Jews already lived in ghettos. The Nazis imposed anti-Semitic policies: making Jews wear the yellow star, pay fines, and risk confiscation of property. Five thousand Jews were sent to forced labor camps and over 150 to European death camps.

When my mother was six years old, her mother died during childbirth when the Germans wouldn't permit a doctor to enter the ghetto. Rachel's father, a wealthy businessman, remarried a beautiful young woman, so Rachel grew up in a step-family of ten kids: six from her parents and four more from her step-mother. Like other girls in her community, Rachel never received an education and was illiterate. She didn't have an easy life, but her father trusted her, and he gave her his money to safeguard for him.

At the age of 18, Rachel married Mordecai Bashiri, who came from a Klezmer musician family originally from Yemen. In the Djerba community, marriages were arranged, and the bride and groom did not meet until their wedding night. When Rachel got married, her father gave her jewelery and gold bars, perhaps to make up for her difficult childhood.

Rachel never liked the life style in Djerba: the lack of higher education for women, and the overly close living arrangements and responsibilities for extended family. She was an individualist and feminist ahead of her time in her support for equal rights and education for women. She knew that it would be better for us to grow up in a different culture with more opportunities. Soon after marriage Rachel expressed her wish to go to Israel, and since my father was a Zionist, their ideas and desires complemented each other.

My parents left their beautiful house, active business, friends, and family with four children and a fifth on the way to immigrate to Israel. I was four and a half years old the day we left. I remember that we woke up and were told to get dressed to go to France for a wedding. When we arrived there, we learned there was no wedding, but instead we got on a ship bound for Israel. My mother went into premature labor on the third day of our voyage and gave birth to my sister, her fifth child.

Upon arrival in Israel my family was sent to a transient-camp (called *Ma'abarot*) in Beer Sheva, where we lived for nine years. The *Sochnut* (the Jewish Agency that helped newcomers settle in Israel) put us in a neighborhood with immigrants (*olim*) from different countries of North Africa, but treated all the groups the same. This upset my mother because she wanted her girls and boys to get the best education available in the Holy Land, including a high level of math and science, which was not available in our neighborhood. She locked us in the house to avoid our being exposed to life style habits of other neighbors of which she disapproved.

My father worked as an employee in a factory. Three more children were born and for the first six or seven years we were poor, but my mother never created the feeling of poverty. I remember my mother always wearing the same yellow skirt without complaint. She would buy second hand clothing, recut it, and make into "new" clothing for us; you could say she was an early recycler. I remember being sent to the grocery to buy stale bread, and my mother would make a creative tasty meal with it.

So important was education to my mother that there were days when we didn't have food at home, but we always had what was needed for school. She made sure that we read, wrote, and did our homework, accepting no excuses. When my father came home from work he checked our homework as well. This may sound exceptional, but the results were exceptional as well.

My parents soon realized that my father's salary was not enough to support or give the best to such a big family, so they opened a shop similar to what my father had in Tunisia. But where would the money come from? My mother gave my father all of the jewelry and gold bars she had saved all those years. As a child I was impressed that our house always seemed clean and sparkling. My mother dressed up for when my father came home for his lunch break. My father treated my mother much better than the average woman of her time. My parents' relationship was loving, with mutual respect, close collaboration, and clear roles.

Despite the success of my father's business, my parents instilled in us modest behavior and a sense of responsibility for doing housework. My mother was a woman of great *chesed* (kindness) who taught us to be generous to the needy. As a teenager I remember going with my mother to deliver packages loaded with food, merchandise, and money to give to several poor families. She taught us about love in a family and between human beings. Today the business is still an active shop that supports at least twenty families in Beer Sheva.

My father trusted my mother in all ways around the house. She was a practical psychologist with common sense to solve problems, and her motto was to find happiness in the small successes of life. Although she was a homemaker, she pushed all of us, boys and girls alike, to get the best higher education in university. Today we are engineers, scientists, doctors, teachers, therapists, economists, and business people. During my master's studies in biochemistry my mother babysat for my little child and was very proud of me when I got my doctoral degree.

When there were no more babies in the house, and everyone was doing well, we encouraged my mother to attend a class near our house to finally learn to read. She had sacrificed so much for our education; now it was her turn. My mother taught us that determination and decisiveness can help one go far. Her ability to envision the future, be assertive, and seek better opportunities impacted future generations. She directed us to focus on education and the important things in life to be part of a healthy community and nation. While I miss my mother Rachel dearly, her teachings live on in all of us.

Chapter 5

## *Butterflies for Freedom and "Next Year in Jerusalem"*
## Israela Meyerstein

Looking at my watch, I couldn't believe it was 10:00 p.m., because the sky was still bright, this evening in early June 1972, during "veisse nacht" (White nights of the Arctic Circle). While the light sky made it easier to find our way to the apartment we were about to visit, we still felt anxious wandering in an unfamiliar city.

We were in Leningrad, (now St. Petersburg) the Soviet Union, as part of our trip, or I should say, mission. For months my husband and I, who were living as students in Israel for the year, had been planning this trip. Idealistically inspired by the Student Struggle for Soviet Jewry, we wanted to do our part. We visited absorption centers in Jerusalem to meet Russian immigrants and get contact information for their relatives, who had been prevented from leaving the Soviet Union. We planned to visit them and give them *chizuk* – moral support.

To prepare for our trip we collected Jewish ritual objects such as kippot, Jewish stars, several prayer books, and even a translation of Exodus into Russian. If discovered, these items would certainly be confiscated. We even packed a special cigarette lighter with an Israeli flag designed on it. By turning the top around and striking it, the lighter played *Hatikvah*. A further "red flag" was that we would be travelling alone as a couple, rarely acceptable in Russia, where mostly group tours were common.

Arriving the day after President Richard Nixon had left, we learned that one week before, Representative Charles Schumer of New York had been strip-searched at the airport after visiting Russian Jewish Refuseniks. We had taught ourselves the Cyrillic alphabet so we could read street signs and not call attention to ourselves, and we obtained maps to help us navigate our way around on the subways.

No, this was clearly not a tourist vacation. We didn't even tell our parents in the United States about it. As immigrants who fled Europe, they wouldn't understand why anyone in their right mind would go there. I guess we were idealistic, inspired by Elie Wiesel's "The Jews of Silence". To us, the slogan "never again" meant that we must protest when Jews were in trouble, something that didn't happen enough during World War II.

In Moscow we contacted and visited several prominent Refuseniks, Jews who were denied exit visas: Vladimir and Marina Slepak and their circle of friends. We were awed by their courage and *chutzpah* (daring). They would go out on their small balcony to access Kol Yisrael on their ham radios, and they conducted a Hebrew speaking group as well. One Russian Jew who took us around in Moscow insisted that we speak Hebrew together with him on the subway. In Minsk we visited an aging, decorated Jewish World War II general, whose apartment was filled with packed cartons. He wanted to be ready to leave immediately if and when his family got permission to leave for Israel.

In Riga we met a group of spirited young Jews who had already lost their jobs in reprisal for applying for an exit visa. On June 6, they invited us to join them for a walk to the Post Office to send a congratulatory telegram to Golda Meir on the fifth anniversary of the Six Day War victory, an event that had galvanized Russian Jewish identity and pride. We felt nervous because any gathering of more than five people was considered to be unlawful assembly by the government, yet we felt obliged to accompany them since they risked everything. We hoped that our American passports would save us if necessary. Fortunately, when the Militia came to break up the gathering, no one was arrested.

And now we are in Leningrad, where we did some daytime sightseeing. Our evening visit that night before leaving the country the next day was our main reason for being there. We were coming to visit Yeva Butman, the wife of Hillel Butman, to offer moral support. Hillel Butman, a Leningrad born engineer, was sentenced to a ten-year prison term for his role in organizing a plot to hijack a Russian airplane to Sweden in 1970. He and other Jews undertook a defiantly symbolic act to alert the world to the plight of Soviet Jewry, who were forbidden to emigrate. Although he was not one of the hijackers, he was arrested and became one of the Prisoners of Conscience.

Approaching the neighborhood, we were struck by the enormity of the apartment buildings. We found the address and made our way to the apartment number we were given. After knocking on the door and telling who we were, the heavy door was opened cautiously. A woman introduced herself as Yeva Butman, Hillel's wife. With her were two other women relatives. She thanked us for coming and ushered us into a simple living room. We expressed our sympathy about her husband being in prison and inquired about his health and wellbeing. Yeva described Hillel as having quiet strength, a strong smile, and an ironic sense of humor. She got emotional as she described the difficult conditions Hillel faced in prison: malnutrition, weight loss, and certainly psychological strain.

Hillel was punished by being kept in solitary confinement after defiantly affixing a yellow star to his prison uniform. While Jewish prisoners were kept separately from one another, they somehow

Chapter 5

managed to yell to each other through the pipes, and even figured out how to smuggle notes to each other and to the outside with the help of other inmates.

Despite the current grim situation for her husband and the other prisoners, Yeva hoped for a future when they would be reunited as a family and be able to go to Israel. We commented on how brave she and her husband were, and tried to reassure her that many Jewish people in the United States were working to get her husband's release.

Yeva introduced us to her six-year-old daughter, and although there was somewhat of a language and age barrier, we managed to ask a few simple questions about school, friends, games, etc. Yeva offered us some light refreshments and we talked for a while, until we decided we needed to go, let them sleep, and get ready for our early morning flight.

I wanted to give them something as a token of our visit and friendship, so I removed a beautiful little butterfly pin I was wearing and gave it to the little girl as a gift. I thought of it almost as a symbol or omen, hoping that someday she would be able to spread her wings and fly to freedom like the butterfly. They thanked us for visiting them, and asked us to spread the message about Hillel to help him gain freedom. We told her we would do everything we could.

The next morning, after an anxious night's sleep, we managed to leave the Soviet Union without incident, eventually making our way back home. When we reported our experiences to the Student Struggle for Soviet Jewry, they greatly appreciated the first hand information, and we continued to be involved, including organizing a huge ecumenical rally in a large Catholic Community Center on Long Beach Island the following summer.

We didn't hear from Yeva Butman again, until one day in 1973 when we received a letter from her telling us that she and her daughter had received a visa to leave and they had made *Aliyah*. We were touched when we read the letter, and even more so when we saw the enclosed photo of her little daughter wearing her butterfly pin and smiling.

*Postscript:* Yeva continued to campaign for her husband's release. In 1979 Hillel Butman was stripped of his Soviet citizenship, set free, and was finally able to fulfill his dream of going to Israel, for which he sacrificed eight years of his life and health. While in prison, he had studied English and Hebrew daily through a textbook, managing to memorize 1000 Hebrew words without the benefit of pencil and paper. He also taught others in prison.

Butman received a hero's welcome at Ben Gurion airport and was greeted by Prime Minister Menachem Begin. Butman stated that: "Our aim was not to transfer a certain number of people to Israel. We wanted to do what Moses did when he led the people out against the wishes of Pharaoh." While many Russian Jews experienced frustrations and even disillusionment as a result of the challenging absorption process, Butman once shared: "My dreams are fulfilled. For me the fact that an independent Jewish state exists is the most important thing. Everything else is commentary." (An allusion to the statement of the sage Hillel, his namesake.)

## *"Next Year in Jerusalem"*

Perhaps no one individual symbolizes the modern dramatic fulfillment of the Zionist dream more than Natan Sharansky, a late-twentieth century Jewish hero. As both he and Israel turn 70 in 2018, he is being awarded the prestigious Israel Prize for a lifetime of achievement and exceptional contributions to Israel in the field of *Aliyah* and the ingathering of the exiles.

When Anatoly Sharansky requested the right to emigrate from the U.S.S.R. and go to Israel, he was refused permission to leave on the grounds of "national security reasons." This denial of human freedom led to his becoming a leading human rights activist and "refusenik." In 1977 Sharansky was arrested on fabricated false charges of spying for the United States. Before being sentenced in a Moscow court on July 14, 1978 for thirteen years of imprisonment in forced labor camps, Sharansky's defiant words to the court were:

…. "I hope that the absurd accusation against me and the entire Jewish emigration movement will not hinder the liberation of my people. My near ones and friends know how I wanted to exchange activity in the emigration movement for a life with my wife, Avital, in Israel.

For more than 2,000 years the Jewish people, my people, have been dispersed. But wherever they are, wherever Jews are found, every year they have repeated, "Next Year in Jerusalem." Now when I am farther than ever from my people, from Avital, facing many arduous years of imprisonment, I say, turning to my people, my Avital: *Next Year In Jerusalem*…..

…..Now I turn to you, the court….to you I have nothing to say."

More than half of the time of Sharansky's imprisonment was in solitary confinement. Terrible conditions there created significant deterioration in his physical health, but he survived mentally by playing chess with himself. After nine years, owing to the campaigning of his wife, Avital, other already released Prisoners of Zion, active international protests, and strong measures by the United States, Sharansky was released on February 11, 1986. He left immediately for Israel, where he continued to fight for the rights of refuseniks to emigrate.

*Avital and Anatoly Sharansky (L), riding with Prime Minister Shimon Peres and Vice-Premier Yitzhak Shamir (R) to Terminal Building, Ben Gurion Airport upon Sharansky's arrival in Israel in 1986.*

In 1995, Sharansky founded the Yisrael BaAliyah party in the Knesset, and from 1996-2005, he filled various ministerial positions in the Israeli government, including serving as Deputy Prime Minister (2001-2003). In 2009 Sharansky was elected Chairman of the Jewish Agency for Israel, a role he held until 2018. During his tenure Sharansky was a strong advocate promoting *Aliyah*. He believed that Israel is the best place for self-actualization for all Jews, and for impacting the future of the Jewish people.

Sharansky's strong commitment to the unity of the Jewish people led him to express his opposition to the freezing of the agreement for pluralism at the Kotel. He felt that such actions will weaken relations with world Jewry and erode the Zionist vision of Israel as a "home for all Jews," a view held by Herzl, Ben-Gurion, and Jabotinsky. He challenged whether the Kotel, a symbol that unites all Jews, should be allowed to become a symbol that divides them. At a special Knesset session, Sharansky vowed that he will "not give up on a single Jew; there is room for all of us here."

*Ingathering Of the Exiles: A Nation of Immigrants*

## *Leaving Mother Russia*
### Words and music by Cantor Robbie Solomon © 1979

They called me Anatole in prison I did lie
My little window looked out on a Russian sky
For nearly nine long years secluded and in pain
And all my people know the charges were a frame

See my accuser standing in the hall
He points his finger at us all
You now must pay the penalty
For the crime of daring to be free.

(Chorus)
> *We are leaving Mother Russia*
> *We have waited far too long*
> *We are leaving Mother Russia*
> *When they come for us we'll be gone*

For all those centuries we called this land our home
We loved the Russian soil as much as anyone
In countless armies our young boys have died for you
But never did you call them "sons" you always called them "Jew!"

We fell in battle for the Tsar
100,000 died at Babi Yar
And yet your monument denies their faith
While on our passports we read "yevrai"

(Chorus)

I send my song of hope to those I left behind
I pray that they may know the freedom that is mine
For in my darkest hour alone inside my cell
I kept the vision of my home in Yisrael
My friend, we know what silence brings
Another Hitler waiting in the wings
So stand up now and shout it to the sky
They may bring us to our knees but we'll never die.

(Chorus)

*Chapter 5*

# The Boy with Two Mothers
## Israela Meyerstein

As a volunteer student social worker at Hadassah Hospital Ein Kerem in late December 1971, I donned my white coat and headed up to the Pediatrics ward. I was asked to visit a young patient who had seemed quiet and somewhat sad. He was hospitalized for a flareup of rheumatic fever and a heart murmur, not an uncommon presentation in Jerusalem, where living in stone buildings with only space heaters during damp and cold winters easily exacerbated such conditions.

In a large, brightly lit room, I saw a husky, but small ten-year-old boy with black hair and dark eyes lying on a hospital bed. I smiled, said hello in Hebrew, introduced myself and asked his name, to which he smiled back and replied: "Yoav." I explained that I had come to visit with him since he is by himself in the hospital. Yoav came from a large family with nine kids that had immigrated from Khurdistan. Part of my assigned task was to discern if there were any concerning psychosocial or familial issues involved.

Like a curious but friendly amateur detective, I asked Yoav to tell me about his family. He started reeling off all the names of his brothers and sisters, ranging in age from 12, 11, 10, 8, 7, 6, 4, 2, and a baby on the way. As he finished, I remarked: "Yoav, if you have a ten-year-old brother, you must be a twin!" But Yoav insisted this was not the case.

Perplexed, I continued, "Perhaps one of you is adopted?"

"No," said Yoav.

Then I asked Yoav to please help me understand how that can be. Yoav matter-of-factly explained: "It's because I have two mothers."

Yoav went on to tell me that his father married his first wife in Khurdistan, but she could not bear children. Then his father took a younger second wife, who bore him eight children, and was now pregnant again. When the second wife became pregnant with Yoav's brother-to-be, suddenly the first wife became pregnant, even though she was much older. That's how the two brothers were the same age.

I began to wonder what kind of family household this could be ... two wives married to the same man, living under the same roof ... in modern Israel? How does that work? Also, what were their housing conditions like with all those children, when the father was a general laborer? I imagined that this family's circumstances were like those of other immigrant families I had visited who lived in tiny Jerusalem apartments, with several children sharing the same bed at night.

Rather curious to understand Yoav's family situation, I got his father's permission to visit the family a week or so after Yoav's discharge. The family lived on a *moshav* (settlement) about a forty minute walk from Hadassah Hospital. When I arrived and knocked on the door, a young, pregnant woman welcomed me in. She was holding a baby, and next to her was Yoav.

Yoav eagerly showed me their house, especially his room that he shared with his "brother from another mother." I was surprised to find a spacious comfortable house with five bedrooms that Yoav's father had built himself. Then Yoav took me into the kitchen to meet his mother, who was just about to take out a large pan of *sufganiyot* (jelly donuts for the holiday of Chanukah) that were warming in the oven. Yoav told me that his mother is the best cook, as evidenced by the wonderful aroma that wafted through the house. The family invited me to join them for a Chanukah snack.

As we sat at the long dining room table fit for a large family, I began to question myself why I allowed my social work mind to become so suspicious. Here appeared to be a well-run, economically-stable family, with well-fed kids and two mothers who shared the work. The older one functioned as a cook and housewife, and the younger one, as the children's nursemaid and caregiver. Relations between them seemed pleasant and collaborative enough. Besides, who wouldn't want an extra pair of hands?

As I returned home with warm memories of the family visit, I knew I had learned an important lesson that would serve me for the rest of my entire social work career: Families come in all shapes and sizes, all kinds of arrangements, often strongly influenced by culture, among other factors. I learned that I should not rush to judgment or assume pathology. It would be wiser to create a larger tent for what is "normal." Moreover, when entering a family's home as a visiting professional, it is useful to be a curious anthropologist and just as important, to be an appreciative, respectful guest.

Chapter 5

## *Embroidered Aliyah Stories:*
## The LEAP Project
## Nicole Rosenberg

I came on *Aliyah* with my husband over thirty years ago from Johannesburg, South Africa. We found it increasingly hard to live with the Apartheid situation there, as did many of our peers who also left the country. We decided to come to Israel where we now live on a *moshav* (farming community) near Ashkelon.

Ashkelon is home to many immigrants from the former Soviet Union, France, South America, USA, Ethiopia, and more. As an immigrant myself, I experienced the tremendous disorientation and culture shock that *Aliyah* can entail. That said, immigrants from Ethiopia face even greater challenges as they come from a traditional rural culture. Many lived in outlying villages, in kraals made of straw and mud with no running water or electricity.

In Israel they had to cope with learning a new language, adjust to the fast-paced techno-urban environment, and overcome the challenges of fitting into Israeli society. Many of the women had little formal education or training, and they felt inadequate, not being able to help their children with homework. They had low self-confidence and self-esteem, and were often lonely. Unable to join the work force, the women often relied on welfare benefits to support their families.

I felt real empathy for the women immigrants living in the neighborhood of Havatzelet Community Center in Ashkelon, a low socioeconomic area with a high concentration of families from Ethiopia. I had a strong desire to help them. I developed a pilot project that received enthusiastic support from Director Sigal Ariely of the Baltimore-Ashkelon Partnership, which provided funding, along with additional support from the Ashkelon Foundation, Ashkelon Women's Forum, and the Ashkelon municipality.

As the official coordinator of LEAP: Ladies Ethiopian Art Project, I encouraged the Ethiopian women to use their traditional embroidery skills to make and sell handicrafts. This approach not only supplemented their incomes, but also restored self-pride in their cultural heritage and upgraded their image in the eyes of their families, their community, and themselves.

We began meeting once a week with twenty women of all ages at the Havatzelet Community Center. Havatzelet Director Shai Damteu supported LEAP and helped me gain the women's trust, no easy task. I supplied the women with embroidery materials, encouragement, and guidance. We drew inspiration for the designs from many sources – both Jewish and Ethiopian cultures, as well as from the women themselves.

The women chatted during the meeting while they embroidered, and continued their craft at home as well. Their products included *Challah* covers, pictures, *mezuzot* (cases that hold prayers on rolled parchment), and more. I helped them improve their technical skills and found a seamstress to hem covers for them professionally. I kept a meticulous bookkeeping system to keep track of who handed in what pieces and what was sold. Our oldest member, over seventy years old, always surprised me. Although she was illiterate she always knew how many pieces she handed in. She added a bean to a bowl every time she handed in a piece and then asked a neighbor to count all the beans.

The project had an added benefit because it became a social support group in which the women shared their experiences and problems, and talked about news of the day while embroidering. Together we discussed how to motivate husbands to help more with domestic tasks, how to provide good food for family members, and other related matters. Often the women would perform the traditional Buna Ethiopian Coffee ceremony at meetings, which provided valued cultural continuity.

When Grad missiles fell on Ashkelon in 2008, the women shared their fears with each other, learned emergency procedures, and turned to the embroidery as a therapeutic stress reliever. The group became an arena for the women to be creative, socialize, and develop a greater sense of community. Some women took leadership roles and eventually led meetings. Over time the women even wanted greater Ethiopian political representation in the Knesset for their needs, and looked forward to the building of an Ethiopian Heritage Center and museum in the community.

## Chapter 5

I often invited women of non-Ethiopian descent to join our weekly meetings to share their new techniques of knitting and sewing machine skills, engage the LEAP women in conversation, and exchange stories and advice with them. Visitors and overseas delegations met the women and bought their work. The sales and the visitors' admiration boosted the women's images in the eyes of their families and friends. One high point was Eli Wiesel's visit in 2007, during which the women presented him with an embroidered tapestry illustrating their journey from Ethiopia to the Land of Israel.

Along with the main embroidery project, we provided the women with free eye glasses, a field trip to Jerusalem, and small gifts at holidays. We involved the Diller Teen Fellow Project of Ashkelon and Baltimore in an intercultural and intergenerational program. The teens interviewed the women about their *Aliyah* stories, which were recorded in Hebrew and translated into English and Amharic. A professional photography book was made for each woman to take home and proudly share with family and friends. This "living history" project highlighted the common Jewish identity of all participants.

What follows is just one of the many fascinating and courageous *Aliyah* stories that were recorded by the teens.

> *I was born in a small village in Ethiopia in 1953. In Ethiopia I suffered from lack of food and water, the strong sun, and a very difficult life. From a very young age my father always told me that the Bible calls Israel a safe haven for all Jews. Because of these reminders I knew that Israel was the best place to go in order to get away from the dangers of living in Ethiopia.*
>
> *My husband was drafted into the Ethiopian army and disappeared. For five years I tried to find him without success, and then I decided to leave for Israel. In order to escape I had to avoid the many robbers along the route who would have taken everything from me, so I had to crawl on the ground to not be discovered. I still have scars on my legs from the terrible conditions on my journey.*
>
> *I was caught and beaten by the Sudanese police, imprisoned, and then sent to forced labor camps for a year and a half.*
>
> *Following my release I made Aliyah with the assistance of Operation Moshe. When I arrived in Israel it was everything I had imagined: clean, beautiful cities, grass and healthy green trees, and good people. I learned Hebrew in the Ulpan, where I received my Hebrew name: Tamar. I speak Hebrew reasonably well and even some English with a good accent. I continue to study and improve in Hebrew and arithmetic, as well as learn reading and writing.*

*I can understand and handle everything I need to know for daily life, so I am content. For fourteen years I worked very hard making shirts in the cotton industry. I have a grown up son, I love the city I live in, and I enjoy a great circle of friends. If you ask me about my life I would say: "Baruch Hashem, things are good."*

The LEAP project has been most gratifying for me as its founder and coordinator. One of our own women of Ethiopian descent, Seged (*Sigalit*), a participant in the original LEAP group, is its proud leader today. The group meets several times a week to make handicrafts of all kinds, socialize, and perform the coffee ceremony at the Community Center. While funds are thin, the project proved to be a great success and more than fulfilled our expectations because the women took a great leap forward.

# PART II

## *Tikkun Olam Values*

"Living is not a private affair of the individual. Living is what man does with God's time, what man does with God's world."

Rabbi Abraham Joshua Heschel

"We make a living by what we get, but we make a life by what we give."

Winston Churchill

"Learn to do well.
Search for justice,
aid the oppressed
be true to the orphan,
plead for the widow."

Isaiah 1:17

"Those who do good things for others are like the stars."

Daniel 12:3

"If you want to feel closer to God, do a mitzvah, any mitzvah."

Rabbi Solomon Schechter

"The State of Israel will prove itself not by material wealth, not by military might or technical achievement, but by its moral character and human values."

David Ben-Gurion

*Part II*

In Genesis it is written that when God finished creating the world, he said it was "very good," and he charged man and woman with taking care of it. Humans, created in the image of God ("*b'tzelem Elohim*"), were to emulate Godly qualities on earth through acts that bring light, holiness, and healing into the world. In Kabbalistic tradition, God's charge to man is to gather the dispersed shards of light, showing that God wants man to be a partner in the spiritual mending of the world. That is the ancient origin of *Tikkun Olam*.

*Tikkun Olam*\* includes *Tzedek* and *Tzedakah*, which are linguistically related. *Tzedek* refers to justice in the larger society and *tzedakah* refers to performing personal acts of kindness for others. The Torah's 613 commandments describe proper conduct towards others and doing good deeds (*mitzvahs*) in the world. While studying Torah is important, without a virtuous life of good deeds, it is not enough. According to Isaiah (1:11-17), "Sacrifices, the Sabbath, and other rituals are abominations if not accompanied by compassion for the needy or concern for truth and justice."

The term *Tikkun Olam* re-emerged in the latter part of the twentieth century when the term was borrowed by evolving political and social movements to advance their progressive values. For some secular Jews, ethical conduct and social action have been their main purpose and pathway to spirituality, instead of through traditional religious practices. A.B. Yehoshua expressed a vision of Israel having a special message and substantial contribution to the world, in terms of narrowing the gap between the first world and the third worlds. He imagined establishing a corps of Israelis (Jews and Arabs) and Diaspora Jews to bring experienced teachers in various fields to poor and needy nations. He felt this would fulfill Israel's mission as a Chosen People of bringing light to other nations. It would also show the world that Jews' ultimate response to the *Shoah*, was to decide to spread hope and progress throughout the world.[1]

For many decades, Danny Siegel, founder of the Ziv Tzedakah Fund, financially supported many individuals and small projects in Israel and America who were doing beautiful Mitzvah (deeds of kindness) work. Calling these people Mitzvah Heroes, Siegel encouraged young people and people of all ages to become heroes in their own lives. Echoing the Ethics of the Fathers (1:15), "Say little but do much," Siegel would often remind: "It's actually not the thought that counts ... it's the doing!" He believes that every individual has a much greater power to

---

\* Hebrew, lit. "Repairing The World"

change the lives of others than he or she thinks possible. People who practice *Tikkun Olam* often discover a new perspective, and a sense of accomplishment, meaning, and purpose. They may discover new talents and greater vigor. Physiologically, the release of endorphins may lead to greater serenity and peace of mind. Rabbi Abraham Joshua Heschel stated: "I am convinced that the sense of meaning grows not by spectacular acts but by quiet deeds day by day."

In Israel many people and organizations are engaged in *Tikkun Olam*. For example, "Latet" (to give), Israelgives.org, is an umbrella organization consisting of 180 non-governmental apolitical agencies that provide 60,000 families with physical, nutritional, and social aid, including 1,000 Holocaust survivors and youth. It is operated with the help of over 13,000 Israeli volunteers. Ruach Tova is another NGO that promotes volunteerism in Israel by connecting individuals, groups, communities, organizations, businesses, and even visitors to Israel with volunteer opportunities, and there are many others.

In 2007, Shari Arison initiated The Good Deeds Day Flagship Project, run by Ruach Tova. Good Deeds Day began in Israel and has become a global tradition of doing good deeds. People from all walks of life, ethnic groups, and ages, volunteer to improve neighborhoods, distribute food to the needy, help in homes for the elderly, clean parks and public spaces, create fun days for underprivileged youth and special needs populations, and do activities with aging seniors and Holocaust survivors. By 2017, participation reached an all-time high in Israel, with almost all of the local authorities, hundreds of schools, academic institutions, youth groups, soldiers and students, and more than 1,700 businesses taking part in projects country-wide. More than 1.5 million Israelis participated in Israel alone, along with hundreds of thousands in 93 countries across the globe. Having so many people do good deeds simultaneously can encourage doing good deeds all year long and be a unifying international force leading to positive change in the world.[2]

I have created a graphic framework as a way of looking at Biblical *Tikkun Olam* values. I have identified six points of the Jewish star, representing what I consider to be some key interrelated humanistic values in the Torah. The framework acknowledges the centrality of life combined with God's qualities of justice and compassion and mercy. While Saving a Life is considered the most important value, it is soon followed in importance by the practice of Justice in society. If you care for the rights of others, you will act with fairness and compassion, in concert with the hallowed principle of loving one's neighbor.

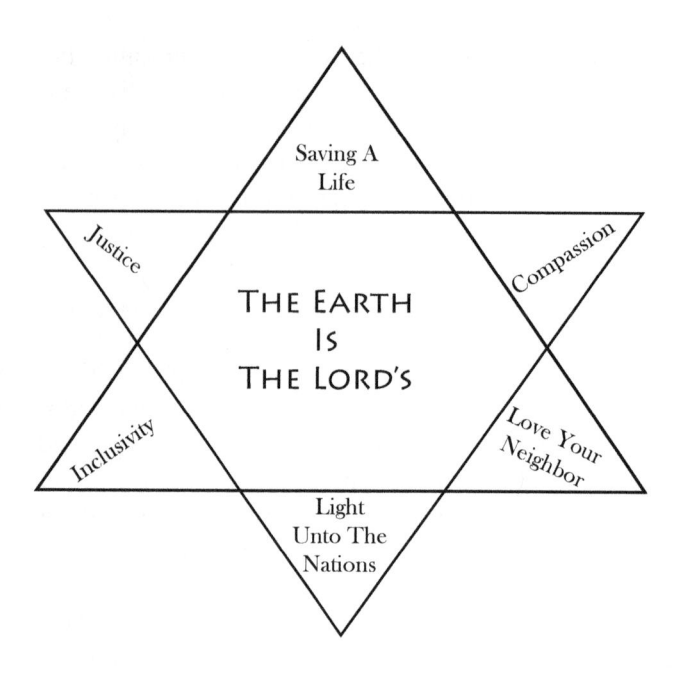

*Part II*

```
         Saving A
           Life

Justice              Compassion

      THE EARTH
          IS
      THE LORD'S

Inclusivity         Love Your
                    Neighbor

         Light
       Unto The
         Nations
```

    If we learn to love our neighbors, we will also be more likely to feel compassion for people who are poor, widows, orphans, disadvantaged groups, and strangers among us. A just society will also make efforts to ensure fairness for all of its citizens, while fostering greater inclusion of those in need, such as elderly, disabled, and disenfranchised people. Finally, the value of being a Light unto the Nations involves embracing all the above values and harnessing Israeli creativity, inventiveness, and humanitarianism. In this way, Israel can truly become a model for other nations around the world. The adoption of these *Tikkun Olam* values should lead to the betterment of society, and hopefully be more conducive to a world of peace.

*Chapter 6*
# THE EARTH IS THE LORD'S: PROTECTING OUR ENVIRONMENT

> "The earth is the Lord's, and the fullness thereof; the world, and they that dwell therein. Praised are You, *Adonai*, our God, King of the Universe, whose power and might fill the world."
>
> A Psalm of David (24:1)

During the Grace after Meals we thank God for food, and for bequeathing to our forefathers a good, beautiful, and blessed land. A *Midrash* describes God telling Adam and Eve that the beautiful creations were done for their sake, along with a warning to not spoil the world, because there will be no one else to repair it: "Pay heed that you do not corrupt and destroy My universe." (Ecclesiastes (Kohelet) Rabbah 7:2). According to the Jewish text Perek Shira, every aspect of the natural world comes from God with a purpose or song, and we are expected to use it wisely and responsibly.

In the Torah a principle called *Baal Taschkhit* forbids unnecessary destruction when one besieges a city: "You shall not destroy its fruit trees. You may eat of them, do not cut them down, for man's life depends on the trees of the field." (Deut. 20:19). The Bible clearly encourages ecological awareness. In Israel, the Society for the Protection of Nature has been in existence since 1953 to preserve the land with its beautiful bio-diversity. Since its inception, Israel has planted nearly 250 million trees through the Jewish National Fund.[1]

The following stories focus on our relationship to, and use of God's world and its natural resources, chief of which is water. Water is not only important in Jewish tradition, but essential to survival. Since its founding, Israel has faced severe water challenges and desertification, knowing only too well what Levi Eshkol expressed: "Water to a country is like blood to a human being." Today, Israel is a world leader in water conservation, sharing its amazing technological advances, such as drip irrigation and desalination. Globally, the absence of water as a resource, resulting from spoiling the environment and climate change, impacts the poorest communities the hardest, affecting public health and education. Desertification leads to increased migration and dislocation of communities. Fortunately, for many African desert countries, the livelihood of their citizens has been greatly improved through Israeli generosity of human resources and technical knowhow.

Any observer of the shifting sands of the desert understands that nature knows no boundaries, especially along Israel's border with its Arab neighbors. In this section, you will read how desperately-needed cross-border efforts around shared concerns have led to collaboration with Israel's neighbors, improving the quality of life for area residents and creating a more hopeful path to more peaceful relations.

## A Refreshing Water Story [2]
### Israela Meyerstein

It is described in Genesis: "There was darkness over the ocean; a rushing spirit of God hovering over the face of the waters." (Gen. 1:1-2). Water was created on the second day, and completed on the third day as the waters were gathered up into oceans, seas, rivers, and lakes, with the top part of the surface becoming dry land for vegetation.

Water surrounds us before birth and revives us. Water is an important recurrent motif in Jewish tradition: a sign of joy, purification, and salvation. Early Israel, an agrarian society, was dependent on God for water and rainfall. There were threats to withhold water if Israel misbehaved, and daily prayers for *Geshem* (rainfall) and *Tal* (dew) in season, as well as songs that celebrate water, such as *"ushavta mayim besasson mimayineh hayeshua* – You shall draw water with joy from the streams of salvation". The theme of water is found in the episode of baby Moses in the basket being rescued from water, as well as with Moses the leader, impatiently striking the rock instead of talking to it in order to get water.

In the Middle East, having enough water is synonymous with survival and is key to development. When water disappears civilization scrambles as desertification, migration and dislocation occur. Today Israel is the only country where desert has receded. In 1948 the desert began fifteen miles from Beer Sheva. Today the desert has been pushed back sixty miles. The thriving city of Beer Sheva is the site of the Zuckerberg Institute for Water Research and the Beer Sheva River Park project. Under Blueprint Negev, the river park is being created out of a dry, garbage-filled river bed, and will become a 1300-acre waterfront with green spaces, twice as large as New York's Central Park!

Golda Meir shared Ben-Gurion's vision of developing water resources to help over one hundred developing countries, the 2.4 billion people in the world, especially in Africa, who face severe water shortages. Israel's water achievements are on par with its military, technological, and societal triumphs. In Israel water is owned by the State (as soon as rainfall hits the ground), and as a result, from the very beginning of the state, there has been an essential government water policy that is administered locally.

As early as the 1930s, under the leadership of Simcha Blass, an immigrant engineer, the National Water Carrier project was begun. This first major project using Israel Bonds, it is Israel's most impressive infrastructure project. Designed in 1939 as a "fantasy plan" to prove that the land could sustain more Jewish immigration to Palestine, the National Water Carrier opened in 1964 to bring water from the north to the south.

From an early age Israeli children are taught to save every drop of water. Public campaigns offer incentives for water-saving technologies, and financial disincentives discourage fresh water use in landscaping. Israel invented many water saving practices such as drip irrigation to revolutionize Israel's and the world's agriculture, and techniques of growing more water efficient crops. Israel has developed technology to seed rainclouds, harvest rainwater, and then reuse it. Dual-flush toilets were first mandated in Israel, along with other hyper efficient appliances. Israel has mastered desalination and sewage treatment and is the world leader in wastewater recycling.

In 1990 there was a drought, followed by another in 2008 in the Sea of Galilee, followed in 2009 by the worst drought in nine hundred years. Yet through many efforts, Israel now has a water surplus. It is a hope that water diplomacy can also bring new life to the peace process. A 2018 Water Knows No Boundaries Conference will bring together scientists from Egypt, Turkey, Jordan, Israel, the West Bank, and Gaza. In addition, the $900 million dollar Red Sea-Dead Sea Pipeline Canal project is a trilateral plan between Israel, Jordan, and the Palestinians to increase the freshwater supply to the region. It is estimated that pending cooperation, it is possible that by 2020 pumped water will be shared, and Israelis, Jordanians, and Palestinians will be drinking the same water to foster overall better quality of life.

## Tevel B'Tzedek: Creating a More Just, Compassionate, and Beautiful World
## Rabbi Micha Odenheimer

When Susmita was 11 years old, her father took her down to the river to go fishing. Susmita and her family of five were part of a fisherman's caste called the Mahji, who lived on the sloping hills nearby the rivers that cascaded down from the majestic, snow-covered Himalayan range. The rivers cut through the hills everywhere in Nepal, rushing towards the lowlands by the force of gravity. The Mahji made special nets and waded into the river among rock formations where the fish liked to feed and rest. The Mahji almost always came home with fresh fish for eating or for trading with their neighbors, who grew rice, corn and wheat, along with mustard seed for oil.

The Mahji made just about everything themselves: their homes were made out of dried mud and thatched branches from the forest, as well as the woven mats on which they sat. They also made the gently spiked "chang" beer and the garlands woven from marigolds and wildflowers to adorn honored guests. Only the metal pots and kitchen utensils, forged by blacksmiths living near the area, came from outside the village.

Susmita's family lived about a half hour's uphill walk from the river. The Mahji were not Buddhists or Hindus, even though over the course of many centuries, they had absorbed practices from both. They had their own customs, language, songs, dances, and ceremonial dress based around the spirit of the river and the power of the fish.

The day that Susmita's father brought her down to the river was a very sad one. He waded into the icy river, placing the net right where the current was sure to sweep something into the net, but after two hours he still had not caught a single fish.

"This is how it is, Susmita," her father said. "There are fewer and fewer fish still here in the river. With the new road, people from other castes have come to fish here. Some have used explosives to kill the fish, and when the fish float on the surface, they are swept into a barrel. I wanted to show you this so you will understand why we have to leave here and go to work in the nearby brick factory."

The brick factory! Susmita had heard about how other Mahji families had started working there at least three years before. Susmita's father had always resisted going because families came back from the brick factory coughing from the smoke they inhaled. One little baby came home sick, and after two weeks, he died. Susmita remembered how sad his mother was for weeks afterwards. Now even Susmita's family

## Chapter 6

was going to the brick factory!

"How long must we work there, father?" Susmita asked.

"For six or even seven months," her father answered.

"Will there be a school for me there?"

Even though Susmita complained about school, the truth was that she loved to see her friends there, and learning to read seemed like something magical. Neither her father nor mother had ever learned to read.

Two years ago, as the number of fish began to dwindle, Susmita's parents didn't have money to buy her the school uniform or books she needed, nor pay the registration fee. They promised to try and to put her back in school the following year, but now they had to tell her: "No Susmita, you won't be able to go to school."

From late fall until late spring, for four long years, Susmita's family was forced to migrate and go to the brick factories. Over the past 30 years, the forests had dwindled in size due to logging. Without the trees to hold the earth, powerful monsoon rains swept the fertile topsoil into the river and downstream to India. Because of climate change, the monsoon season became shorter, and the torrential downpours meant that the water couldn't be absorbed into the earth quickly enough to recharge the springs that the community depended on for water during the dry season.

Sadly, farmers in the hills couldn't grow enough to feed their families for more than six months a year. Entire families were forced to leave the village and live in crowded, dangerous city slums or they migrated to other countries. Susmita even heard about two girls her age who left the village, were drugged and smuggled across the border, and forced to work against their will in a brothel in Mumbai.

Instead of enjoying their spacious ancestral home in the village, Susmita and her family now were crowded into little factory-owned hovels with hardly any room to stand up. Everyone in the family, including her five year old little brother, had to work 10, 12, 14 hours a day. There were no toilets, so they had to go in a field which soon became dirty. There was no clean water either, so stomach ailments were common, along with coughing from the smoky kiln air. Sometimes the family worked all day making bricks, and then a burst of rain turned all their work back into mud – a total loss, since they were paid by the brick. Susmita dreamed longingly of her friends, her school, and her bed at home surrounded by fresh air, and the songs of night birds that lulled her to sleep.

Several years ago something changed in the village. Our Israeli

*The Earth is the Lord's: Protecting Our Environment*

organization, *Tevel B'Tzedek* came to the area and teamed up with a Nepali organization to help the people grow enough crops and allow them to sell the surplus. This way the village could become self-sustaining and people would no longer have to go elsewhere out of hunger.

*Tevel B'Tzedek* is a Hebrew word that means "The earth in justice". It reflects Biblical teachings such as the Jubilee year and equitable distribution of resources. I founded *Tevel B'Tzedek* (Tevel) to resemble a Jewish Peace Corps. I wanted to influence a generation of young Israelis to help the very poor and prevent ruination of the environment. We searched for university-trained professionals who knew how to make things grow, and took them to remote corners of the globe. Tevel became a novel way to engage Israeli tourists, backpackers, and other volunteers (from among the thousands who travel to Nepal after army service) in worthwhile *Tikkun Olam* projects. Starting in 2007 with 15 volunteers, Tevel has attracted some 800 volunteers who have helped improve the lives of 40,000 Nepalese living in slums and villages.

At first a rumor was spread that we had missionary intentions, but the villagers came to understand that we were not missionaries at all. Instead of wanting to change people into something else, we wanted people to become self-reliant and stay in their own village, with their own culture.

"We know what exile is," one of the Israeli volunteers told Susmita. "We know how vulnerable people are when they don't have a home to call their own. We don't want that to happen to you – or to anyone."

Since its founding, Tevel has dotted the landscape of that Nepalese area (population 15,000) with 13 small teaching farms. There, hundreds of farmers have learned about new crop-growing techniques, irrigation, and organic farming. Hundreds of women have been organized into women's groups, where for the first time they can share their burdens and hopes in public, as well as borrow money from a collective fund. They also learned to read and write, keep a ledger, tackle health issues, and learn early childhood development skills. More than that, they've learned leadership skills for the first time.

Susmita's father told her that Tevel was the only organization that sent experts to actually *live* in the village. As a result the farmers learned such practical things as the importance of using good seed, how to start a nursery, how to protect cauliflower from the special moth that attacks its leaves, and how to grow tomatoes during the monsoon season in plastic greenhouses.

The Israeli volunteers organized youth groups that connected with

*Chapter 6*

villages in other districts, and helped the young people express their values and achieve their hopes. Together with Nepali volunteers, they brought new ideas to the women's groups and the teachers' groups that they had helped organize. They also introduced methods to collect spring water and rain water – hundreds of thousands of liters – so that every drop could be used. Now, throughout the winter, vegetable gardens can be cultivated. The next challenge for the villagers was how to market produce.

Tevel's plan was to create a cooperative collection center that would buy fruits and vegetables from surrounding villages. This way, Susmita's grandmother, for example, could sell her surplus of cucumbers that she didn't need for eating. By pooling their produce together, the villagers' cooperative could hire a truck to drive the produce to Kathmandu for sale at the big marketplace. Together with our Nepali partners, we brought more projects to the village such as: Commercial beekeeping, the growing of mushrooms and ginger, and even fish farming in the reservoirs to irrigate the vegetable plots.

Two years after the organization came to the village, Susmita's father said: Enough of the brick factory! Too much good is happening in the village now. A year later, the last of the families in the brick factory called it quits. But the greatest accomplishment for the villagers and for Tevel was that the women and the young people were becoming leaders in the village. When elections were held for the new village council, Susmita's mother was elected, despite being from the Mahji caste.

"We are going to organize," Susmita's mom said, "to take control of the river, so there will be no more dynamiting, and no more unrestricted fishing. We want the fish to return."

And Susmita herself? She is now part of a two-year service program sponsored by the Israelis, which allows her to work in her own village, among her own people. It seems as if hope, along with the fish, has begun to return.

## A Still, Small Voice Grows Stronger in the Arava Desert
### Rabbi Michael Cohen

A small notice appearing in the International Jerusalem Post weekly newspaper in February 1996 caught my attention. It announced the opening of the Arava Institute for Environmental Studies at Kibbutz Ketura, and gave the email address of the founder, Dr. Alon Tal. Given my interest in the environment I wrote to Alon to see if I could be part of the Institute during my upcoming eleven-month sabbatical later that year. After extended correspondence, both Kibbutz Ketura and the Arava Institute took the chance of allowing us to come that fall.

There is much I could say about the first magical year of the Institute. All I will say for now is that the Institute was, and is, the place of so many of my interests and passions: peace, the environment, multi-cultural education, kibbutz, desert, and the best of Zionism. Twenty years later we found ourselves back at Kibbutz Keturah on our fifth visit.

Kibbutz Ketura was founded in 1973 right after the Yom Kippur War by members of the Young Judea youth movement who brought with them a Zionism infused with the American ideals of democracy and pluralism. Unlike most kibbutzim in Israel today it still remains a community based on the egalitarian principles of the kibbutz movement. It is located in the Arava Valley, part of the Syrian-African Rift, one of the great tectonic fault lines of the earth. Dramatically exposed are the different magmatic, sandstone, and limestone layers, quietly telling the geological history of Mother Earth.

At the Arava Institute I teach a class called "The Bible as a Key to Environmental Thought." In the class we explore the many Biblical messages which speak to our shared human responsibility to take care of this planet.

From the opening chapters of Genesis, which over and over speak about the importance of diversity, to the command to rest on Shabbat, which can very easily be understood as a message to leave the earth's environment alone, to the commandment of *Baal Taschkhit*, "Do not destroy," which becomes the proof text of "recycle, reuse/repurpose, reduce, and refuse," the Bible is full of contemporary environmental messages for us today.

I begin most days with a bicycle ride through the Kibbutz orchards, past the 40 megawatt solar field, and then arrive at the desert border with Jordan. I was fortunate to travel a lot growing up, and so I always had a fascination with maps and borders: drawing maps was something

*Rabbi Michael Cohen teaching students of the Institute near the biblical oasis of Yotvata (Numbers 33:33; Deuteronomy 10:7) just down the road from Ketura. (Rebekah Sanchez Cruz, photographer)*

I loved to do. So it is natural for me to be drawn to that spot.

There are other reasons why I love riding my bike there. For one, it is peaceful and quiet. It is no accident that in the Jewish, Christian, and Islamic traditions the desert is a place of quiet contemplation and revelation, where, as it says in the Bible, "the still small voice" (1 Kings 19:11-13) can be heard. The other reason I am drawn to that spot is that the border there does not go in a straight line but makes four ninety degree turns that frame the fields of Kibbutz Ketura. It is a sign of compromise between Israel and Jordan.

When it came time for the Peace Treaty between the two countries to be signed in 1994 (at a spot along that same border further down the Arava valley), there had been changes made to the Armistice Line of 1949, which could have prompted Jordan to demand that those parts of the Ketura fields remain in Jordan. Rather, as a sign of being a good neighbor, Jordan let the border literally reflect a give and take. It remains a quiet model of compromise when it comes to land disputes between countries in this part of the world.

Along the border there are the official border markers that have been placed every 500 meters. In addition to the markers, there is barbed wire fence that also demarcates the border. Being that this border is in the desert, there is a lot of sand, or more precisely, sand dunes. Sand dunes are not static but move with the desert winds. They also don't know or care about fences and borders. So it is not unusual for the official border to be swallowed up and buried by the moving sands of the Arava desert. It is one of the reasons why we say at the Arava Institute that: "Nature knows no borders." And if nature can transcend those differences, so can people, which is part of the work of the Arava Institute.

The Arava Institute is an environmental and academic institution in the Middle East, dedicated to preparing future leaders of Israel, Palestine, Jordan, and countries around the world to find solutions to the most pressing regional and global challenges of our times. The Arava Institute has five trans-boundary research and development centers focusing on key areas of water management, renewable energy and energy conservation, sustainable agriculture, ecology, and sustainable development. Some of the topics studied include: solar research, geohydrology, on site grey water treatment, reverse osmosis desalination, oil spill reclamation, stability of sand dunes, climate change, biodiversity and food webs, medicinal plants, and endangered species.

While the focus of the Arava Institute is environmental studies, cross-border environmental cooperation and exchanges of knowledge and technology occur regardless of political conflict. We also address the "camel in the tent", the Palestinian-Israeli conflict, through a weekly Peacebuilding Leadership Seminar. Mandatory for all of our students and interns, we create a safe, structured place for challenging discussions and environmental leadership dialogue about the Middle East. The student body is a diverse mosaic of Israelis, Palestinians, Jordanians, people from North and South America, Europe, and Asia. By bringing together people from diverse multicultural backgrounds to work together toward important goals, a common striving for peace and sustainability shines through.

The present Arava Institute offices were built in an old turkey coup of the kibbutz, and use a curved wall design, much like the dwellings of nomads in the desert. The Nomadic lifestyle is according to the rhythm and flow of nature, which tends to be more curved. The wisdom and insights of those who lived in the desert millennia ago and understood nature as a manifestation of God's presence have left their imprint in many places, including the Bible and the offices of Arava Institute for Environmental Studies.

How curious that the Arava Institute's home base, Kibbutz Ketura, has the same name as Abraham's second wife Ketura. According to the Rabbis, Ketura is another name for Hagar. It was in the desert that an angel first spoke to a human, the pagan woman Hagar, after she and Ishmael were expelled from Abraham's household and left to die in the desert. The Rabbis have made a *tikkun* (textual edit/repair) based on the multiple mentions of the spring of *Beer-lahai-roi*, where they found themselves. That edit, based upon those other mentions of the well, suggests that there was more contact between Abraham, Isaac, Ishmael, and Hagar than what appears on the surface, allowing for a reconciliation reading and understanding of the text.

    The behavior modeled in Biblical times inspires the work we do at the Arava Institute on Kibbutz Ketura: Repair relationships between Jews and Arabs, as we also repair our shared environment and home together. The activities at the Arava Institute are daily reminders that hope can also be lived as a shared reality today.

## Water Knows No Borders
### Sophie Clarke

A bright orange halo of sun shines over the Dead Sea as Maya steps down from the minibus. She is excited to go on her first Youth Water Trustee trip sponsored by EcoPeace Middle East, a regional environmental organization that brings together young people from each side of the Jordan River and Dead Sea to learn about shared environmental issues, cooperate in problem solving, and hopefully become leaders.

Maya notices another girl about her age, not from her school group, wearing a beautiful blue hijab, who is approaching her. Maya begins talking to the girl, but the girl doesn't seem to understand Maya's fluent Hebrew. Maya begins to feel somewhat anxious about how this day will go if she and the kids she is supposed to become friends with do not even speak the same language.

A woman walks up beside her and asks Maya in Hebrew what she'd like to say to the girl. "Could you ask her what her name is?"

In a lilting Arabic tone, the woman explains to the girl that Maya was trying to get acquainted. "Why don't you ask her yourself?" the woman suggests to Maya. The conversation between the two girls begins awkwardly, pausing for translation breaks, but soon it's as if the translator is not there at all.

Both girls sit down at a green picnic table overlooking the shimmering blue sea and chat over some bread and spreads. Maya learns that the other girl, named Hiba, is from the Jordanian side of the Dead Sea. Just like Maya, she goes to the Dead Sea all the time for vacation, but she'd never crossed to the other side before. Maya is shocked to learn that Hiba had to apply for a visa a month in advance for this trip.

Soon, Shira, the Good Water Neighbors trip leader, interrupts their lively conversation: "Maya! Hiba! Come join us! Good morning everyone," Shira says, speaking in Hebrew and then pausing for the translator to repeat her words in Arabic for the other half of the group. "We're going to start with some games and then go for a walk around the area of the Dead Sea. The Palestinian group will be joining us soon; they were held up at their checkpoint for a few hours earlier this morning and are running a little late."

Maya and Hiba raise their eyebrows in confusion. Surely they had the same visa process as the Jordanians? Why were they questioned for coming on an environmental trip? Maya felt a little flutter in her stomach. All her life she'd been told that Palestinians were angry at

## Chapter 6

Israel and hated Jews. Maya hoped that the Palestinian group wouldn't blame her for holding them up at the checkpoint. On the other hand, she never met a Jordanian before this morning, and Hiba didn't seem angry over her lengthy visa process, so maybe there was hope.

Shira invites the group to follow her to an open grass field next to the picnic area to form lines for races. Competitive at first, the races end in fits of laughter, as speed-skipping across a field is very hard to do with a straight face. Hiba feels pleased that the Israelis are finding the same things funny as she does.

Maya notices that a new group of kids have arrived. Shira exclaims: "Wonderful! Everyone is here now."

All the girls welcome the Palestinian group: "Thank you for joining us after your long morning."

Everyone gathers in the shade around the large palm tree. Shira continues: "Today we are going on a nature hike around this area of the Dead Sea and Ein Gedi. Each small group will learn about a section of this hike and then practice leadership skills by presenting your ideas to the group." Shira starts reading out the teams. "Hiba, Maya, Nadeen." Maya and Hiba squeeze each other's hands, and look up for their new teammate. A girl with long curly brown hair and deep brown eyes walks over to join them.

"I hope they like me," Nadeen thinks to herself as she walks towards the girl in the bright blue hijab and kind green eyes. Nadeen's heart flutters a little as she sees the second girl in her group who has fair skin. She knew that Israelis would be here, but suddenly she's nervous.

"What if this girl hated Palestinians as much as she'd been told Israelis did?" Nadeen takes a deep breath. She had never met an Israeli before, but she felt that she should form her own opinion. She walks toward the girls, sits down on the grass and introduces herself. Her spoken Hebrew is a bit broken, because it's not always safe to speak Hebrew in her city as people might become suspicious.

Soon, however, their conversation finds its flow, and the three converse comfortably across Arabic and Hebrew to plan their presentation. Their task is to explain how the Dead Sea is shrinking. Before long, their script is written, with speaking parts divided up equally. The group sets off on their hike through the dense and lush palm trees, out into the enormous desert hills. Panting under the desert sun, they scramble up the orange rocks to reach the top of a hill overlooking Ein Gedi and the Dead Sea. Maya begins to slip as her foot catches on loose stones, but Nadeen grabs Maya's forearm to steady her so she won't fall.

*The Earth is the Lord's: Protecting Our Environment*

"Thank you!" exclaims Maya. "*Shukran*? Is that 'thank you' in Arabic?"

"Yes it is!" replies Nadeen. As they reach the top of the hill together, they are awestruck by the natural beauty surrounding them: bright orange valleys, golden yellow hills, and the pure, clear blue of the Dead Sea below. They're so engrossed in the nature and with each other that Shira has to call loudly several times to catch their attention and tell them to begin their presentation.

"The Dead Sea region is internationally known for its unique geographical, biological, and historical value." Hiba announces.

"It is the lowest point on earth and the world's saltiest water body," follows Maya.

"And it's known for its unique plants and animals, which bring visitors from around the world to the area. But it's drying up at a very fast rate," says Nadeen.

Their presentation flows smoothly, and they pause only for the brief translations.

"The main reason the Dead Sea is disappearing is the lack of water coming into it from the Lower Jordan River. Industries are taking water to extract minerals, and all of our countries are taking water for drinking and farming, so less and less water is reaching the Dead Sea. Also, climate change is making summers hotter and evaporating more water from the Jordan River and the Dead Sea every year. The Dead Sea has already lost over 1/3 of its surface area, and its sea level has fallen over 25 meters and is continuing to drop by over one meter per year. This is causing massive sinkholes on the coast and other irreversible damages to natural life in the area."

"We are all stakeholders in this: Palestinians, Jordanians, and Israelis all benefit from having a healthy Jordan River and Dead Sea."

"As people who live on this land, we have a responsibility to look after this unique part of the world as there's nothing like it anywhere else. We also have the power to stop it from drying up! Across the region we must prevent further damage from climate change and encourage our local leaders to have a more sustainable approach to conserving water in this area. Have hope! We can fix this! Thank you," they say together, hands held with smiles across their faces as the rest of the group applauds.

It is time for everyone to return to the green field where they left their bags in the morning. The girls pull out their phones and immediately begin adding each other's Facebook, Snapchats, and Instagrams. They have such similar pictures of food, parties, sunsets, and friends, that

*Chapter 6*

anyone might think they all lived in the same place and culture.

Shira calls across the field. "Nadeen, time to go!"

With hugs and tears in her eyes, Nadeen boards her white minibus. Maya watches as her friends drive away. Maya reflects on the fundamental Jewish value of *Tikkun Olam*, repairing the world. She believes that by improving the physical environment we can also improve our human environment as well.

"But how can we repair the world if we don't repair ourselves?" she asks herself.

She takes a deep breath. The girls she met today are just like her. They care about their environment; they also just want peace so they can live a normal life with their families. Like them, she wants to work to make sure that this area will be just as beautiful for their children as it was for them today.

"Maybe this is what *Tikkun Olam* really means. Maybe it's a common value shared not just among Jews, but among all people and religions. Perhaps I need to step out of my community and understand the problems faced by others as well."

Maya continues to ponder all she had learned during the camp. Israel may have clean water, but her neighbors may not be in as good a situation. Maya realizes that *Tikkun Olam* demands caring about others as well. She smiles, feeling lucky to be part of a country and a culture that not only embraces these values, but is also passionate about caring for the environment and water in the region. She realizes that water, unlike countries, has no borders. Then she reaches for her phone to text her new friends.

*Chapter 7*

# SAVING A LIFE ABOVE ALL: PIKUACH NEFESH

"A person who saves a single life, it is as if that person saved an entire world."
Talmud, Mishnah Sanhedrin 4:5

"Do not stand idly by while your neighbor's blood is shed."
Leviticus 19:16

The Rabbis taught that each individual is a miniature universe, so that saving one person is like saving the world. Conversely, destroying a single soul is like destroying the whole world. Because Judaism regards life as holy, we are obliged to protect it, and not "stand idly by" when someone is being harmed, but rather feel responsibility for others' lives. *Pikuach Nefesh* refers to the duty to save life, even if doing so means violating the Sabbath, eating forbidden foods, and eating on Yom Kippur (Pesachim 25a). The only laws that cannot be violated to preserve a life are those prohibiting murder, idolatry, or sexual immorality. (Yoma 85b, Sanhedrin 74a).

After the flood God promised Noah to never destroy the world again, sealing his promise with a rainbow. God's final message to Moses at the end of Moses' life was: "I have set before you life and death, the blessing and the curse; therefore choose life that you may live, you and your seed." (Deut. 30:19).

Golda Meir once said: "We can forgive the Arabs for killing our children. We cannot forgive them for forcing us to kill their children. We will only have peace with the Arabs when they love their children more than they hate us."

While Hamas often glorifies martyrdom, during the 2014 war the IDF set up a field hospital on the Kerem Shalom border crossing to treat wounded Gazans. Several months after the war, the granddaughter of Hamas Prime Minister Ismail Haniyeh was in critical condition, and Israelis saved her life.

Historically, when Jewish lives were at risk, they were often not valued or saved by others, but our tradition instructs us to take the noble path of observing this most important commandment to save life. The stories in this chapter tell of extraordinary acts of opening one's heart to the suffering of human beings and saving lives. The Israeli

Defense Forces (IDF), one of the most ethical armed forces, observed from the Golan Heights the suffering of neighboring Syrian civilians, and chose to act as good neighbors. Israel's field hospitals are of the highest level and can arrive and be assembled almost immediately in disaster areas around the world, giving help when most needed, long before others arrive.

Thousands of Palestinians receive medical treatment in Israeli hospitals each year. Hadassah Hospital, founded by Henrietta Szold, has had a mission of healing since the early years of the *Yishuv* in pre-Israel Palestine. Hadassah Hospital offers high quality medical care without regard to nationality or religion. Christians, Jews, Muslims, and other nationalities are treated without bias, and over 30% of their pediatric patients are Palestinians. Hadassah also provides the Arab world's only Bone Marrow Registry that serves 400 million Arabs worldwide.

Because Israel has experienced terrorism and significant trauma, Israel has had to develop advanced methods of coping and restoring functioning. Magen David Adom, Natal, Ambucycles, and Zaka, are just some organizations that intervene in life-saving situations. Believing in the sanctity of an individual's life may also be why Israel has embarked on life-saving missions in so many countries around the world through various organizations such as IsraAID, the IDF, United Hatzalah, Mashav, and many others. Israeli doctors volunteer their talents by travelling around the world to help poor children without access to health care, and bringing them back to Israel for free surgeries of various kinds, including treatment of burn victims. The value of saving a life extends to all people, because every life is sacred in God's eyes.

## A Good Neighbor Policy to Save Lives [1]
### Former Deputy Chief of Staff
### Major-General Yair Golan

In everything that we do, I would like to believe that there is an ethical as well as a practical dimension, and that the two need to be integrated. In my eyes the ethical dimension is principal, and everything we do at the practical level should be in keeping with our ethical values to the greatest extent possible. The saying, "Cast your bread upon the water" (Ecclesiastes 11:1-2), calls on people to do good for others without expecting anything in return, although one can always hope and believe that good deeds may lead to positive results.

During February 2013, I was the Commanding Officer of the Israel Defense Forces (IDF) Northern Command as the bloody civil war in Syria was (and still is) raging. Looking over the border from the northern Golan Heights, we saw indescribable human suffering. We asked ourselves: How can we sit idly by if it is possible to do something? What might be done?

Our decision to help Syrians wounded in the civil war came about by chance. One day the commander of the Golani Reconnaissance Unit was patrolling the border and saw rebel soldiers on the other side. The soldiers were moving eastward towards the fighting and had gathered the wounded in need of medical care near the border fence because that area was secure. When I received that information, I said: "We must help them."

We decided to erect a field hospital at Outpost 105 in the northern Golan Heights near the Syrian border to administer medical care to the hundreds of wounded civilians and rebels from the Civil War. When it was determined that more intensive medical care than we could provide on-site was needed, we referred the most severely wounded and chronic cases to our hospitals in northern Israel.

The message to our soldiers was: We save lives because we are not indifferent to suffering. Yes, they come from an enemy country, and even though the hospitalizations cost us millions, we are engaging in proper humanitarian behavior and providing help makes us feel more human. As Jews we have had our own disasters throughout history and we were not always helped. Therefore it is our responsibility as a "Light unto the Nations" to demonstrate this humane obligation.

Our efforts in the Syrian crisis expanded since 2013 and became "Operation Good Neighbor," with the goal of providing humanitarian aid to as many people as possible while maintaining a policy of noninvolvement in the conflict in Syria. The primary recipients are the 200,000 residents in southwest Syria, families living near the border, one third of whom are displaced persons or refugees, and one half who are under age 18.

The IDF provides pipes for water wells, ovens for bakeries, generators, and school equipment. The IDF has also distributed hundreds of tons of food, basic supplies, flour for bakeries, baby formula, diapers, shoes, and cold weather clothing and other necessities to prevent starvation and death. Since the aid began the quantity of food has increased tenfold. The IDF provides medical care and equipment as well. Over 4,000 people, including 100 orphans, have been transferred from our internationally managed field hospital near the border to Israeli hospitals, and medical supplies and equipment have been given to over 600 Syrian children and mothers.

Although Syrians are taught to view Israel as "Satan," those receiving care in Israel are positively impacted. In the words of one woman: "Israel is the only country that has done something like this for the Syrians. It is a humanitarian country. We were told they are our enemy, but we came and saw with our own eyes what they are giving to us and believe that they are friends."

Already three decades ago we realized that Israel has the capabilities to contribute significantly in disaster situations in our neighborhood as well as around the world. Perhaps it is the Israeli temperament: We arrive at a site that is in complete chaos and we know how to manage. We can handle authority, know how to improvise, we get organized more quickly than others, and we are good problem solvers. For example, the earthquake in Haiti (2010) caused extensive damage to infrastructure, turning the capital to dust, so we offered to come to their aid. We realized that we needed to dispatch both an evacuation and rescue team, medical staff, as well as come equipped with a hospital. Networking through El Al Airlines, we organized a jumbo cargo plane, and got approval for landing on the one runway that remained open at Port-au-Prince airport.

We arrived with no contact person, yet we were still able to mobilize quickly. Within twelve hours we took in our first patient and we were the only hospital operating on the entire island for the first fourteen days following the disaster. Of our staff of 240, two thirds were medical staff and the rest were evacuation and rescue personnel. Included were nurses who had left their children behind at home at short notice, doctors, and hospital department heads who just dropped everything and were ready to work under difficult conditions (i.e. living in tents, treating patients in intense heat and humidity, and with aftershocks occurring all the time). Our Israeli chef prepared meals to preserve morale and help us cope with the devastating sights we witnessed, until we passed the torch to the U.S. Army, who came with a hospital ship.

Japan, unlike Haiti, had excellent preparedness for natural disasters, but the 2011 Tsunami was a crushing blow with 32,000 fatalities, villages destroyed, and boats landing on top of mountains. The Japanese were proud and initially reluctant to accept help, but eventually did.

At one point I gave a talk to the Staff of the Japanese Government Institute for Disaster Area Response Training, describing how difficult it is to deal with disaster because nature is unpredictable, and that we (Israel) would do everything we could to help. The Japanese, ordinarily quite reserved, stood opposite me openly crying. When you can touch people on a personal level, cultural differences fall away, and I believe that they were moved by my identification with them.

As Head of the Home Front Command, I have proudly participated in providing help in various missions around the world in disaster zones. From the earthquake in Mexico City in 1985, to the flooding in the Philippines in 2015, to the earthquake in Nepal, the State of Israel has been sending relief delegations abroad for thirty years. What is amazing is that almost everywhere we go, we are the first to arrive and our contribution is the greatest in the period closest to when the disaster occurs. While we do not have the capability of the United States, we excel at arriving quickly and offering the necessary help in an efficient manner.

As a result of the speed and quality of Israel's humanitarian emergency interventions in disasters, the United Nations World Health Organization recently (2016) recognized Israel as providing the world's best field hospitals, and they are completing their review to give Israel a Type 3 ranking, the highest possible, which would place Israel first to be called to handle future disasters.

The IDF field hospitals have the capabilities of an advanced, permanent hospital that can be set up almost anywhere in less than a day. The hospitals have double the number of required inpatient beds and operating rooms, and the hospital ethically treats anyone in need, regardless of race, color, or creed. Moreover, the hospital can be self-sufficient in its services so as not to be a burden to the country that is already burdened by disaster.

If you ask, "What's the gain in these efforts by Israel?" Could it be a useful form of international diplomacy? We know that it doesn't change Israel's image in the world, especially with Syria, who is technically still at war with us. However, we are in effect saying to the Syrians: "You can live alongside us as neighbors, without fighting."

## Chapter 7

I believe in "Cast your bread upon the waters." If one day there will be a government there, and on both sides of the border there will be people who say to themselves, "We know from the past that we can gain from these mutual ties," that will be our reward. We must take practical steps and get involved, because it is the right thing to do, and also to hope for the day when we have a different relationship with the massive Arab world surrounding us.

We must not abandon our hopeful vision of life, which in my eyes, is the only way to live. It is this sense of purpose that arose, grew stronger, and strengthened the Jewish people throughout history. And it was the Zionist vision that insisted on rebuilding. Because of what we've been through, we understand and we know how to help.

## *Saving Children's Hearts*
## Dr. Shaanan Meyerstein

Summer 2003 – The line of waiting families seemed to never end. It extended out the door, through the hallway, into the pediatric ward, down the stairs, and out into the main hospital courtyard of the Mnaje Mojo Hospital (Swahili for "one coconut"). Here in Stone Town, Zanzibar, a tiny Muslim island off the coast of Tanzania, access to medical care was extremely limited. The hospital had little suitable equipment, and its staff was overworked and stretched thin. Malnutrition, malaria, and poverty were rampant, and like other countries in the region, there was a scarcity of resources including access to clean water, electricity, and basic medicine.

The chaotic corridors teemed with people who came in response to an announcement on Zanzibar radio earlier that week, inviting parents to bring their children suffering from heart problems to be examined by heart specialists from abroad. I wove my way through the overflowing crowd, walking past groups of mothers, fathers, and children who were sprawled out on blankets on the ground, until I finally reached the small room at the end of the corridor.

As I opened the door to the small pitch-black room, I saw a small light coming from a computer monitor in the back of the room. At the top of the right hand corner of the screen were the words: SAVE A CHILD'S HEART. Two white men, Israeli cardiac surgeons from the Save a Child's Heart organization, sat huddled together focusing intently on the monitor. Nearby on a bed sat an African woman wearing a burka, holding an infant. The only medical equipment in the room was a portable echo cardiogram machine manufactured in Israel.

Dr. Amram (Ami) Cohen, a charismatic, American-born Pediatric Surgeon who immigrated to Israel, first conceived of the idea for SACH while serving in the United States Military in Korea. It was there that he saw impoverished children in need of heart operations and described himself as "having been bitten by the bug of helping the helpless." After making *Aliyah* in the 1990s, Dr. Cohen was contacted by an Ethiopian doctor about two children who would die without immediate heart surgery. Wolfson Medical Center, where Dr. Cohen was the Head of Pediatric Cardiac Surgery, agreed to take the children, and Ami's family cared for them in their own home. His mission became saving children born with congenital heart problems living in the poorest conditions around the world. He would bring these children back to Israel for urgently needed surgeries, treatment, and follow up care at no cost to the families. Since its inception in 1995, SACH staff members have treated over 4,500 desperately ill children from the Middle East, Africa, Eastern Europe, and Asia. Nearly 50% of SACH cases come from the Palestinian Authority, and others include cases from Iraq and Syria

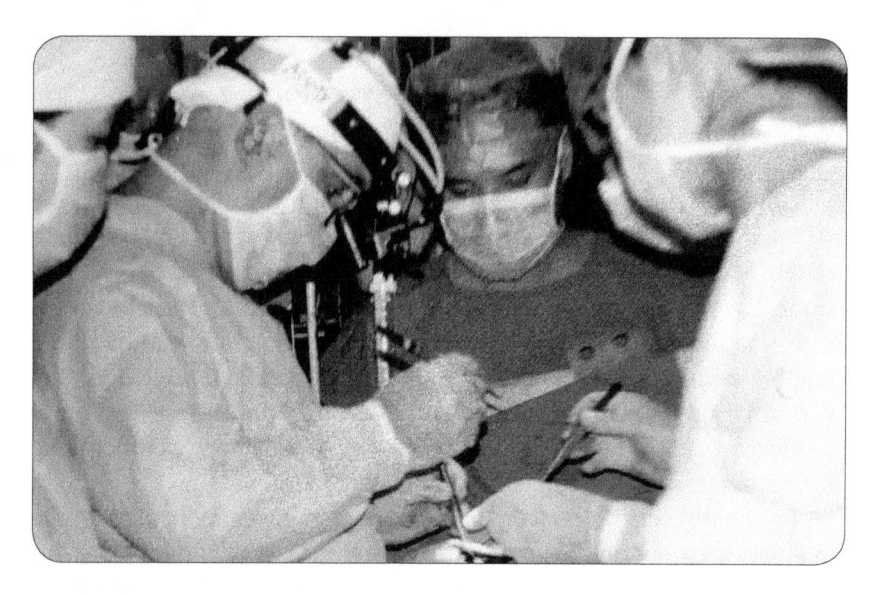

In addition to the surgeries in Israel, SACH has an outreach training program for medical personnel from participant countries. To date, almost one hundred medical personnel from developing countries have been brought to Israel for in-depth clinical training, and SACH staff travel overseas to educate and perform surgeries in cooperation with local personnel. The organization's ultimate goal is to enable other countries to become self-sufficient in performing cardiac surgeries on their own soil.

As the day proceeded, from time to time the two physicians peered out of the exam room to check how many patients remained to be seen. This was a long week as the Israeli doctors committed to examining every single child who showed up at the hospital. This example was set by Dr. Cohen early on in the organization's existence when he travelled to countries in order to screen potential cardiac candidates. The hardest task was deciding who to help since the need was so great. In his words: "I cannot hear myself say to the parents that we do not have enough money to save your child." Dr. Cohen left a tremendous legacy that has survived him and continues to this day, although he himself died tragically during a medical mission in 2001.

As the doctors began to examine the next few patients, I was puzzled that the children looked familiar to me. Suddenly I realized that I had met them exactly one year prior when I observed their open heart surgeries in Israel. I visited them while they were in the SACH Children's House. At the time, when I said goodbye to those kids, never in my wildest dreams did I think I would see them again in their native land, and certainly not looking as healthy as they did.

What a blessing to see the faces of children who arrived in Israel skin and bones, weak and blue from lack of oxygen, some on the verge of death due to complications from their heart problems. It was remarkable to now see them having gained weight, appear so energetic, and able to participate in normal children's activities. It was easy to identify the post-op children because when the doctor finished examining them, these little kids said "*todah rabbah*" ("thank you very much") and "*lehitraot*" ("see you again") in Hebrew, words they learned during their stay in Israel.

Despite amazing turnarounds, there were agonizing moments as well, such as a seventeen-year-old girl who had symptomatic uncorrectable congenital heart disease. While the doctors said it was a miracle that she had lived so long, sitting with the families as they empathetically explained her prognosis and their inability to reverse her condition, left me in tears. I reflected that if only these kids had access to regular health care, perhaps their lives could have been spared through early detection and intervention.

As an aspiring physician, I was fascinated to watch these expert doctors at work. They graciously explained to me how to read the echo machine, and how to properly auscultate a patient's heart and lungs to pinpoint the exact nature of the heart defect. It was amazing to witness how after just a few seconds of listening to the heart, even before looking at the echo, the doctors were able to diagnose a particular kind of heart murmur, a broken valve, a missing ventricle, or a diseased artery.

To me, SACH represents the best in Jewish values and Israeli society: health care workers volunteering their time and clinical expertise, while Jewish donors provide significant financial support for the organization. Yet perhaps the most amazing aspect of my experience in Zanzibar with SACH, was watching how when the doctors examined a child, they were blind to race, religion, and economics. All they saw on the echo machine was a ticking human heart that desperately needed repair. At that moment I felt privileged to be in the presence of holy acts of *Tikkun Olam*. I felt blessed with a mixture of gratitude and pride to have witnessed first-hand a small part of Israel's mission in the world.

*Chapter 7*

## *Henrietta Szold: Mother of Hadassah*[2]
## Israela Meyerstein

Henrietta Szold has been called the "mother of Hadassah," because she founded this worldwide women's organization designed to save lives and promote the health of women and children in the *Yishuv*, pre-state Israel, then Mandatory Palestine. Today Hadassah is a world class hospital with two campuses in Jerusalem. Known for its cutting edge clinical medicine and research, Hadassah treats patients regardless of their religion or ethnicity. While Szold initiated these efforts, she could not have accomplished them without the assistance of many others, especially women.

Henrietta was born in 1860 in Baltimore, Maryland, the oldest in a family of eight daughters. Her parents immigrated to the United States in 1859 from Hungary for her father to become the pulpit Rabbi of Oheb Shalom Synagogue in Baltimore. Her father was a brilliant scholar who could be fiery and eloquent in his sermons, but otherwise patient and gentle. Henrietta learned scholarly thinking from him, and how to appreciate Judaism as a way of life that encourages noble acts to service to others. Many of his ideas shaped her beliefs. From her mother, Henrietta acquired a strong sense of duty and a practical, intellectual mind that focused on details.

In her loving family home, wide-ranging discussions took place around the dinner table about current affairs, theology, and what is a Jew's ultimate mission. The young women were encouraged to speak up and have opinions. Her father's sage advice to Henrietta was to adopt a central idea, never depart from it, and then relate everything to that idea. Henrietta took three ideas: the value of education, practical Judaism as a way of life, and Zionism.

In the 1880s the Russian government began an official reign of terror and repression towards Jews, which led to a mass exodus, with many poor Jews landing in Baltimore. Henrietta's father took her down to the docks to meet the immigrants, even inviting them into their home for dinner. The Russians, in their thick accents, spoke with zeal about establishing a Jewish homeland where Jews would not be subject to pogroms.

The Russians asked Henrietta to help them learn English, so she created an evening school to teach them about America and learn English. Raising money to rent rooms and buy supplies, Henrietta became the teacher, superintendent, and janitor for the first Russian Night School in the country, teaching about 150 adults in the first semester.

As much as Henrietta helped the Russians, they also inspired her about the need for a homeland for Jews in Palestine where Jews could be safe and free, with Judaism as a way of life at the core. In order to make that happen, it would take education, Zionism, and Judaism. Even before reading Herzl's book, *Der Judenstat*, (*The Jewish State*), Henrietta began describing a vision of a Jewish state in Palestine that would gather Diaspora Jewry and revive Jewish culture.

Following the trauma of her father's death in 1902, Henrietta pursued courses at the Jewish Theological Seminary in New York. After a sad relationship breakup in 1909, Henrietta's mother proposed a trip to Europe to console her daughter. Since Henrietta had always dreamt of going to Palestine, she added Palestine to the itinerary.

The beauty of Palestine took her breath away: The sunsets and moonrise, the hills, the sky, the yellow and green fields, the flowers, the fruit trees, and the vegetables. Yet the poverty was heart-wrenching, the filth everywhere, and medical help almost non-existent. Henrietta and her mother were shocked and touched by all the poor children with flies around their eyes that caused trachoma, leading to the prevalence of blind beggars in adulthood.

Henrietta's mother suggested that Henrietta organize her women's study group in New York to become involved with the much needed practical work in Palestine. She told Henrietta: "You have studied enough! It's time for action." In that powerful moment, her mother gave Henrietta a precious seed – her Hadassah seed. It was during this trip that Henrietta solidified her life's mission: Saving lives through improving the health, education, and welfare of the *Yishuv*.

Returning to the United States with vivid and strong impressions of the extraordinary beauty and the grinding poverty in Palestine, Henrietta told others about the needs there, and how her visit to Palestine had strengthened her Zionism. Inside her, the seed her mother gave her began to sprout.

Henrietta energized her women's group to become involved in health work for the women and children of Palestine, a task that would require significant fundraising. She hoped that Zionism was a Jewish cause that could reinvigorate the group with new meaning and purpose. During Purim 1912, a group of six women Zionists met to found the national organization. They decided on the name "Hadassah," taking the motto from Jeremiah 8:22: "Healing the daughter of my people." Their goals were to spread Zionism in America, and promote health for women and children in Palestine.

Henrietta proposed they begin by sending a visiting nurse to Palestine. Through good fortune Henrietta met Nathan Straus, the owner of Macy's, and he agreed to pay four months of salary and travelling expenses for one nurse, and the group would raise the rest. Another funder supported a second nurse, and within three weeks they hired two nurses and sent them to Palestine. Henrietta arranged treatment for victims of trachoma, set up a nurses' station, and during World War I, outfitted an American Zionist Medical Unit with ten doctors, two nurses, and a supply of drugs.

Henrietta began a speaking tour to set up more Hadassah groups in Philadelphia, Baltimore, Boston, and other cities around the country. The membership grew to two thousand women in 27 cities in America. By 1919 Henrietta was asked to go to Palestine to oversee the operations of the Medical Unit there. Hadassah was able to fund hospitals, medical schools, dental facilities, x-ray clinics, infant welfare stations, soup kitchens, and other services for Palestine's Jewish and Arab inhabitants.

When Henrietta's mother died in 1916, Henrietta was age 59. In 1920 she began life all over again by moving to Jerusalem to direct the Hadassah Medical Organization. She set up a whole social services and educational system. Henrietta found that running the social services department of the *Yishuv* was very demanding work, filled with politics, frustration, and long work hours, from 5:30 a.m. until midnight.

In 1933 at age 73, Henrietta immigrated to Palestine to work with *Youth Aliyah* to help organize the rescue of children from Nazi Germany to Palestine. She met each child at the train station and welcomed them home, like an *Ema* (mother).

In 1934, Henrietta participated in laying the cornerstone of Hadassah University Hospital on Mount Scopus, and opened the first school of Social Work at Hebrew University. While a lot of work, it was a great success, due to all the support from the United States and from the physicians, nurses, and others in the *Yishuv*. The project emanated from the very spirit of Judaism: the commandment to save lives. Henrietta considered herself only a symbol, because Judaism and Zionism never depend on one person, but on the people and the land as a whole.

Henrietta had other academic accomplishments, such as helping to compile the First Jewish Encyclopedia, and being the first editor of the Jewish Publication Society for 23 years. She liked to reflect that the themes of her life's work were saving lives, education, Zionism, and Judaism. Perhaps that's what earned her the title of "Mother of Hadassah," healing the daughter of my people.

*Postscript:* Henrietta Szold died on February 13, 1945 at Hadassah Hospital at age 84, and is buried on the Mount of Olives in Jerusalem.

## Chapter 8

# JUSTICE: CREATING A MORE EQUITABLE AND COMPASSIONATE SOCIETY

> "Justice, justice, shall you pursue, that you may thrive to occupy the land that the Lord your God is giving you."
>
> Deut. 16:20

> "Let justice roll down like a river, righteousness like a mighty stream."
>
> Amos 5:24

> "You have been told what is good and what God requires of you to do. Only to act justly, and love mercy, and walk humbly with your God."
>
> Micah 6:8

> "You should stand up when you see an injustice."
>
> Rabbi Joseph Telushkin,
> The Book of Jewish Values

> "When one loves *tzedakah* and justice, the earth is filled with God's lovingkindness."
>
> Psalm 33:5

It is said that when God created the world, He reflected: "If I create the world on the basis of mercy alone, its sins will be great; on the basis of judgment alone, the world cannot exist. Therefore, I will create it with a combination of judgment and mercy, and may it then stand." (Genesis Rabbah 12:15).

Qualities of justice and compassion may very well be the basis of all other values, because if you respect and care about the rights of others, you will act with fairness and compassion. Being fair in your dealings with others is the just thing to do.

Rabbi Joseph Soloveitchek, a great twentieth century leader, stated that "human dignity and social justice" are implicit in the concept that man was created in God's image. (Besdin 1979:19a). Every person is equal in God's eyes, and Justice is one of the three pillars of the world, along with truth and peace. (Rabbi Simon Ben Gamliel, Deut. Rabbah 5:1).

## Chapter 8

The Jewish search for justice has existed in a long continuous chain from Abraham through Moses to current day *Tikkun Olam*. Early in the Bible we read the story of Abraham pleading to God not to destroy the city of Sodom if even ten just men could be found. (Gen. 18:23-36). Moses was a person who could not stand by and watch injustice. He intervened with a brutal Egyptian overseer who was whipping a Hebrew slave, with two Israelites who were fighting each other, and he rose to defend women shepherds who were being mistreated.

Today what we call "charity," the Bible viewed as mandatory justice and a sense of obligatory responsibility for the world. In early Israel the twelve tribes lived under a system of "distributive" justice, according to the Biblical injunction that no one should remain hungry or unclothed, not widows, not orphans, nor strangers. Therefore it was considered a societal responsibility to prevent poor vulnerable people from falling because once they fell, it would be harder, if not impossible, to lift them up. For the prophets the justification for having the land was to create a just society.

The stories in this chapter address different aspects of the important concept of justice and equality, a cornerstone of democratic society. One story addresses the gaps between rich and poor, suggesting ways of redistributing food to create greater fairness, especially for those who have less, and shows how the efforts of one individual can make a difference. Another story focuses on the crucial importance of preserving democracy and fighting through legal channels to uphold women's and human rights. One story describes social involvement and support as a way of strengthening and positively affecting the health and wellbeing of women, particularly young mothers, as well as their children.

Finally, a story about advocating for religious pluralism describes the need to recognize and uphold women's religious rights to freely observe their religion by having access to full participation in meaningful Jewish rituals.

## Leket Israel: From One Good Idea to Feeding Thousands
### Israela Meyerstein

Observing the problems in the world around us, it is easy to notice the gap between the haves and have-nots. Most of the time, we feel powerless to make any change. After all, what can one person do against the enormity of hate, poverty and tragedy in the world? We might even dream up the perfect solutions in our heads. If only I had the money, power, influence – I could really make a difference – but I'm too small by myself. But when someone decides that they can and will do something about it, it can grow into tremendous change that helps thousands.

In September 2000, Joseph Gitler, a lawyer from New York, made *Aliyah* with his wife and young family. A few weeks later, the Second Intifada broke out. By the end of 2002, times were tough in Israel. The years of suicide bombings and terrorist attacks led to an economic crisis as tourists stopped coming and businesses stopped investing. One third of Israeli kids were living below the poverty line, and many families were struggling daily to put food on the table.

Joseph saw the increasing poverty and wanted to do something to help. He spent December of 2002 visiting non-profit organizations and charities in Israel and asked them what they needed most. The answer he got over and over again was more food. They were so busy helping homeless and elderly people, battered women, youths at risk, and Holocaust survivors figure out how to make ends meet financially, that they couldn't also worry about how to feed them.

Despite the increasing economic difficulties, Israel's supermarkets were still full of food. When there is such abundance, as in most developed countries, only the nicest looking fruits and vegetables make it to market. Food that doesn't have the right shape or label or color, despite being perfectly healthy, is thrown away. Caterers at event halls and cafeterias always prepare more food than they need to avoid the possibility of running out. As a result, perfectly good surplus food often ends up in the garbage at the end of the night. After witnessing trays of food being thrown away after a Bar Mitzvah party, the solution became clear to Joseph. He realized that the best way to feed those in need was with the huge amount of food that would otherwise be going to waste.

Joseph took inspiration from the role models of *tzedakah* (charity) and wisdom he saw in his parents and in-laws and from Jewish tradition that is concerned with how we treat food and poor people. Leket is rooted in the ancient Jewish mandate to nourish all sectors of society,

## Chapter 8

taking inspiration from two Jewish principles. The first is *leket,* the Biblical commandment to leave the sheaves of grain that fall from your hands during harvest for poor people and strangers – "When you reap the harvest in your field and overlook a sheaf in the field, do not turn back to get it; it shall go to the stranger, the fatherless, and the widow – in order that the Lord your God may bless you in all your undertakings." (Deut. 24:19, JPS translation).

The second is *Baal Taschkhit,* the ethic of not wasting that which is useful. In the Bible it states: "This is the way of the pious, those who love peace and are happy at the good fortune of others … They will not destroy even a mustard seed in the world and they are pained by all ruination and spoilage they see and if they are able to rescue, they will rescue anything from destruction with all their strength." (Sefer HaChinuch 529:2).

In January of 2003, Joseph flew to Canada to visit and learn from the Second Harvest food bank, then came back to Israel and got started. For the first few weeks, it was just himself and his car and a few volunteers, calling up catering companies, picking up excess food at the end of the event and driving it to soup kitchens and shelters. Then more volunteers started joining him and they were able to rescue more and more food. One night, Joseph was almost left behind in a catering hall's parking lot because the car was so full of food!

Soon Joseph and his team of volunteers began knocking on doors at corporate cafeterias and collecting their leftover food. Then a farmer called and offered the persimmons that he could no longer sell because they had fallen off the trees in a storm. Joseph recalled, "I'll never forget that first week, we had no clue what to do." They started calling families, youth groups, and everyone they could think of. Because it was during Chanukah vacation they were able to gather 500 volunteers and rescued eight tons of fruit.

As Leket grew, then known as Table to Table, it soon became far too much for Joseph to operate out of his car. After he had five refrigerators in his garage and couldn't fit any more, operations moved to the first warehouse. By 2004, Leket bought its first truck.

Now, well over a decade later, Leket Israel is the largest Food Bank and Food Rescue network, feeding hundreds of thousands of Israelis in need every week. Each year, over 50,000 volunteers help rescue thousands of tons of fruits and vegetables and millions of cooked meals from farms, food suppliers, Israel Defense Force (IDF) bases, corporate cafeterias, hotels, wedding halls and more. The prepared food is brought directly to those who need it while a fleet of trucks bring the rest of the food to logistics centers where it is sorted, packed and sent

## Justice: Creating a More Equitable and Compassionate Society

*Leket volunteers help to rescue fruits and vegetables still in the fields.*

out to hundreds of non-profits throughout Israel. Leket runs nutrition workshops to help teach those in need how to eat healthily on a limited budget and educates the public about reducing food waste. Other food banks from around the world often come to learn best practices from Leket's experience.

The food provided by Leket is so much more than a meal. It is the freedom for an elderly Holocaust survivor to not have to choose between having enough to eat and being able to afford their medication or their heating. It is the gift to a high school for at-risk youth to be able to feed their students a hot lunch. This enables the students to stay in an educational after-school program until 5:00 p.m., instead of being dismissed when the school day ends at 1:30 p.m. It is the ability of poor parents to give their children nutritious fruits and vegetables that they wouldn't otherwise be able to afford. It is the extra energy that a crisis counselor can devote to helping the battered women in her shelter when she does not have to worry about how to find enough food for them.

Leket is the model of a modern Israeli organization with over 100 employees and hundreds more volunteers under Joseph's leadership as founder and chairman. The next time you see injustice, remember Joseph and Leket Israel's example. In his words, "When you want to get something off the ground, you'd better be willing to do everything. And of course I did have to do everything at the beginning. There's no job at Leket that exists today that I haven't done, from food raising to fundraising, from public speaking to collecting food to getting my hands in the muck."

"My favorite motto is 'no schnitzel (fried chicken breast) left behind.'"

Joseph's activities and actions at a national level have brought the issue of food waste and rescue to the public discourse. For these activities and for showing dignity to its food recipients, Joseph was honored with the Ruppin Academic Center Honorary Fellowship Award in 2017.

Making a difference doesn't have to be glamorous. It doesn't have to solve everything. But being part of the solution is a whole lot better than not trying to solve it at all. Here are some takeaway lessons:

1. Find the issue that shouts out at you that no one else seems to see or is willing to solve.

2. Research what can be done to help.

3. Rely on the giving spirit of the Jewish and Israeli people.

4. Start small, do what you can, and if what you're doing is valuable, be assured that more people will join you and it will grow.

## *Fighting For Equality, Personal Liberty, and a Just Society* [1]
### Sharon Abraham-Weiss

Israel is a land of diversity, and like most developed nations, it has its haves and have-nots. Traditionally the haves come from one background and the have-nots from another. I am from the other. I was born in Israel's South, in Eilat. The South is not just Eilat's glitzy hotels and sun-drenched beaches. It has often been referred to as Israel's forgotten backyard. Those of us who grew up there were not expected to join the elite from the center of the country. I never wanted to believe the people who said that my part-Indian descent disqualified me from prospering and making a difference. I fought that perception; and I know better than most that fighting for civil rights means fighting for disadvantaged people.

My other grandparents were Holocaust survivors from Poland. That reality burned two things into my mind from a very young age. First, that the Jewish people need a home, and second, that this Jewish national home must offer justice and fairness to all its inhabitants. One of the lessons of the *Shoah* is that atrocities happen when the voice of justice is silenced. I want to live in a society that sets an example of how minorities ought to be treated. My grandparents' story taught me what can happen in a society that fails to speak up for justice. Personally growing up as a minority in Israel only drove this message home more.

My parents were divorced when I was fourteen and my mother had to go through the Rabbinical Court in order to have it finalized. I remember feeling shocked as my mother's freedoms and independence were being stripped away in the name of *Halachic* law (Jewish law), a system of law in which women are inherently unequal to men. The same year, all of the students in my school were offered elective courses – one for the boys and the other for the girls. While the boys were invited to take sailing lessons, the girls were given the option to take home economics, a course designed to teach young girls how to navigate in the kitchen. My demands to switch to the sailing lessons, which seemed much more exciting and interesting to me, were denied, confirming for me society's predetermined trajectory for a woman. It was through these experiences that I began to understand the systems in place that prevent marginalized people in Israel from reaching their potential.

I soon became committed to promoting and protecting the rights of women in Israel, first through volunteering with a public hotline dedicated to promoting women's rights in the workplace, eventually co-founding Women Lawyers for Social Justice (Itach Maaki), and finally heading up ACRI – Association for Civil Rights in Israel, which I truly believe is the voice of those who otherwise go unheard.

Working at ACRI, the country's largest human rights organization, has been both a dream come true and the biggest professional challenge of my life. ACRI's storied history goes back more than four decades, during which some of the most important advances in civil liberties and human rights in Israel were achieved, thanks to the dedicated people working at ACRI. Since its inception, ACRI has brought precedent-setting litigation to the Supreme Court on a range of issues, including the freedom of and from religion; women's rights; criminal justice; equality for the LGBT community; migrant workers' rights; and human rights in the Occupied Territories.

Our organization mirrors all the faces in Israel, a diversity that is often mistakenly overlooked. Looking in on us in Israel from the outside, it is easy to imagine that everything happening here is somehow related to the conflict with our neighbors. That's not altogether true. Israel is a land of law, but also of contradictions. We affirm equality for all citizens, yet as a citizen body, we have elected governments that chip away at that equality. In Israel we are proud of our culture that insists on "speaking our minds," yet we stand by as laws are promulgated to silence dissenting voices. We extol the idea that everyone is created *b'tzelem Elohim* ("in the image of God"), yet there are those who are marginalized if they fall outside the accepted Israeli consensus.

Fighting for civil rights in Israel entails many unique challenges. Contrary to the United States, Israel does not have a Constitution which embeds equality within the legal system. Instead, the bedrock of Israel's legal system is a series of Basic Laws, which legislate the role of principle institutions in Israel and protect civil rights. Absent from this group of laws, however, is the right to equality, which poses a severe threat to the protection and promotion of this essential right. Here at ACRI, that doesn't dissuade or deter us. We remain committed to the understanding that injustice anywhere is injustice everywhere, and protecting our precious democracy here in Israel means first and foremost protecting our right to equality.

Two of ACRI's signal achievements illustrate this commitment: the Supreme Court decisions in the cases of Alice Miller, and of Adel and Iman Kaadan. Alice Miller was an immigrant from South Africa who came to Israel with a pilot's license in hand. When she joined the Israel Defense Forces in 1993, her application to enter the prestigious air-force pilot training course was turned down because she was a woman. With

ACRI's help, she petitioned the Supreme Court to compel the air force to accept her, and she won. This decision established gender equality as a fundamental principle in Israeli law.

ACRI represented Adel and Iman Kaadan in their petition to be allowed to buy land in Katzir – a village near Umm El-Fahm. Adel, a registered nurse, and Iman, a teacher, wanted to raise their children in a community that enjoys the same benefits and safety as are afforded to the small Jewish settlements in the region. Their request was denied out-of-hand on the grounds that the Kaadans are Arabs, while the land in question was leased from the Jewish National Fund and intended exclusively for Jews. ACRI's lawyers argued that denying the couple's request on the grounds of their ethnicity amounts to illegal discrimination. The Court agreed: four votes to one. In a way, this case was Israel's *Brown v. Board of Education*, the 1954 Supreme Court decision in the United States that made racial segregation of the schools illegal.

Through my work I feel privileged to follow my chosen path to defend the fairness, equality, and personal liberties guaranteed in Israel's Declaration of Independence. Because every person is created in God's image and is equal in God's eyes, I choose to oppose Israeli lawmakers who betray that democratic vision. I do this with the confidence that, as Martin Luther King Jr. said, "The arc of the moral universe is long, but it bends towards justice." I do this work because equality is not only a universal right but also a hallowed Jewish value.

*Chapter 8*

# *The Language of Social Change*
## Professor Julie Cwikel

The first time I understood a four-syllable word in Hebrew, I knew there was hope that someday I might someday be able to speak this language, so different from English. The word was "to turn around" or *"le-his-toh-vev."* I was a passenger in a car driven by my friend, Inez, herself a new immigrant from the Netherlands, who asked the guard at a hotel parking lot in Jerusalem if we could just turn our car around. I vowed that someday I too would casually throw out long and complicated words in Hebrew as easily as snapping my fingers. I still remember the challenges that learning to communicate, lecture, and work in a non-mother-tongue language held for me as an immigrant.

My *Aliyah* to Israel happened in fits and starts. After graduating from high school in Berkeley, California at age 16 in 1971, I decided to take a six-month break to learn Hebrew in an *Ulpan* (language school) on Kibbutz Hanita on the Lebanese border, with a childhood friend for companionship. We worked in the citrus groves for 4 hours a day and studied Hebrew for 4 hours a day. Little did I know that Hanita had an illustrious history as one of the strategic *"migdal and choma"* (tower and stockade) settlements, established in 1938 by direct order of David Ben-Gurion as a way to build up the *Yishuv* (pre-state settlement of Israel). Hanita is also adjacent to archeological ruins, including a Byzantine church with a mosaic floor. It seemed that everywhere in Israel ancient and modern history exist side by side.

Remarkably, my own family history turned out to be entangled in Hanita's establishment. A distant relative, Kurt Bengen, had come to Israel in 1932 from Berlin, driving his mother's Daimler luxury car that he then traded for a car and a tractor. Settling in Nahariya, the closest town to Hanita, he changed his name to David Ben Gaon and was hired by the kibbutz to till their fields, creating "facts on the ground". Unfortunately, he was killed by Arab gunmen as he was returning home on Erev Passover, 1938. We discovered this family connection among documents sent by our Berlin relatives in 1939, as they tried to obtain visas to get out of Nazi Germany. Sadly, the family did not manage to escape.

After studying pre-med for two years at the University of California, Santa Cruz, I returned to Israel in 1973 with a group of young people *(a gar'in)* to start a new kibbutz in the Golan Heights. The Yom Kippur War (October 6, 1973) caught me, along with most of Israel, unprepared. In the painful aftermath, the experience strengthened my conviction that I wanted to remain in Israel. I stayed to finish my university studies, not in medicine but in social work at the Hebrew University in Jerusalem. After completing a PhD in Public Health from the University of Michigan, I decided that the rest of my career would straddle these two worlds: social involvement and health. I returned to make *Aliyah* in 1986, propelled by Jewish values, including Zionism and a desire to build this country. I worked with immigrants from the former Soviet Union, South America and Ethiopia, never forgetting my own struggles as a new immigrant. Many of my graduate students were also immigrants, and some did their research relating to the unique experiences of immigrants in Israel.

*Professor Julie Cwikel*

I observed that the mental health of women in the Negev was at risk from both social and physical insecurity, such as the threat of missiles from the Gaza Strip. Diverse immigrant groups with less access to education and paid employment faced struggles to meet basic needs, a situation which adversely affects health. Women from patriarchal cultures such as the Negev Bedouin and the Ultra-Orthodox have higher rates of post-partum depression. I established a women's health studies center that serves as an umbrella organization to sustain programs addressing the diverse health needs of women in the Negev. These included Jewish residents of towns, kibbutzim, moshavim, and development towns, Bedouin Arab women, new immigrants, and women of different ages of the life cycle. The center also supports research on women's health, preventive health care, and stress reduction.

I brought new models to the Negev derived from similar programs in the USA. When we first proposed the idea of a women's counseling center based on feminist values in psychotherapy, our colleagues in the psychology department were skeptical, not seeing the relevance or the need for women-centered skills in mental health treatment. Today, ten years later, some of these same doubting psychologists are working here at "*Isha Be-Shela*," (roughly translated as "a woman in a place of her own"), the women's counseling center of the Negev.

Throughout the Negev we provide high quality psychotherapeutic services to women and men (yes, using women's therapeutic models

*Chapter 8*

that emphasize democratic values and gender sensitivity). Treatment by therapists from diverse backgrounds is offered on a sliding scale, with no waiting list, and available to all. Women coping with grief, trauma, chronic illness, aging, loss, anxiety, and depression find a place where psychotherapists help to provide solutions, support, and paths to growth. We also offer training to upgrade the skills of our mental health professionals. Here is a story that illustrates the counseling at *Isha Be-Shela* (all names and identifying information have been changed).

*Hagit, age 23, emigrated with her family from Ethiopia when she was six years old. A second year psychology student, she is the first in her family of eight children to attend university. Hagit was referred to Isha Be-Shela because of a strong social phobia that prevented her from making presentations in class and showing her true skills and abilities. Together with her psychotherapist, a short treatment using cognitive behavioral interventions was devised that helped her explore the dysfunctional thinking that activated her anxiety. She was encouraged to learn alternative skills and try them out in a gradual, anxiety-reducing fashion. Eventually, she made an excellent presentation about her family's immigration experiences.*

Another population that we support are new mothers in their transition to parenthood in a program called *Mom to Mom*, the center's longest running initiative. We use a volunteer force made up of mothers age 28 to 70, who make home visits to new mothers in their infant's first year of life. Soroka University Medical Center nurses refer women who seem isolated, upset, or withdrawn, and we follow up by inviting them to join *Mom to Mom*. The program contributes to the parenting skills of new mothers, while also providing a volunteering option for many who want to give back to their communities. Both programs have helped hundreds of women from all walks of life, many of whom are immigrants. Here is a story about an immigrant we have helped.

*Katrina emigrated from Russia at the age of seven, and has been living on her own since age 15. She dropped out of high school, but managed to finish a course in accounting. Married to Avi, who works as a delivery boy at a pizza chain, Katrina works in the billing department of a supermarket. Katrina was referred to Mom to Mom by the public health nurse, who noticed that Katrina barely picked up or talked to her healthy baby girl. Katrina was matched with Michal, one of our veteran volunteers, who reached out to her and established a trusting relationship, helping Katrina acquire basic mothering skills. When Katrina announced that she was pregnant with her second child, Michal moved heaven and earth to make sure that Katrina received economic support and extra supplies for the new baby. Slowly, Katrina learned to play and sing with her daughter. Now Katrina is able to successfully mother her two small children.*

As a full professor of social work and the founder (in 1999) and director of Israel's Center for Women's Health Studies and Promotion at Ben Gurion University of the Negev, I oversee cutting-edge research and intervention programs to promote women's physical and mental health. I have brought new programs to the Negev, a region that was lagging behind in women's health and mental health issues, perhaps because of its geographical distance from the mainstream central areas of Israel. My work has allowed me to contribute to greater equality for women in Israeli society.

Israel is truly a nation of diverse immigrants, whose inner riches and talents, if supported, can contribute to the benefit of all. The bottom line is that if you believe in *Tikkun Olam,* it is possible to develop the language, programmatic, and academic skills to be effective in bringing about positive social change. The task can be summarized in two words: *skills* and *commitment*. "Skills" in Hebrew has five syllables ("*mah-yu-man-nu-yot*") and "commitment" has four ("*meh-chu-ya-voot*"). And now, I can say them both in one sentence!

*Chapter 8*

## Women of the Wall: Seeking Social Justice, Gender Equality and Religious Pluralism
### Nechama Namal

In December 1988, seventy women gathered at a feminist conference in Jerusalem. They went to the Kotel (Western Wall) with a Torah scroll to conduct a prayer service. The women were scorned and attacked – both physically and verbally – by onlookers who were not comfortable with women wearing ritual garments, praying out loud, and reading from a Torah scroll. While the service was foreign and incomprehensible to the angry viewers, it was not against Jewish law. The ultra-Orthodox claimed that the women violated "the custom of the place," meaning not practicing in the ultra-Orthodox manner. This experience led to founding Women of the Wall of Jerusalem in 1988.

Although Israel projects an image of gender parity, such as electing a female Prime Minister early in its history, drafting women into the military, and the early Kibbutzim having an egalitarian ethos, personal status issues such as family law, marriage, divorce, and the courts, are under the purview of the country's religious establishment, which has created the most difficulty for women.

Women of the Wall aims to bring about greater gender equality and pluralism because they yearn to make the world a better place. WOW has effected revolutionary cultural change in Israel with its focus on girls and women: Emboldening them to fight for the 4 **T**'s: Freedom to wear a **T**allit, wrap **T**efillin, (phylacteries), pray out loud in a group **T**efillah, and read from the **T**orah scroll. Protesting against public silencing at the Kotel, WOW encourages women to speak out against the exclusion of women in the public sphere.

Since the end of the Six Day War in 1967, when the united city of Jerusalem came into Jewish hands, the Israeli government gave complete control and management over the Kotel to the Western Wall Heritage Fund, an ultra-Orthodox governing body. Under its rule, a partition separating men and women went up, and women have been prohibited from fully expressing themselves through religious acts which bring them spiritual satisfaction.

During the founding of the State of Israel Prime Minister Ben-Gurion acknowledged that Orthodoxy was Israel's de facto religion. But could he possibly have imagined that the situation would devolve into discrimination against non-Orthodox pluralistic expressions of Judaism in Israel and in the larger Jewish world?

Girls in Israel, from a young age, are treated with second-class

## Justice: Creating a More Equitable and Compassionate Society

*The Kotel, also known as the Western Wall.*

status at the Western Wall. When they attend a Bar Mitzvah ceremony of a male relative at the Kotel, they witness the fanfare surrounding the boy as he enters the Western Wall plaza accompanied by drums, a *chuppah* (canopy), loud and gleeful singing, and a parade of family and friends. The boy is handed a Torah scroll to read from and dance with, freely passing it to all the joyful men around him.

Meanwhile, the Rabbi of the Western Wall and Holy Sites who also heads the Western Wall Heritage Foundation, has refused to let women have access to even one of the more than 200 Torah scrolls held for "public use" on the men's side of the Western Wall. Thus girls experience the sad reality of gender inequality: At the Kotel only males count, and women are made to feel inferior and dismissed. On the women's side, there is no music or parade – the silence is deafening. Only 2% of young girls celebrate a "Bat Mitzvush," simply a party for their 12$^{th}$ birthday, that lacks religious depth or Jewish meaning.

Rare and extraordinary is the young woman who requests a coming of age ceremony at the Kotel. When this occurs we proudly support these brave girls and their equally strong mothers and grandmothers. We create an experience completely visible to the public, to raise the consciousness of all present. The atmosphere is positive, affirmative, and unforgettable for the young woman, creating a solid bond between the young lady, Judaism, Jewish tradition and the State of Israel.

WOW goes to great lengths to provide a Torah scroll for the girl's first *Aliyah* (call to reading of the Torah scroll) so that she can hold it, kiss its cover, read from it and dance in circles with the Torah, creating a festive and joyful mood. The Bat Mitzvah girl is surrounded by like-minded women to demonstrate that their womanhood is cause for immense celebration.

WOW provides lectures in Hebrew and English for thousands of people in Israel and abroad: elementary school students, teens, young adults in pre-army programs, university students, synagogue communities and urban kibbutz members. WOW representatives speak throughout the Diaspora to Bar/Bat Mitzvah-aged students, Confirmation classes, Hillel communities, women's philanthropy groups, synagogue communities and Jewish Federation groups.

WOW offers mentoring for girls to learn about Jewish ritual and meaningful ways to participate in tradition. WOW kiosks in public places such as the Carmel Market provide an opportunity for women to don a tallit or wrap tefillin or perform another Jewish ritual for the very first time. At the High Holidays, a shofar-blowing workshop and women's Selichot services are offered. During Hanukkah and Purim WOW leads services on the women's side of the Western Wall, alongside the official national ceremony on the men's side. WOW also trains women how to lead Rosh Chodesh and holiday prayers, empowering women to make the most of their ritual lives.

WOW receives support from women and men all over the world who sponsor rallies, petition their local Israeli representatives or politicians, and compose personal blogs and op-ed pieces on social media. Many women wear beautiful WOW tallitot, which have the four matriarchs' names (Sarah, Rebecca, Leah, and Rachel) embroidered in Hebrew on the four corners of their tallit.

WOW advocates for women's rights at home, attending Knesset committee meetings and appearing at the Supreme Court to petition the Israeli government to dismantle the stranglehold of the ultra-Orthodox. WOW attempts to educate decision makers of all levels about the repercussions of the interwoven Religion and State relationship, and how it negatively impacts people by increasing intolerance and divisions in society.

Already in 1989 the Supreme Court ordered the Israeli government to build a separate prayer space at Robinson's Arch at the southern end of the Western Wall. Despite this ruling, harsh treatment of WOW has continued there, and we have had to go repeatedly to the Supreme Court for intervention on our behalf. In 2013 the District Court ruled that since Women of the Wall possessed no viable alternative prayer space, they could pray freely in the women's section of the Western Wall. Despite this, the ruling body of the Kotel continued to ignore the court ruling.

This disturbing situation led to three years of negotiations in which Women of the Wall, the Reform and Conservative movements in Israel and North America, the Jewish Agency, led by Natan Sharansky, and the Jewish Federations of North America came to an agreement with the Israeli government for an expanded pluralistic prayer space that would be aesthetically pleasing. It would be equipped with liberal prayer books and Torah scrolls, with a common entrance and clear signage so that people entering the Kotel plaza could freely select in which space they would be comfortable praying, and that space would be governed by members of the liberal negotiating alliance, including Women of the Wall, and not the ultra-Orthodox ruling body.

Passed by a majority vote of the Knesset on January 31, 2016, this hopeful, respectful, and inclusive measure had the potential to create good will and unite the Jewish people in Israel and abroad. However, no implementation occurred, and eighteen months later, the cabinet reversed its own decision as the Prime Minister bowed to ultra-Orthodox pressure and canceled the very agreement he initiated.

As of the publication of this story, the Kotel agreement has not yet been implemented, but rather frozen. WOW petitioned the Israeli Supreme Court on January 14, 2018 to force the Israeli government to keep the promises of the Kotel agreement. Clearly, creating real cultural change for girls and women is work remaining to be done.

*Chapter 9*

# GOD LOVES ALL HIS CREATIONS: ON BEING INCLUSIVE

"You shall not curse the deaf and you shall not place a stumbling block before the blind."

Leviticus 19:14

"Educate a child according to his way."

Proverbs 22:6

"Do not cast me off in old age; when my strength fails me, do not forsake me."

Psalms 71:9

"You shall rise before the aged and show deference to the old."

Leviticus 19:32

"If you can't get up for an old woman on the bus, you can't be an officer in the IDF."

Moshe Ya'alon, former Israeli Defense Minister

When God lovingly created the world, He made it gloriously "bio-diverse," with many different species. There is even a special blessing that expresses the sentiment of appreciating differences: *Meshaneh Habriyot:* "Blessed art Thou, King of the Universe, who makes wondrous creations different one from another." Since all are precious in God's eyes; therefore we must treat all members of society with care.

Mahatma Ghandi stated: "The measure of a civilization is found in how it treats its weakest and most vulnerable members." People with disabilities suffer in multiple ways: from the disability itself, from cruelty they experience when others don't accommodate and arrange for special needs (i.e. such as a special ramp for wheelchairs), or when people with disabilities are not treated with respect, love, or support. The same is true for elderly and frail members of society. The Bratislaver Rebbe believed that the prosperity of a society is directly related to its treatment of the elderly. Our tradition strongly emphasizes the value of respecting and honoring the aged. We must emulate God's qualities of love for all people.

In Israel today nearly one tenth of the population has some kind of disability. While they still face barriers to full participation, there are constant efforts by many individuals and organizations to integrate people with disabilities, the elderly, and those with special needs into Israeli society to make it a more inclusive culture. In 2012 the Knesset ratified the Convention on Rights of Persons with Disabilities, and in 2014 an amendment was added to provide better accommodations and integration of students with learning disabilities into Israeli universities. Today many programs work toward insuring that no member of Israeli society is left behind. Cutting edge rehabilitation services, special education, medical care, and innovative community programs seek to support and include people with disabilities and the elderly into society to the greatest degree possible.

In the following stories you will be inspired by wondrous moments when children with severe disabilities shine and participate in Bar Mitzvah ceremonies like other Jewish kids. Israel's truly unique army has found a way to include people with disabilities to serve their country, develop their talents, and prepare for participation in society. In another story you will learn about a wonderful organization that enlists volunteers who offer kindness, problem solving, and a supportive community to help the elderly, Holocaust survivors, newborns, disabled veterans, and terror victims, and other vulnerable individuals, to name a few of those served. Last is a story about helping severely disabled individuals from early childhood to adulthood to access state-of-the-art health services delivered with love to their families, who find renewed hope and healing.

*Chapter 9*

# *I Saw Elohim Today*
## Rabbi Judith Edelman-Green

As guests and family members enter the makeshift prayer hall at Beit Sefer Nir in Ashdod, they see a space artistically decorated with crepe paper to create a festive atmosphere. There is a buzz of anticipation as an important Bar Mitzvah ritual is about to occur. The young celebrants are seated in the front row, awaiting their big day. They are smiling for pictures, giggling with friends from school, and fiddling with their *tallits* and special *tallit* clips that their art teacher has helped them make. Dressed in their best clothing, the children are both excited and nervous. They glance around at the many guests in attendance, then look at their parents for last minute reassurances.

As the service proceeds, momentum builds up leading to the Torah reading. As the Torah scroll is paraded around, people step forward to kiss it with their book or tallit fringes. In a short sermon the Rabbi tells the congregation: "Today we have present a moving ingathering of the exiles, with children whose families have made *Aliyah* from India (Hodu), Ethiopia (Kush), and the former Soviet Union." The Rabbi continues to explain that in the Bible Aaron held out his hand to bless the people, but today "we will reach out to these children with both hands." The Rabbi invites the congregation to clap and throw candy in appreciation after each child's *Aliyah* and before the Bar or Bat Mitzvah goes to his or her parents for a joyful/tearful hug and kiss.

So far the service resembles any other Bar Mitzvah, but this one will be somewhat different and quite special. Out of sensitivity, the Rabbi modifies the traditional commandment of "stand" to "rise" before the Torah, as Tomer, a boy with severe cerebral palsy begins an unsteady walk, aided by his father, up the access ramp to the *bima*. (podium) Leaning on the *amud* (reading stand) for support, the young man takes a deep breath before reciting the traditional blessing to usher him into adulthood, surrounded by supportive teachers, family, and community. Each child has been asked to create a personal blessing to thank God for something. At the end of the Torah reading, Tomer recites a second blessing thanking God for "planting the life of this world into our being." Tears of pride flow in his parents' eyes and in the congregation for his incredible determination.

Next Anton is called up to the Torah. He stands next to a felt board divided into four sections. On one side are the blessings illustrated with picture symbols. He quickly moves the cards into the right order, and the congregation responds with "Amen." Creative learning materials are used to allow even the most disabled child to participate, including recording the child's message and having the child press a lever to play it at the ceremony.

Mimi follows, wearing a crown of flowers on her head. She manages to say the blessings out loud by memory, with some gentle support from her teacher. Mimi smiles joyfully, while her mother, dressed in traditional Ethiopian garb, sheds poignant tears with the other parents. Mark and Ilya, two twin brothers with autism, are called up to the Torah. During the prayers they hold hands tightly with one another.

Now it is Nadav's turn. His entire family is present, including his brother in Army uniform. Nadav stands up, then walks past the *bima*, the Rabbi, and the Torah. For a moment it is unclear where he is heading ... is he about to leave the room? But then, Nadav goes to sit down at a computer and begins to give a blessing in his own way. One finger at a time, one letter at a time, he types the *bracha* for being called up to the Torah: *Bet, Resh, Vav, Chaf*...When he finishes each line, the computer teacher from his school presses a button, and the computer "speaks" the *bracha* out loud, or more correctly, Nadav "says" his blessings. As the letters appear, there is a hushed silence. No one needs to prompt Nadav as he "knows" and "speaks" the *bracha* by himself. When he types an incorrect letter, he corrects it by himself.

The gathered community sits in stunned silence as the word for God-*Elohim*-appears on the screen. No one remembers to breathe, until the Rabbi prompts the congregational response. The faces of the Bar Mitzvah teacher, the Rabbi, and Nadav's mother and father say it all: *We Saw Elohim Before Our Eyes*. At the end of the second *bracha*, we call out "Amen." Nadav rises from the computer and stands next to the Torah as it is being read. Then he sits back down at the computer to type the *bracha* for after the reading. Nadav's father could not hold back the heavy sobs of gratitude.

The service continues with the children singing solos and prayers taught by the music teachers. In this choir, everyone belongs...standing or singing is not a requirement. What a message of inclusion! A delegate representing Ilan, an organization that works with disabled children, offers gifts and words of encouragement. Speeches are followed by hearty "*Mazel Tovs*" and a congratulatory brunch at the conclusion of services.

A beautiful blessing in Judaism is: *Baruch Atah Adonai Eloheynu Melech Haolam, Meshaneh Habriyot.* (Blessed are You O God, Who makes creations differently).

In Proverbs 22:6 it says: "Educate a child according to his/her path."

## Chapter 9

That path may be typing on a computer, using a felt board, holding a picture, or speaking at one's own pace. But today was extra special: Nadav actually typed Elohim's name; we were the witnesses and we saw Elohim as we never had before!

The ceremony described above is one of twenty such annual joint celebrations orchestrated and financed by the Conservative Movement's Bar/Bat Mitzvah Program for the Special Child.

Since 1995 well over 1500 disabled and impaired youngsters have been included in the ritual of celebrating a Bar or Bat Mitzvah. The children suffer from a range of disorders, including mild or moderate retardation, autism, Down Syndrome, hearing impairments, deafness, attention deficit disorder, and severe learning disabilities.

We believe that although a child may be limited physically or mentally, he or she need not be limited spiritually. The project was created to fill a void for those disabled and impaired children who were being overlooked by their own local synagogues. Begun as a pilot project in Holon, this experience helps them feel included like regular kids. Services are offered to children in forty "special needs schools" by a staff of twenty exceptional special education teachers and school psychologists who involve families in a national program funded in part by the Ministry of Education and largely by American charities and the Conservative Movement.

The children study Jewish subjects for two hours weekly over a period of six months at no extra cost to the families. One aspect of their preparation involves performing a mitzvah project, just like other Bar Mitzvah kids do. This requirement provides the opportunity for the children to give to other people, a rare experience for disabled kids. The children visit an army base to deliver baskets to soldiers, an exciting and inspiring experience for both the children as well as the soldiers, who themselves are required to do a mitzvah project while serving in the army. When a group of children in wheelchairs visits an army base, the soldiers take them on a tour of the base, give them army uniforms to wear, show them jeeps and tanks, and share a festive meal and conversation together.

This hope-full project is offered to children from religiously diverse homes. Because the service includes girls and mixed seating, Orthodox families who are uncomfortable are offered the option of having their service in the school instead of a synagogue. Winning approval from the schools, which are religiously neutral, took time and effort. However, the resultant participation of Orthodox, Conservative, Reform, and secular families from all ethnic backgrounds is itself a triumph of religious pluralism in Israel, for which I was awarded the Liebhaber Prize for Religious Pluralism and Tolerance in 2003. Most families are convinced of the project's worth by how much their children love their experience and how it increases their self-esteem. The smiles of pride and accomplishment on the children's faces tell the most important part of the story.

Chapter 9

## No Soldier Left Behind: Special in Uniform
### Lt. Col. Tiran Attia

Israel is a country where national military service is a central part of life and culture, a rite of passage when high school graduates take their first steps of independence, a way of showing pride and loyalty to country, and a place where friendships and future connections are made. Those missing out on the process can feel much more than just not belonging ... they can feel truly left behind.

Receiving an exemption from military service because of disability or special needs can be a devastating experience: A time of sadness, anxiety, and loss of purpose, especially in families with a long and heroic military tradition. This was the situation in Israel until about twenty years ago, when a small group of senior officers launched "Special in Uniform." Founded by Major General (Res.) Gabi Ophir, Lt. Col. Ariel Almog, and Lt. Col. Tiran Attia, Special in Uniform looks beyond the surface of the disability to the person within, and to their strengths.

We are told that when the ancient Israelites continued their journey in the wilderness with the set of new commandments (after Moses shattered the first ones), they were instructed by God to carry the broken tablets in the holy ark along with the new ones. This was meant to teach us that God cares about those broken in body and spirit, loves all of His creations, and that each soul is divine, holy, and unique. Special in Uniform reflects these values and redefines what it means to be a "hero." The Hebrew word for hero is *gibor*, and from that root comes from the word *le-hitgaber*, to overcome challenges and adversity.

Special in Uniform partners with the Ministry of Education and Social Welfare and Jewish National Fund. Currently there are 350 members of Special in Uniform serving at 22 army bases alongside 30,000 typical soldiers. While typical basic training is not practical for many of the Special in Uniform soldiers, instead they learn skills of group formation, learning bus routes, dealing with changes in plans, and in particular, managing their own medications. Each Special soldier is given an orientation and assessed for his or her unique strengths, and then offered further training in certain areas of skill, moving from "special" to "specialist." Suitable jobs are found, such as preparing protective kits, packing field gear, work in the military store, emergency depot, warehouse, print shop, kitchen, or shipping department. Higher functioning soldiers with analytic skills are trained in special intelligence and air force units, software quality assurance, the Air Force fire department, or canine units.

## God Loves All His Creations: On Being Inclusive

*Israel's President Reuven Rivlin in 2017 recognized 30 soldiers who are enlisted through the Special in Uniform program of the Israel Defense Forces for their hard work and devotion.*

Special in Uniform helps soldiers grow and gain life and work skills so that they can transition into civilian life and become part of the workforce. Soldiers are offered a curriculum in academics, daily living skills, social and occupational skills, with the goal of helping them function independently and becoming productive members of Israeli society. Groups, workshops, and therapeutic coaches help teach problem solving skills, how to handle changes, and ways of cultivating a more positive self-image. After the army Special in Uniform helps the young person find a meaningful job match in civilian life.

One soldier, whose father served as a pilot in the Air Force, was trained in helicopter maintenance, so that both father and son wound up serving in the Air Force, a source of pride to both. Another soldier transitioned into a Tech company that supplies parts and designs for clients like Hewlett Packard. He checks mechanical parts to make sure they are packed properly. The grateful young person said: "Special in Uniform gave me the foundation and ability to be an independent person," and his grateful parent expressed: "Thank you for helping make this possible for my son."

One very special shining star of Special in Uniform is Major Riki Golan, with twenty years of service as a ranking and highly respected officer. Now a spokeswoman for Special in Uniform, Riki's job is to consult with and help officers integrate "special" soldiers into their units. Riki's own experience prepared her well for her work. As a result of being born premature at 27 weeks and being deprived of oxygen, she developed cerebral palsy and impaired muscle control, which affected developmental milestones. Despite being told that she would never walk, her perseverant parents advocated for her, provided appropriate medical care, constant encouragement, and determination to never give up, a valued quality of the Israel spirit.

Riki comes from a long line of military heroes, so she had a strong desire to serve her country. When she was initially exempted from military service for "medical reasons," even volunteering, she felt heartbroken, frustrated, and defeated. Her self-esteem took a big hit. However, Riki was a *giborah*, a brave heroine, and she refused to give up. She persisted and eventually got accepted. Then she rose through the ranks to participate in the rigorous officer training course, setting an amazing example for others. Riki became an advocate to raise awareness about the abilities of people with disabilities. Her dream is to show people with disabilities that they also can succeed.

Special in Uniform's motto is: "When everyone is included, everyone wins." It makes the army, a central institution of Israeli life, a place for everyone. In fact, the IDF is the only army in the world that recruits disabled individuals. While a disabled person may feel their chances are limited, Special in Uniform tells them a different message. According to Lt. Col. Tiran Attia, Special in Uniform's Director: "Special in Uniform has had a positive ripple effect – the soldiers' families are positively influenced, their neighbors see the abilities and capabilities of these soldiers, and eventually that ripple widens out and touches everyone in Israeli society." Through inclusivity and equality of opportunity for the disabled, Special in Uniform has had a profound influence on Israeli society's perception of individuals with disabilities.

Recently, a new parallel program called *Roim Rachok* ("Looking Ahead") which works collaboratively with Special in Uniform was created to specialize in integrating high functioning young adults on the Autistic Spectrum into the IDF. *Roim Rachok* capitalizes on the strengths of people with autism, such as visual acuity and the ability to notice tiny movements and changes, skill in detail oriented work, a knack for precision and repetition, long concentration spans, tolerance for repetition, and high motivation. These skills have usefulness in aerial reconnaissance, studying satellite images, and sensitive quality assurance work.

*Roim Rachok* offers an intensive six month college pre-army course with training in communication skills and writing, independent life skills, and significant emotional support. The program has helped over 100 soldiers gain social experience, leadership, independence, and a feeling of contributing to their country, while the Israeli army has also stretched and grown through the process as well.

## Yad Sarah: Volunteering to Build a World of Caring
### Adele Goldberg

"The world is built with *chesed* (kindness)."

Psalm 89:3

I feel proud to be a part of Yad Sarah, an organization that cares for society's most vulnerable: the elderly, Holocaust survivors, newborns, the injured, disabled, children with special needs, recent immigrants, army veterans, and terror victims. Started originally in the 1970s in the home of Rabbi Uri Lupolianski as a *gemach* (a free loan service), Yad Sarah became a nationwide nonprofit in 1976.

The original Yad Sarah model consisted of one neighbor helping another, lending equipment such as wheelchairs from their own homes. It was open 24/7, including Shabbat and holidays. As patients waited for their equipment, the less formal environment helped them feel more comfortable sharing details of their lives and hardships with volunteers. One young woman who borrowed equipment was upset that she was not in a position to thank the organization through a donation, but volunteers reassured her that it was fine. One day, years later, she called to say that she had saved a few shekels a week for years, and now could express her appreciation.

Today, Yad Sarah has more than 100 branches throughout Israel, with 6,000 caring, dedicated volunteers, who transform the lives of more than 400,000 people every year, while saving the Israeli government healthcare system millions of dollars. One of the largest volunteer organizations in the country, Yad Sarah meets some of the most critical needs in Israeli society – from providing elder care, home hospital health care, lending medical equipment and dental care, to advocating for disability rights, cultivating volunteerism, and community building.

Yet Yad Sarah is much more than a collection of services. It is a hub of healing, dignity, and opportunity, especially for society's most vulnerable and underserved. It is highly respected for the ways it brings help and hope to all of Israel's people – young and old, Jews and Arabs, religious and secular.

Yad Sarah's kindness and professionalism lead to thousands of beautiful and inspiring stories – here are just a few!

*An elderly couple was being abused in old age by their guardian, who made uninformed decisions about medications, forced the frail wife*

## Chapter 9

*out of bed against doctor's orders, and antagonized the home care aides. The husband was fearful about his wife's condition and treatment, but afraid to defy the guardian. He sought help from Dr. Mickey Schindler, one of Israel's most influential leaders on the legal issues of geriatric rights, and the Director of Yad Riva Legal Aid for the Elderly – a division of Yad Sarah. Dr. Schindler intervened immediately, filing charges and obtained a restraining order against the guardian. The wife received the medical care she needed and now lives with dignity.*

\*\*\*

*A young mother dying from breast cancer longed to be home with her family in her remaining time. Yad Sarah lent the necessary equipment to make her comfortable, and helped her attend her son's Bar Mitzvah before she passed away. Shortly thereafter, we received this note from the woman's mother: "It is the most difficult thing in the world for a mother to watch her child suffer, but Yad Sarah made it a bit easier on me. You have meant the world to us and I am eternally grateful."*

\*\*\*

*Yad Sarah's dental clinic typically serves older adults. Recently, Yad Sarah got a special request from Alyn Hospital to treat several children with disabilities. The Clinic manager found two pediatric dentists, outfitted the mobile unit, and organized the visit. Alyn said it was a "magical day" in which "the children received wonderful care and attention."*

\*\*\*

*Veronica walked into the Play Center with her three-year-old son, Oren. He has epilepsy and recently underwent brain surgery. For the first time in months, Veronica breathed a sigh of relief and hope. At Yad Sarah she watches Oren happily participating in therapies, meeting new friends, and playing with specialized equipment while building skills.*

\*\*\*

*A young man, who suffered leg damage in a car crash, continued to experience great pain after discharge from the hospital. He had difficulty getting to work and taking care of his family. When he came to the Yad Sarah House in Jerusalem, experienced volunteers and retired medical professionals patiently showed him the medical equipment he needed and how to use it. They loaned him the items – knee braces, a wheelchair and leg extensions – for just a few shekels, and guided him through rehab.*

*When he returned to his apartment, he felt as if Yad Sarah came with him. Volunteers visited regularly to check in on his progress, chat about events of the day, and help him and his wife care for their young children. Now, fully recovered, the young man stops by the Yad Sarah just to say hello and express his gratitude. He says: "If these walls could talk, they would sing." It would take music, he feels, to express the beauty of his experience as a client of Yad Sarah.*

\* \* \*

*A beautiful woman, who'd had an easy, pampered life, suddenly had to care for a parent with Alzheimer's. She felt like a reverse Cinderella, who used to be a princess but turned into a servant. Yad Sarah's caregivers program gave her much needed emotional support to help her understand her new role and responsibilities, to problem solve, and cope with the stress.*

\* \* \*

*One young woman needed constant oxygen tanks, more than her insurance would provide. Yad Sarah provided tanks and refills so that she could visit friends, go to doctor appointments, and pray at the Kotel. One of our volunteers even gave the woman her personal cell number to call if she ever needed another tank.*

\* \* \*

*A woman with a spinal congenital disability worked at a job where she had to sit for hours on end. She required fitness and strength exercises, but couldn't find a program that accommodated her work hours – until she found Yad Sarah. Yad Sarah offers many fitness classes, physiotherapy, art therapy, and yoga, at many convenient times, so women with physical limitations can integrate their work and family life with their need for rehabilitation services.*

\* \* \*

*A young couple was struggling to care for a severely ill daughter, who required a feeding tube. Lifesaving surgery was available but it was a 12-hour flight away, and her feeding tube wouldn't last that long. The woman's father turned to Yad Sarah, who prepared two specialized feeding devices that would each last six hours, and delivered them to the family so that they could make the journey.*

\* \* \*

*A mother of three children became blind at age 30. She began using multiple services and programs offered by Yad Sarah. Not long after, she*

*Chapter 9*

was injured in a terrible car accident and became a quadriplegic. She said: *"My personal journey has been filled with enormous difficulties, but I can honestly say that I have a fulfilling life today. Yad Sarah helped me to rehabilitate physically and emotionally, provided intellectual stimulation, and a caring social network. It would be very hard to imagine my life without Yad Sarah."*

There are so many more stories about Yad Sarah and its exceptional, trained volunteers, who help the lives of many people. The volunteers themselves, especially the elderly ones, find significant purpose and gratification as helpers. The goal of each volunteer is for the person they helped to leave the encounter with a solution to their problem, more hope, and a smile.

## ALEH: An Inclusive Community Creating Better Lives for Individuals with Disabilities
### Elie Klein

As with many other successful social movements, Israel's disability care revolution began with a group of parents seeking a better life for their children. In 1982, these pioneers decided that they would "do whatever it takes" to give their children with varied complex disabilities the best available care and the opportunity to grow and develop to their fullest capabilities. With grit and determination, they laid the foundation for the network of care their beloved children required. "We rented an apartment, hired a special education teacher and solicited a group of dedicated volunteers to assist us," recounted one of the committed parents.

Before ALEH, many of these children had to spend their lives in hospitals, with no opportunities for rehabilitation, education, or the love and warmth of a home. Now, thanks to ALEH's dedicated professional staff and volunteers, they enjoy all of the specialized services they need to live a quality life, including residential living, medical care, rehabilitative and therapeutic treatment, special education, vocational training opportunities, and social and cultural activities.

Three decades later, ALEH has blossomed into Israel's foremost network of state-of-the-art facilities for children with severe, complex disabilities, providing over 750 children from around Israel with high-level medical and rehabilitative care in four residential facilities in Jerusalem, Bnei Brak, Gedera, and the Negev. The beauty of ALEH is that children with complex disabilities are able to live in much the same way as their nondisabled peers.

The mission of ALEH is based on the belief that all individuals, regardless of the severity of their disabilities, have the right to benefit from the best available care to reach their full potential. In an effort to influence mindsets and create a more caring and inclusive society in Israel, ALEH has developed numerous programs involving families, schoolchildren, university students, the Israeli Defense Forces, and volunteers from abroad. The guiding philosophy is that young residents should not feel like patients, but regular children their age, so they attend school, participate in vocational programs, and enjoy activities, such as swimming at the beach or touring Israel.

It was this ideology that made devoted father and Israeli war hero, Major General (Res.) Doron Almog fall in love with ALEH and dedicate his life to helping individuals with special needs develop to their fullest

## Chapter 9

potential. A decorated soldier, Almog was the first Israeli paratrooper reconnaissance commander on the ground in the 1976 Entebbe Raid, one of the most heroic chapters in Israel's history and one of the greatest rescue operations of all time. Later, Almog participated in Operation Moses, which brought thousands of Ethiopian Jews to Israel during the 1980s. As the head of the IDF's Southern Command from 2000-2003, he protected Israel's southern border from infiltration by terrorists from Gaza.

After retiring from the IDF, in 2005 Almog joined forces with ALEH, a place where his son, Eran, who was born with severe autism and intellectual disabilities, truly felt at home. After Eran lost his battle with Castleman's disease in 2007 at the age of 23, Almog helped reestablish ALEH's Negev facility in Eran's memory, transforming it into a rehabilitative village unlike any other in the Middle East, perhaps the world.

Located in Israel's southern region, the ALEH Negev-Nahalat Eran Rehabilitation Village is a multifaceted facility that provides children and young adults with complex disabilities the opportunity to live a rich and productive life in a safe environment. Acting as chairman of the village, Almog has worked with the ALEH professional staff to create an inclusive community that provides a continuum of loving care for individuals with disabilities, from infancy and childhood through adulthood.

In 2016, Almog received the Israel Prize, the country's most prestigious civilian award, in recognition of his contributions to Israeli society in caring for Israel's special needs population and bringing a crucial change in societal perception of individuals with disabilities. At the award ceremony in May 2016, Israeli Education Minister Naftali Bennett praised Major General Doron Almog as an Israeli hero, saying to the effect, that Almog risked his life for the security of Israel, commanding the IDF's most elite units. Then he dedicated his life to Israeli society, fighting on behalf of the most vulnerable members of Israeli society. He fought bravely for his son, as he fought fearlessly to free the hostages at Entebbe.

When accepting the prize, Almog said: "This prize belongs to my son, Eran, who was born with severe limitations. He never spoke and never called me 'Dad.' Yet, he was the greatest teacher of my life. Eran is the one who taught me to have compassion for the weakest members of our society. It is for them that I work, and will continue to act throughout my life. This award also reflects that the State of Israel has in some way grown up. Previously, no one talked about children with special needs. Now they are being brought out of the shadows and into the light, and attitudes towards those with disabilities are changing, although there is still much work to be done."

Rabbi Yehuda Marmorstein, Director-General of the ALEH centers added that as a courageous leader, Almog "lives by the motto 'Leave No Man Behind.' He will always be our Major General, and we will fall in line beside him to fight for a state and future society that is more accommodating and tolerant of the needs of individuals with disabilities, so that no child with disabilities will be left behind."

No one is impacted more by ALEH than the families of residents. The Klein family immigrated to Israel a decade ago, largely in search of help for their son, Shalom. Born seemingly normal and happy, by age sixteen he was labeled profoundly intellectually disabled, and became entirely reliant on a wheelchair and the assistance of others. Following years of frustrating searching and evaluations, the family found the best care, community, and family support at ALEH in the Negev.

The parents were touched by the warm professional care and the involvement of so many volunteers: men, women, even high school students. One of the volunteers from abroad who helps Shalom with hydrotherapy exercises in the pool, shared that: "While on land, Shalom can't move, in the water he enjoys the moving around and feels free." Shalom's mother reflected: "ALEH provides the long-term care he desperately needs. He has begun to thrive and our family is blooming in the Negev."

ALEH has also become known as a place where miracles occur. Young Shira was born with Cytomegalovirus (CMV) and spent nine months in intensive care. On her first night home, Shira stopped breathing and her mother realized that the family was inadequately equipped to help her. Shira arrived at ALEH in critical condition, and the first goal was to stabilize her. With the staff's efforts, physical therapy, and a lot of faith, much has improved. While at nine months Shira was unable to eat on her own, crawl, or even sit up, now she is a determined and capable four-year-old. Starting to walk, she is integrating beautifully into the nursery school. Although it was hard for the family to place Shira outside her home, they are comforted by watching her amazing development and happy state. While Shira is not in her family's home, she is at home in ALEH.

More than ALEH's world renowned reputation for promoting disability inclusion, ALEH is also a model of a beautiful community in which children and adults of all disabilities, whether Jews, Christians, Arabs, or Bedouins, are treated equally with love as human beings. The

*Chapter 9*

*ALEH Twinning Bar Mitzvah with 80-year-old Larry Feinstein.*

ALEH staff is similarly a mix of the different ethnicities that compose the spectrum of Israeli citizenship, who work together with common purpose. "Loving Thy Neighbor" is practiced and put into action here. There is an understanding that everyone, regardless of ethnicity, has a precious soul. ALEH has been called a place where "angels are loved and cared for by angels."

In the words of Shira's mom: "The staff at ALEH is doing holy work … like a miracle."

## Chapter 10

# LOVING THY NEIGHBOR: BUILDING FRIENDSHIP AND COOPERATION

"All Jews are responsible one for another."

Babylonian Talmud Shavuot 39a

"You shall love your fellow as yourself."

Lev. 19:18

### *A Prayer for the World* [1]

Let the rain come and wash away the ancient grudges, the bitter hatreds, held and nurtured over generations.

Let the rain wash away the memory of the hurt, the neglect.

Then let the sun come out and fill the sky with rainbows.

Let the warmth of the sun heal us wherever we are broken.

Let us turn away the fog so that we can see each other clearly.

So that we can see beyond labels, beyond accents, gender or race.

Let the warmth and brightness of the sun melt our selfishness.

So that we can share the joys and feel the sorrows of our neighbors.

And let the light of the sun be so strong that we will see all people as our neighbors.

Let the earth, nourished by rain, bring forth flowers to surround us with beauty.

And let the mountains teach our hearts to reach upward. Amen.

(Rabbi Harold S. Kushner)

Hillel, the first century C.E. sage, was asked to teach the Torah "on one foot" He replied: "Whatever is hateful to you, you shall not do to your fellow human beings." (Talmud Shabbat 31a). This major principle of the Torah became the popular Golden Rule: "Do unto others as you would have others do unto you." Because each person is lovingly created in God's image, (Gen. 1:27) each person is important and valuable, regardless of their education, abilities, or status in life.

The unwillingness to recognize the sanctity of every human being

## Chapter 10

can lead to doing dreadful things to one another, from discrimination, to exclusion, to slavery, and murder. Very early in the Bible we witness the dangerous sinfulness of hard heartedness, as in the story of Cain, who murdered his brother, Abel. When confronted by God, Cain responded in a challenging manner: "Am I my brother's keeper?" Hard heartedness can lead to *Sinat chinam* (gratuitous hatred), and standing idly by when someone is being harmed is viewed as the equivalent of murder.

The Torah describes offenses against human beings as offenses against God and spells out our duty to love and help our fellow human beings. (Miketz 421:1, 44:17). Loving Your Neighbor begins with seeing the likeness of God and the humanity in every person. It involves showing respect, disagreeing civilly, and treating all people with dignity. If you believe in loving your neighbor you won't be prejudiced, take advantage, or deceive, covet, steal, or kill. Believing in the brotherhood of man extends to concern for mankind as a whole, not just one's own people. It also means concern for strangers and refugees.

Israeli President Reuven Rivlin reminds us that sovereignty means we have an obligation to stick up for Jewish values and work against discrimination or any kind of racism. Sovereignty that sanctions intolerance is incompatible with healthy democracy, so it is incumbent upon Jews, Christians, and Arabs to be vigilant against discrimination and follow the ethical instructions of the prophets.[2]

In this chapter you will read courageous and heartwarming stories about Israelis and Arabs trying to overcome barriers and work together against gratuitous hatred and towards becoming good neighbors. Through education and cultural programming, neighbors who are strangers can learn more about each other's culture and language, so as to be able to work together better. A final story tells about efforts by Jews and Arabs who reside in the same area, to dialogue, stick together, and speak out against terrorism, while trying to build cooperation and friendship. These efforts which seek to stretch the human capacity for forgiveness, are vital to rebuilding better relationships between neighbors.

## In The Galilee There Are Stones
### Rabbi Yoav Ende

In October 2015 frightening headlines told about a 13-year-old child taking a knife and trying to murder another 13-year-old child who was riding his bike to the grocery store. Such news challenges our ability to be hopeful and optimistic about our future. Only hatred and generalizations could drive a 13-year-old boy to become an agent of death who would murder a faceless enemy in Allah's name, instead of seeing the other 13-year-old boy as someone with whom to play soccer.

Dear God, where are we? And what of our hope and our future? For those of us who believe in peace, who not only preach pluralism, but also practice it on a day-to-day basis in the Galilee, such events severely threaten our vision for the future.

\*\*\*

I live on Kibbutz Hannaton in the Lower Galilee. To me it is like living on the frontier of Israel. Our community is a pluralistic and intentional one, where we attempt to create safe space for dialogue about what it means to be Israeli, and how to achieve a more democratic, egalitarian society. It is a place where we self-consciously try to bring this model and life practice together. We offer a *Mechinah* (preparatory) program for high school students, *Tikkun Olam* for youth groups, pre and post-army leadership training, and advanced learning for Rabbinical students. Our staff lives and works on the kibbutz.

My neighbors on the east are the residents of a Muslim village, Kfar Manda. Most of the residents were once *falachim,* loosely translated as farmers. To the west of Hannaton, there is a village called Bir al Mahsur, a Bedouin Muslim village. Not too far down the road, on the way to my children's school, is another Bedouin village. When the new "children's intifada" started a few days ago, some of the residents of Kfar Manda began holding demonstrations in the village and throwing stones from the roads. Not just any road, but the road my wife uses every day to travel to and from work. It's the road I use to take my children to the doctor and the road that leads from my neighbor's village to our kibbutz. The junction at which they were throwing stones is less than a minute from my house!

I have set the scene for you. Here is my dilemma: My neighbors were throwing stones to harm me, not just to land on the road, not just to scratch the windshield of my car, but to harm me. What is confusing, however, is that I also have friends in this same village,

## Chapter 10

where I do grocery shopping and mingle with my neighbors, people I know by name and who know me. My students volunteer there each week in a school for special needs children and teach Hebrew in the local community center in the village. And after months of trying, we organized a joint soccer team for our children and theirs, and last week they started practicing together.

Right now, however, I feel unwelcome and unsafe in this village. I check police reports before driving by. Has this become the reality of my neighborhood? Residents of the Galilee are familiar with this type of cognitive dissonance. It's not the first time that stones have disrupted our normalized lives. We are forced to consider: which reality and set of emotions will win out? And which values, which vision will triumph this time?

I spoke with my friends from Kfar Manda, some of whom are local lay leaders, and asked them to explain what was going on. "Why are people throwing stones from the road?" I asked.

"Martyrs," they answered. *"Al-Aqsa."*

"What do you mean, *Al-Aqsa?*" I replied. I could hear the shrugs of their shoulders in their silence. "You have to put a stop to this," I said. "You must get control."

Their response? "We wish we could, but in the meantime, you might not want to come here."

Me? I refuse to give up. I want to build a connection with my neighbors that will eventually win out over those who seek to destroy it. Am I naive? Yes. And is my vision, despite my naivety, still a possibility? Yes. Is it all up to us in the end? YES. In short, if we as individuals do not continue to try to live together, our future is indeed very clear.

This same week, I also got a call from another friend who lives in Zarzir, the Bedouin village on the way to my children's school. "Yoav, we have to organize a joint rally of Jews and Bedouins," he said. "Let's call it 'We Refuse to Become Enemies'."

I said to him: "Fantastic idea! Let's do it. We're in!" We had sixteen hours to organize.

What happened? At first people were afraid to come, asking "why, what good would it do? Others had even stronger opinions: "Arabs and Jews refuse to be enemies? Why bring Jews into it? It's the Arabs who are causing the trouble." However, we succeeded in gaining support, and on the main street of Zarzir we voiced our vision for the future.

Not every resident of Zarzir and Hannaton attended, but many did. Does one rally negate terrorism? No. But a rally generates positive energy, not just for the participants, but for the people who drive past it, for the people who hear about it on the news. One rally in the Galilee can shift the thinking of one person who can shift the thinking of another, and little by little this wave of good energy may overcome this current wave of terror.

Today other good things are happening here in the Galilee. We run a program called "You can't ignore it," a series of meetings involving 200 Bedouin, Jewish, Muslim and Druze participants: *Mechinah* participants and their peers from Kfar Manda, Bir El Maksur, and Zarzir. The focus of our first meeting was to find commonality among young adults through music, dance, and food. As people get better acquainted, subsequent sessions are led by a moderator to permit deeper discussion about politics and ethics. Meetings aim to create a home-like atmosphere to facilitate conversation. All sessions are conducted in Arabic and Hebrew, with translators available to assist.

Such joint programming in the Galilee provides an avenue of hope, a glimpse of an alternative possible future. This vision is different from the media's, which often shows only the ugly side of our shared reality here, focusing on conflict and violence. We don't ignore what's happening in our country, but we try to counter the TV and internet images with real-life positive interactions to guide and inspire us to recognize our shared values of humanity and inclusion. As one of the school principals from Kfar Manda declared: "We won't let those images of hatred control us." It is said that leaders sign agreements, but people build peace. We know that we cannot wait for the reality to change; rather we must work towards creating the reality we want to live in by meeting with our Arab and Bedouin neighbors.

Recently a group of thirty children in second and third grade from Bir el Maksur came to spend two days of fun at Hannaton with peers, playing soccer, jumping rope, doing art and more. In the evening there was a gathering of parents from Bir el Maksur and Hannaton parents, and the children slept over at the kibbutz. On the surface, this could be a regular neighborhood meeting, but the truth is, a gathering like this is almost a small miracle: That our neighbors would feel secure enough to allow their young children to stay here, many for the first time away from home, is truly a blessing. We don't take for granted their feeling welcome in a Jewish community, or that there is so much good will expressed by both sides.

After years of building relationships with different communities in Kfar Manda, we had a meeting with the Imam of the oldest and biggest mosque in the village, just a mile away. The Imam and visiting Rabbis

*Chapter 10*

spoke about God, humanity, and extremism which masquerades as religion. We didn't reach answers, but at least we opened the door and began the conversation. We finished the meeting with a joint prayer for peace.

* * *

So yes, in the Galilee, there are stones. But while some are used to destroy, most are used to build. We work together to break down walls of antipathy. Little by little, we build the foundations of living together as neighbors. And yes, sometimes the little we've succeeded to build crumbles in an instant, because to destroy only takes one minute, no more. But as Rabbi Nachman said: :If you believe it can be destroyed, you must also believe it can be fixed."

And so, we take to fixing once again. This is our plan in the Galilee.

## Rays of Light:
## Learning and Volunteering with Neighbors [3]
## Zimra Vigoda

My name is Zimra Vigoda. I was born in Budapest, Hungary in 1968. My parents emigrated from communist Hungary in 1972 with me, my three-year-old brother, two suitcases and 100 dollars. My father, a Neolog rabbi ordained in Budapest, found a position at a Reform congregation in Brooklyn, New York. I was raised in the Reform movement on the tenets of liberal Zionism and *Tikkun Olam* (Repairing the World). I spent 11th grade in Israel on an exchange program and was enchanted by the country's energy and the concept of Jewish self-determination. Upon completing graduate school in 1994, I made *Aliyah* to Israel.

During my first month in Israel, I met the man who would become my life partner and the father of our four children. In early 2000, we moved to the Negev region where about 30% of the population is Arab Bedouin, a part of the Palestinian national minority in Israel. As my children grew, I became increasingly disturbed by the social segregation that existed between the Jewish majority and the Arab Bedouin minority.

Although Israel is a diverse society, it was sad to realize that one could grow up in the Negev and never have any meaningful contact with the "other", a situation that leads to stereotyping, fear, discrimination, marginalization, and inequality. My previous enchantment with Jewish self-determination was slowly becoming complemented with an understanding of the immense responsibility entwined with having majority status. I wanted my children to grow up living by values of tolerance, mutual respect, and empathy for everyone's humanity. I believed in "loving thy neighbor," and wanted to see it practiced.

In 2009, a random encounter with another mom at a children's fun house introduced me to the Hagar Association: Arab Jewish Education for Equality. The bilingual Jewish-Arab educational framework was established two years earlier by a small, brave group of parents who wanted a different reality for their children. The following year, I enrolled my two younger children. Today, 10 years after the school was founded with 40 preschoolers, Hagar is proud of a student population of 310 children ranging in age from one to twelve and an active Jewish-Arab community of over 1,000 staff, parents, grandparents, and neighbors.

Hagar is a springboard for social change and one of only five integrated schools in all of Israel and the only one in the south. At

## Chapter 10

Hagar, half of the children and half of the educational staff are Arab and the other half are Jews. As a public school, Hagar is bound by the Ministry of Education curriculum. The nonprofit Hagar Association adapts the curriculum to fit its mission as a catalyst for developing empathy and confidence in who each child is and where s/he comes from, along with the ability to reach out to others.

Hagar's unique pedagogical approach is based on problem-based learning, and teachers participate in monthly training sessions to learn to adapt material for our two-native-speakers in the class approach. In addition we employ *Sweet Tea With Mint*, our anthology of stories about holidays in the three Abrahamic religions, which the Ministry has approved for use in all schools in Israel, to teach our students about our commonalities and the potential to create the future we dream of living in.

Beyond my work with Hagar, I have worked in diverse non-profit organizations for fifteen years. From 2009-2016, I was an active member of the AJEEC-NISPED* resource development team. Since 2002 AJEEC-NISPED conducts an Arab-Jewish Volunteer year, bringing together leaders from both communities for a year of joint volunteering and learning. Having started in Beer Sheva, today the program is national with groups in various mixed cities. The program is implemented together with the Israeli Scouts Movement that recruits and supports the Jewish participants as part of the Year of Service program prior to their obligatory military service.

The program is open to Arab high school graduates. They volunteer in educational institutions and social services for thirty hours per week (over four days), with a fifth day devoted to in-service training and a sixth to psychometric testing preparation. The number of volunteers participating in the program has increased steadily over the years. In 2011 there were 660 volunteers and by 2016, there were 1,640. Among Bedouin Arabs, the number of volunteers quadrupled from 356 in 2011 to 1,367 in 2016. In addition, twelve young people have volunteered as pioneers to expand the program to Lod, and further expansions are planned for Jaffa in 2017 and Ramla in 2018.

Listen to the words of a young Jewish participant in the program.

*"I am sitting across from a girl who is exactly my age. She speaks in Arabic and most of our communication involves hand gestures.*
*Considering the security situation today, it's reasonable to assume*

---

* Arab Jewish Center for Equality, Empowerment and Cooperation – Negev Institute for Strategies of Peace and Development

*that if I saw someone who looked like her on a bus or on the street, I wouldn't want to get too close.*

*But the room we are sitting in today is an "Island of Sanity."*

*I am from the Scouts group and she is from the Bedouin partners, who volunteer together with us during this year of National Service. The two of us are learning how to be together, respect each other's cultures and differences, find common humanity, and become more friendly neighbors.*

*There is a huge disconnect between the feelings here in this room and the insanity often raging outside. True, we don't agree on everything. We don't need to, and I assume that we will never agree on everything, but both of us share the hesitance about walking around these days and both of us grieve for the deaths of too many innocent people.*

*Despite the pain, fears, and at times anger we feel toward the other side, we are still able to look at one another in the eye. We will not allow the situation raging outside to control us.*

*I won't lie, it isn't always easy. It isn't easy to learn not to blame, or to learn to listen, to control one's emotions, to put one's anger aside for the moment and to be grateful for the opportunity to sit in this circle where Jews and Arabs can sit together and talk. I truly understand how important it is for me to be here.*

*I am certain that peace won't arrive tomorrow. I don't know how it will come. And I am not going to pretend that I will bring peace.*

*I remind myself that across from me sits a girl exactly my age. She is wearing a hijab and a long dress when it is 30 degrees Celsius outside. The peace that is between us I can bring by myself, with her. After all, she is my neighbor.*

## Chapter 10

## *Israeli Jews and Arabs Stand United at the Junction*
# Lydia Aisenberg

In the shadow of ancient Tel Megiddo, a site where thirty layers of different civilizations have been uncovered, and still more await recovery, I watched hundreds of Israeli Jews and Arabs join hands at the side of one of the busiest roads in the country, Route 65. The three-generational human chain held signs pointing to an off road dialogue tent that had been erected on a small hill between the main road and Tel Megiddo. The dialogue tent was constructed by Jews and Arabs living in the Megiddo-Wadi Ara region under the auspices of the Givat Haviva Center for Shared Living, a campus promoting positive encounters between Arabs and Jews in the region and further afield.

The dialogue tent had been hastily erected in response to the recent wave of terror in which four Israelis standing at a bus stop along the highway were run down and stabbed a few days earlier. The anger, frustration and total bewilderment were almost palpable among the older generation gathered at the roadside. The Hebrew and Arabic messages on the roadside banners proclaimed that Jews and Arabs refused to forego a shared, peaceful life together; others called for partnership, equality and security for Jews and Arabs.

"Too little, too late," was a comment heard from one of the Jewish middle-aged banner wavers. "So why have you come today then?" asked an Arab twenty-something standing next to him. "Because I just couldn't stay home and do nothing," was the immediate answer. The younger man gave an understanding nod, then they shook hands before turning back to face the road and energetically wave to the passing motorists and point to the dialogue tent on the hill, where circles of white plastic chairs were arranged neatly on a grassy verge in the shade, hoping some of the drivers would make a pit stop of support on route to their destinations.

There were those that did stop. Every time the traffic light at the junction changed, scores of cars came roaring by on both sides of the highway. The majority of those who reacted to the signs gave hand waves, honked horns, and gave thumbs up signs. A handful made rude gestures, and one young driver in a black car slowed down to yell abuse, most of which was drowned out by the calls of Shalom or Salaam from the demonstrators.

Passing between the people, a traditionally dressed Arab lady from the Wadi Ara village of Biyadah, held up an enormous banana leaf upon which she had inscribed, in Hebrew and Arabic, words of encouragement toward better understanding and tolerance between Jews and Arabs. In the noon heat, the leaf began to curl, hiding her important message. A number of Jewish children and their mother, asking her what she had written on the slowly closing up leaf, helped her unfurl the sides so that all could see, read and hopefully be lifted and strengthened by her words of encouragement.

"We are trying to present hope, faith and a joint responsibility in the face of the terrible fear, hatred and racism," said Givat Haviva executive director Yaniv Sagee, a member of a nearby kibbutz. Standing next to him was his wife Dalia, a teacher at the *Bridge Over the Wadi* Jewish-Arab bilingual school founded by the Hand in Hand organization situated in the Wadi Ara Muslim village of Kfar Kara. Through seminars, cultural events, tours, and cross-community projects, and a recent annual Conference in March 2017, we attempt to foster goals of Jewish-Arab dialogue, restorative processes, civic equality, and mutual responsibility. We hope to submit our proposal, "A Roadmap for a Shared Society" to the Knesset in December 2017, and have plans for a joint industrial park as well.

I (Lydia) have been involved as an informal educator in the International Department of Givat Haviva's Jewish-Arab Center for Peace for twenty-five years, working on joint projects in the Wadi Ara region. I came to Israel to volunteer in 1967 and have lived ever since and raised my family at Kibbutz Mishmar Haemek.

Givat Haviva, started in 1949 by the National Education Center of the Kibbutz Federation, aims to build an inclusive, socially cohesive society by engaging "divided communities" to work together towards common goals, based on principles of equality, cooperation, empowerment, and understanding in areas of education and tourism. Mohammad Darawshe, Director of Shared Society, Shared Living, at Givat Haviva, believes in sharing cultural traditions and creating opportunities to demonstrate that cooperation is possible. Despite the mutually exclusive narratives of our two peoples, living in the Jewish state of Israel should offer equal rights for all of its citizens. The Givat Haviva International School offers a boarding program to develop committed young leaders to work in conflict resolution in their own communities.

Life in this region is complicated but we aim to be good neighbors. One example of a "divided community" is the village of Barta'a, located about five minutes from Route 65. Village families wound up divided as a consequence of the 1949 Armistice (Green) Line: East Barta'a remained under Jordanian control with over 4,000 Palestinians until

1967, and West Barta'a has over 3,000 Arab-Israeli citizens.

Barta'a has become quite a commercial center. In 2000, I led a bus tour for older members of our Kibbutz, Mishmar Haemek, on a visit to "the other side of the world" to meet and connect with our Palestinian neighbors and discuss their view of life post-Oslo. In a warm gathering it turned out that the father of one of our elder kibbutzniks had been best friends with the father of one of our Palestinian hosts before 1948.

These two communities have no checkpoint, fence, police, or army, but also have had little interchange since the Intifadas. The Megiddo Prison, built by the British Army during the British Mandate, is situated directly on the opposite side of the road where the demonstration took place. Hundreds of Palestinians are imprisoned there. It was here, directly under the watchtowers of the prison, just a few kilometers from the 1949 Armistice Line, that in June 2002, a Palestinian terrorist driving a car packed with explosives slammed into the side of a green Egged public bus, killing 17 Israelis, seriously injuring many more. A large memorial created in steel by the father of one of the victims sits a few meters from the roadside, a laser printed image of each victim on the 17 *yahrzeit* (memorial) lanterns adorning the main structure.

While on the other side of the road, rays of sunshine glistened on the memorial to the dark days just a decade ago, the Israeli Jews and Arabs who stood together this week at Megiddo (Armageddon), sat together in the dialogue tent and talked in discussion circles on the grass, eventually drifted off home with fervent hopes in their hearts of better days ahead.

*Chapter 11*

# COMPASSION FOR THE POOR, THE VULNERABLE, AND THE STRANGER

"Has not one God created us all?"

Malachi 2:10

"If all the sufferings and pain in the world were gathered on one side of a scale and poverty was on the other side, poverty would outweigh them all."

Exodus Rabbah 31:14

"There will never cease to be needy people in your land, which is why I command you: Open your hand to the poor and needy kinsman in your land."

Deuteronomy 15:7-11

"*Tzedakah* is equal to all the other mitzvot combined."

Babylonian Talmud, Baba Bathra 9A

"The poor person standing at the door does more for the householder than the householder does for the poor."

Leviticus Rabbah 34:8

The Torah recognized that there will always be poverty in society. For that reason, the Torah mandated that the solution to poverty should be built into the social structure and not rely only on individuals' generosity. By creating a requirement to feed, clothe, and house the poor (non-Jews as well as Jews), the near poor, and the desperately poor, those vulnerable members would be cared for. The Torah instructs: "If there be a needy person among you … do not harden your heart and shut your hand against your needy kinsman. Rather you must open your hand and lend him sufficient for what he needs." (Deuteronomy 15:7-8).

Ancient Israel, an agrarian society, established guidelines describing what farmers and landowners must do for the poor, such as leaving a corner edge of their field un-reaped. (Leviticus 19:10). It was specified to leave over grains, stalks, vines, olive trees, and fallen fruit for the poor: "When you shake the fruit from your olive tree, do not go over them again; they shall go to the stranger, the fatherless, and the widow. (Deuteronomy 29:19-21).

The Torah also required *kvod ha'ani* – respect for the poor. It was forbidden to insult the poor or accuse them of being undeserving, for in God's eyes, all people are equal and should be cared for. The Torah recognized the serious emotional impact of poverty and was concerned about the poor person's sense of shame or embarrassment having to beg or ask for help. Hence the injunction: "Do not close the door in the face of borrowers." (Babylonian Talmud, Gitten 496-509). Maimonides states that one must not refuse help when one is needy, because *Tzedakah* is more than just kindness; it is society's obligation.

God is said to especially protect the vulnerable: the orphan, the widow, and deaf, blind, and elderly people. The Torah emphasizes: "You shall not mistreat any widow or orphan for they lack protectors." (Exodus 22:20-23). An individual who tramples on the rights of the weak is seen as an enemy of God and humanity, as in the following words: "If you afflict them in any way and they cry out to me, I shall surely hear their cry. My wrath will become hot and I will kill you by the sword, your wives shall be widows and your children orphans." (Exodus 22: 21-23).

Due to awareness of a woman's more vulnerable position in society, the *ketubah* (marriage certificate) and inheritance rules in Judaism were modified in order to protect the wife and give her some security in case of divorce. In Talmudic times, taxes were collected to help the needy, and Jews were commanded to give 10% of their earnings to the poor along with an additional percentage of the harvest annually, so as to create a more equitable and compassionate society.

It is said that *Tzedakah* is equal in importance to all the other commandments combined. Maimonides identified eight degrees of *Tzedakah* in his Mishneh Torah, (Laws of Gifts to the Poor, 10:17). The highest degree is to strengthen the hand of a poor Jew by finding a job for the person, or making a gift or a loan to enable the person to earn a living and become self-sufficient (Shabbat 63a). The next highest degree is to give anonymously.

Our sages taught that real *Tzedakah* is giving needy people what they lack: "If he has no clothes, clothe him; if he lacks housewares, buy them for him; if he or she hasn't gotten married, help him to do so." (Maimonides, Laws of Gifts for the Poor, 7:3). In other words, restore a person's livelihood and dignity. The act of giving what others need involves transcending one's own preferences, in an effort to truly understand another's perspective. For this reason, acts of loving kindness, called *Gemilut chesed*, can be more important than just giving money.

*Compassion for the Poor, the Vulnerable, and the Stranger*

While the stranger or sojourner often becomes "the other" in society, the Bible instructs us that: "The stranger who dwells with you shall be treated as your native born, you shall love him like yourself for you were strangers in the land of Egypt." (Leviticus 19:33-34). "If your brother becomes impoverished and his hand falters besides you, you shall strengthen him, whether he is a stranger or a native, so that he can live with you." (Leviticus 25:35). Because we are all children of God, including non-Jewish residents who wish to live in peace with us, we are told to welcome the stranger (*ger*) and extend hospitality.

The stories in this chapter highlight the importance of addressing problems of poverty and the suffering of those who are vulnerable. One story tells of a man who made it his mission to feed schoolchildren who lack food at home, as well as to provide a warm place for them to come after school. Another story describes a family medicine clinic specifically established to treat and support poor refugees from Africa. The story about IsraAID tells of their extraordinary humanitarian work in disaster zones, as well as providing relief to refugees fleeing conflict zones. Finally, drivers escorting Palestinian children and their mothers for medical treatment from checkpoints to Israeli hospitals and back, are doing a double mitzvah: The drivers provide free transportation and absorb the costs, and the Israeli hospitals render skilled care to show compassion to strangers.

*Chapter 11*

## Fat Meir's Kitchen
## Ruti Glasner

Welcome to Fat Meir's kitchen, where we have been providing hot meals for children in need in Israel's Bat Yam community since 2003. We are guided by the Biblical commandment to care for the hungry, the orphan, the poor, and the disadvantaged among us. Every day our kitchen delivers hundreds of sandwiches to schools, feeding children who "forgot" their lunch or lack food at home, and serves hot lunches to children at our kitchen. You may ask, how did this start?

Fat Meir's real name is Meir Shoef. He was born in 1944 in Bulgaria and came to Israel in the middle of the War for Independence. Meir has spent much of his life volunteering and helping people, believing that *Kol Yisrael aravim zeh b'zeh* – All of Israel is responsible one for the other. As a teenager and later in military service Meir became active in the Maccabi youth movement and worked for thirty years in real estate, while he and his wife raised a family of three children.

In 1971 Meir joined the "Bnei Brit" Bat Yam chapter. In the 1980s he volunteered to teach Hebrew to immigrants from Ethiopia and help them in other ways as well. He started a choir and guitar/mandolin band that performed in hospitals and retirement homes, as well as founding a student scholarship fund for IDF orphans. Meir loved volunteering and performing good deeds that lifted others' spirits and brought joy to people.

At the end of 1999, Meir unexpectedly had a severe stroke that paralyzed half of his body. He could hardly talk and had to learn to walk again like a baby. Through physical therapy over three years he regained speech and strength, but was left with a drooping eye and was unable to work.

Meir knew that to recover, he couldn't just sit around the house watching TV or go out to drink coffee all day. Instead he decided to give back to the community, so for three years Meir worked at Beit Hashanti, a place for homeless youth who were kicked out of their homes because their parents couldn't take care of them.

At the homeless shelter located near Shuk Hacarmel, Meir saw hungry people fighting for food. Some would even sift through garbage looking for food and eat rotten tomatoes. When he learned that 300,000 Israeli children were going hungry he decided that he would devote himself to helping poor and hungry kids. That is when he decided to open Fat Meir's Kitchen as a soup kitchen for hungry children so they would have at least one hot meal each day.

## Compassion for the Poor, the Vulnerable, and the Stranger

*Meir in the kitchen.*

We went to a flea market to get an old oven and refrigerator. We invited kids from a nearby school to come to the kitchen after school. We started by making about twenty sandwiches a day, and soon we were making 200 sandwiches a day. After meeting with the social workers in the nearby school, other schools heard about us. We began serving many schools, and now make about 700 sandwiches a day.

Fat Meir's kitchen has a reliable staff of volunteers who are young and old, and from around the world, who come to help. These young people have energized our project. Several organizations and donors give us money, chefs, supplies, and food. In order to raise funds needed for operating the kitchen, some of the best gourmet chefs in Israel volunteer and come to teach cooking classes open to the public. The classes raise funds to provide more kitchen appliances, food, and recreational resources for the children. The funds help provide Bar Mitzvah parties for families who can't afford the cost. The kitchen also supplies computers and internet for the children who don't have a computer at home. Somehow we manage to get by, but could always use more support.

I, Ruti, am Meir's "right hand" in the kitchen, making sure volunteers know what to do, organizing food donations, helping the chefs who do workshops, and keeping the workshop attendees satisfied. My husband

## Chapter 11

Gabi and I have been volunteering for over six years. Twice a week we go to coffee shops just before closing time to get leftover cakes, burekas, and rolls. Gabi goes to the bakery at 3 a.m. to get pita bread. We begin early at 6 a.m. making and delivering hundreds of sandwiches to local schools. For some of the kids, their morning break may be the first food they eat that day.

I used to be an art instructor helping people with disabilities, and was a *shaliach* at Camp Ramah Nyack for thirty-five summers. Gabi is a retired gym instructor. Sometimes my grandkids come to volunteer with me when they have school vacation. This makes me feel grateful that the next generation is continuing these important values.

Our other regular volunteer staff includes Mili, a group tour guide, who cooks lunch at noon for about two dozen children daily who come to the kitchen after school. We purchase raw ingredients to cook meals from scratch so they are nutritious, healthy, and most importantly, tasty. We believe that food helps children learn better and grow. Mili also manages the funds, gets companies to donate products for use in the sandwiches and meals, and makes sure that every shekel is used correctly for the benefit of the children.

Around one o'clock the children start to arrive, where they find nicely set tables waiting for them. They eat and converse politely with each other, just like children do at a proper family dinner. Besides the needed and delicious food, the most important thing the kitchen staff provides is attention and warmth. An ordinary soup kitchen is no place for kids, because children need more: They need a place to come after school, to stay around, do their homework, and play. "We love it here," says one of the girls, "because we have fun."

Some of our other regular volunteers include Soli, age 67, Yossi, age 70, and Miri, age 49, and Shai, age 77, along with high schoolers Natanel and Danny, who are doing their community service here. They describe the homey feeling they experience the minute they step inside Fat Meir's kitchen. Lastly, Young Judea Helpers come as part of their year course, along with Ukrainian participants in the Masa program. There is a feeling of partnership and community that motivates everyone. All of us, and especially Fat Meir, believe that the strength of a society is rooted in shared mutual responsibility. And we have experienced firsthand that the giver receives as much and more than he or she gives.

## Refugee Clinic
### Dr. Bernie Green

Entering the Tel Aviv Central Bus Station is like arriving into another world: exotic, bustling, and energetic. Around the bus station live thousands of refuge-seekers from Africa, mostly Eritrea, Sudan, and Somalia, who have undergone a treacherous journey through hostile countries, fleeing from ethnic conflict and civil war.

I have been a volunteer at the Refugee Clinic there for seven years. It is one of two medical centers providing health care for this population. In January 2013 the Health Ministry significantly improved the facilities available for refugees by opening up Terem, an emergency medical center. Here a team of full-time doctors, X-ray and ultrasound facilities, lab, and basic medicines have become available. Refugees from all over the country, from Metulla in the north to Eilat in the south, come to the Tel Aviv Central Bus Station to receive medical care.

The volunteer doctors look after chronic medical problems. Most good health systems are based on Family Medicine, which provides a wide net of services, as well as referral of cases that need to be seen by other medical specialties. Because the family physician becomes acquainted with patients and their families, ideally there is continuity of care.

At the Refugee clinic, however, we face many challenges. A major one is the cultural differences in medicine between the Western medical model and the East African model. East African tribal medicine is often based on beliefs that illness is caused by the patient's body being invaded by hostile spirits. The tribal doctor can tell just by looking at the patient, which ritual tea ceremony will free the body from the hostile spirits. In the beginning, when I asked my patients what symptoms they have, and told them that I wanted to give them a physical examination, they sometimes looked at me as if I was stupid. What? Can't you tell what is wrong with me just by looking at me?

There are a lot of somatic symptoms, due in part to the different cultural frame of reference. For example, the patient may relate that when he blinks his right eye, he feels a pain in his big toe. Another patient may describe a sensation of electric currents running through his body. There is no medical explanation for this, but the patient believes there is a connection. The tribal doctor doesn't need to deal with specific anatomical or physiological facts, which frees him up to prescribe generalized treatment, which often acts as a placebo (cure by suggestion).

## Chapter 11

Many patients have medical problems that have troubled them for years. I have to try to understand the problem, decide on the appropriate interventions, referral, or treatment in a situation where options are limited. Many of my patients suffer from post-traumatic stress syndrome following their journey on the way to Israel. I have had patients with gunshot wounds, and women who are pregnant due to rape. Many patients' symptoms are a combination of physical and emotional problems. Helping these people with such difficult problems is certainly a challenge.

Until recently, even basic communication with the patient was difficult, so we had to use other patients waiting in the reception area to help us translate. Now we now have better access to translators. I had one case of an Eritrean patient speaking Tigris that was translated into Amharic by an Ethiopian. Then it was translated into Arabic, and eventually into English. By the end I had no idea what the medical problem was, but it was an amazing example of cooperation across cultures.

I often have to be creative as a physician when prescribing medications. We have medicines that have been donated, but each session I have to check what is in stock in order to prescribe accordingly. Otherwise I will give a prescription to buy the medicines. However, what do you do when a mother doesn't have the twenty shekels to buy antibiotics for her child with an ear infection? Diabetic patients coming each week to receive expensive insulin, may not have access to a refrigerator to store the life-preserving medicine. Many of the diabetic patients that I see run around with a level of sugar four times the normal level with very few repercussions, while a similar Western patient would be hospitalized with that level of sugar. And what do you do with a twenty-year-old man with kidney failure who has no chance of receiving dialysis?

On the other hand, we have our successes as well. A forty-year-old refugee with severe high blood pressure, resulting in a ruptured aorta (a major central artery), was hospitalized and operated on successfully. He then developed a heart block (the electrical system that regulates the heart beat stopped working), and a pacemaker was implanted. He received tens of thousands of shekels of medical care. In Eritrea he surely would have been long dead. When he comes to the clinic to receive four kinds of blood pressure medicine, it gives me great pleasure that I can provide him with the critical medications from our donated medical cabinet. Terem provides excellent work and emergency care, but in addition we need to provide a basic primary care system for the refugees with continuity of care, general examinations, specialist referrals, and social work services.

You may ask me why I do this work? As Jews we have often throughout history been in the position of being refugees and being dependent on the tolerance and help of the local community. Judaism has a tradition of being empathic to the weak and vulnerable. When I think of my family, my wife, children, and grandchildren, I feel blessed. I also feel the need to give back. There are many passages in the Bible about this, and one of my favorites is a quote from Shemot 23:9 (Mishpatim): "You shall not oppress a stranger, for you know the feelings of the stranger, having yourselves been strangers in the Land of Egypt."

Chapter 11

## *IsraAID: Humanitarian Help for Strangers Everywhere*
## Yotam Polizer

Scenes of natural disasters around the world such as earthquakes, hurricanes, floods, and fires are routinely shown on television. Most people feel horrified watching lives being disrupted, uprooted, and destroyed. Injured survivors are traumatized and need medical help, practical relief, and psychological support to begin to recover from such overwhelming circumstances.

Not infrequently, on the television screen, amidst the chaos and rubble or floodwaters, one can notice volunteers wearing IsraAID tee shirts. These dedicated men and women have come from Israel to provide rescue and comfort. It is little Israel again, with teams from across the globe, who offer search and rescue operations, emergency medical aid, relief supplies, post-traumatic psychological support, and rebuilding of communities.

What may not be visible on television, however, is what happens after the initial chaotic period of intense and urgent need (the first 48 hours, several weeks or longer) is over. By then, the majority of funding has been spent and the international volunteers have left. IsraAID, however, remains there on the ground to work towards longer-term recovery. IsraAID partners with local government agencies in communities, with the goal of rebuilding self-sufficiency for the future.

How did IsraAID come into being? In 2001 a group of Israeli activists got together and established IsraAID as a forum for international aid. Since Israelis travel the globe extensively, many of whom are already doing humanitarian work, the forum became an umbrella organization to further motivate and support such activities. Today IsraAID is an independent humanitarian aid organization helping people in need worldwide. IsraAID has a nine-million dollar budget, is funded by Israeli and North American donors, partners with organizations, and is supported by businesses, foundations, and UNICEF. With a staff of 300 and 1600 volunteers, IsraAID has helped in 31 countries and 10 states in America. In 2016 IsraAID opened its first office in the United States.

IsraAID has intervened following earthquakes in Peru, Haiti, Nepal, Japan, and central Italy; in typhoons and cyclones; Ebola in Africa; and Washington State wildfires, to name a few places. In natural disasters, such as the devastating earthquake in Mexico City, IsraAID volunteers were among the first to arrive. They came within 48 hours, bringing food, water, sanitation, and psychological aid. There they collaborated with other Jewish relief groups on the ground doing search, rescue, and recovery operations.

Most recently, IsraAID has been extremely busy helping in the disasters of hurricanes Harvey in Texas, Irma in Florida, Maria in Puerto Rico, and the wildfires in California. IsraAID teams stay longer when needed, after the media attention and donations have waned. It is not uncommon for the IsraAID team to remain in a community for several months and even years, as in Haiti, which was a "game changer" because of the extensive damage and long-term need.

Israelis have expertise in water filtration and water technology, along with skills cleaning debris and giving post-traumatic care from their own experiences with terror attacks. Israelis have a way of organizing quickly, cutting through bureaucratic layers, and possess leadership skills learned in army service. They can coordinate, communicate, and identify gaps in needed services with efficiency.

Entering a disaster area to help the most affected community, IsraAid often partners with the local Jewish community when there is one, and enlists their help in rescue and recovery efforts. When the Jewish community is the most affected by the disaster, as happened in Houston, IsraAID partnered with it and the Yazidi community, a persecuted religious minority from Iraq, as well as with military veterans. Connecting with Diaspora Jewish communities has become a central part of Israel's ethos, employing young American and Israeli Jewish volunteers through a fellowship program. A derivative benefit is that this younger generation experiences and can participate firsthand in Israel's *Tikkun Olam* work in the world, such as caring for the stranger and those most in need.

Sometimes the disasters have been man-made, such as the Syrian Civil War, in which unspeakable carnage and cruelty have been unleashed onto civilians, killing, injuring, and displacing tens of thousands from their homes. The fleeing refugees travelled for hours, paying smugglers to take them on the dangerous six-mile trip from Western Turkey to the Greek Island of Lesbos, hoping to reach Europe, while risking drowning and hypothermia at sea. On the island of Lesbos, a real life and death drama played itself out.

As the boats neared the shore, IsraAID workers rushed into the water to steady the boats and help the most injured, wrap babies into blankets, and offer medical aid. Refugees arrived dazed, crying, and traumatized. The volunteers worked together to reassure the weary and frightened travelers, telling them: "You've arrived and are safe. We are here to help you get through this." Quickly surveying the situation, the IsraAID workers provided immediate medical care to those most in need, along with emergency oxygen, defibrillators, and medicines. They distributed blankets, water, food, and warm clothing to the refugees who came with almost nothing.

The refugees, largely Muslims of all ages, were surprised to hear Israelis speaking Arabic, and it may have been the first time they have encountered Jews. At times Israelis wound up helping people who technically came from enemy countries, but none of that mattered on the beach in Lesbos. Care is offered to all human beings, regardless of race, religion, nationality, color, or language. One IsraAID worker reflected that he is motivated to do this work because he recalls the journey of his relatives, Holocaust survivors who were desperately seeking refuge when countries closed their doors to them.

The refugees may also have been surprised to see Israelis and Palestinians, and people of different faiths (Jews, Muslims, Christians, and Druze) working together as a team. Because Israelis and Palestinians have experience with trauma, they understand it and can work well in stressful situations. Beyond the physical trauma, IsraAID provides psychological support to address refugees' emotional needs for comfort and helps them begin to cope with their situation. The volunteers' consistent "being there" helps people feel safe and empowered.

Beyond disaster relief and refugee rescue, IsraAID has been involved in an increasing number of international development projects, with a focus on agriculture, medicine, and mental health. IsraAID has also helped communities in Africa gain access to clean water, and is training Ugandans in basic water technology to improve health and quality of life. In South Sudan IsraAID is offering vocational training to 10,000 youths and school dropouts, with a goal of involving them constructively in their communities. Through the trades, electronics, computing, and other fields the youths are being and feeling helpful in building the new country of South Sudan.

As IsraAID's Co-Chief Executive Officer, together with my close partner and friend, Navonel Glick (Voni), we are very proud of the humanitarian work we do, honoring the important values of showing compassion to poor, the vulnerable, and the stranger. Our motives as Israelis are to actively help, and because of our backgrounds and many pragmatic skills in crisis situations, we can do something.

## White Knight on Four Wheels
## Lydia Aisenberg

It is 7 a.m. with the heat and humidity already on the rise, as two young Palestinian mothers and their children walk through a narrow, wire-mesh tunnel leading from the Jenin side of the Jalameh check point to the Israeli side. Their children are seriously ill. One is an eight-year-old girl with cancer, a silk scarf tied tightly around her smooth head, and a little boy, not yet two years of age, struck by a crippling kidney disease.

Both children are undergoing treatment at Rambam Medical Center in Haifa. The young girl is on her way to Rambam with her mother for a checkup after a course of radiation, and the little boy is on his daily trip from Jenin to Haifa and back again. Six days a week his mother brings him through the checkpoint cradled in her arm, a small carry bag with clean clothing and some food slung over her other shoulder.

Years of suicide bombings and terror attacks have necessitated security checkpoints upon entering Israel, and Palestinians are not allowed to drive private vehicles into Israel. However, the Palestinian Authority does send many hundreds of sick children and adults from the West Bank to receive treatment in Israel, but nobody on either side of the checkpoint takes responsibility for their transportation from checkpoints to the hospitals, or for return journeys at the end of the day from the checkpoint to the Palestinians' homes. The journey from Jalameh checkpoint to Rambam Hospital takes about an hour.

The car park on the Israeli side of the Jalameh checkpoint is abuzz with activity. Scores of men, mostly in their mid-30s and above, are gathering on the curbsides waiting for their employers to collect them. Others jump into already waiting vehicles and head off to another work day in construction or agriculture in the Jezreel Valley. Late afternoons the scene is reversed as the workers and the sick return the way they came, back through the checkpoint into Jenin and surrounding villages on the other side of the Green Line running over the Gilboa Mountain and across this corner of the valley. A Palestinian explains that on a good day it takes around 45 minutes to travel from his village to the checkpoint, 20 minutes to get through and ten minutes from there to his workplace, a factory near Afula. On not so good days, if there are problems at the checkpoint, it might take several hours or more.

A tall, distinguished-looking gentleman with closely cropped white hair and beard, sparkling eyes and a broad smile on his face, gets out of a large white van and greets the two young mothers and sick children.

## Chapter 11

His name is Amatzia Dayan, a seventy-something member of Kibbutz Ein Hashofet, a tour guide by profession, and volunteer driver for *Derech Hachlamah* – "On the road to Recovery" organization. For the women and their children he is a shining white knight on a horse, well, on four wheels anyway.

*Derech Hachlamah* was founded several years ago by Yuval Roth. He recruited friends as volunteer drivers, and today there are about two hundred such volunteers. *Derech Hachlamah* has driven over 90,000 kilometers (55,000 miles) in 2010 alone to help Palestinians access health care in Israel.

Fifteen years ago, Yuval Roth's brother was serving his annual reserve duty in the West Bank. He was murdered by Palestinian terrorists disguised at religious Jews who picked up the hitchhiking reservist. Roth joined the Bereaved Families Circle and when a Palestinian member of that organization who was being treated in an Israeli hospital asked for help with transportation to and from the hospital, Yuval Roth didn't hesitate. In that moment *Derech Hachlamah* was born.

These days Palestinians are met by volunteer drivers the likes of Amatzia Dayan, and their roster is organized and sent out by Roth; both men are really unsung heroes. "Everybody does whatever they can but it is a costly business with petrol prices being what they are," explains Amatzia as we head for Haifa, with the young mothers and children settled on the seats behind us. The toddler is already fast asleep, and the little girl is beginning to nod off on her mother's shoulder.

"The strain on the organization is enormous as more and more patients appeal for help with transportation, whether to Rambam or hospitals in the center of the country," explained Amatzia, who constantly glances in the driver's seat mirror to see that all is okay with his passengers. In extremely basic Arabic, Amatzia explains that there will also be someone waiting to take the family home at the end of the day. There might be a shortage of conversation, but there is certainly no shortage of smiles and head nodding all the way to Haifa and Rambam.

"I help wherever I can, nothing political, purely for humanitarian reasons," said Amatzia Dayan, pulling in to the driveway of the Rambam Medical Center to drop off the children and their mothers. Papers need to be shown, bags need to be checked, and goodbyes need to be said. The young patient from Jenin clutches her mother's hand as Amatzia is about to re-enter the vehicle. "*Todah rabbah*" (thank you very much) they both call out in Hebrew, and wave as they enter the building together with the other lady, her son fast asleep on her shoulder.

At four o'clock in the afternoon another "good person" will be waiting there to take them back to the Jalameh checkpoint. At at 7 in the morning the next day, another will be waiting to return the boy to Haifa for his life saving dialysis once more. Palestinians at the checkpoint view Amatzia and Yuval as "*anashim tovim*" (good people), so *Derech Hachlamah* is truly a way to recovery in all ways.

*Chapter 12*

# LIGHT UNTO THE NATIONS: TECHNOLOGY FOR THE GOOD OF MANKIND

"I will set you a covenant to the people, for a Light unto the Nations…"

Yeshayahu 42:5-7

"Don't tell me you can't do it; tell me how you're going to do it."

David Ben-Gurion

"If an expert says it can't be done, get another expert."

David Ben-Gurion

The original mandate to become a "Light unto the Nations" comes directly from the Bible. The covenant with God required the Children of Israel to follow the Torah commandments of faith, morality, and behavior, so as to be a shining example for the nations of the world. Ben-Gurion, Israel's first Prime Minister, chose the menorah, a symbol of light, as Israel's national emblem to symbolize Israel's purpose in the world.

Israel has become a veritable "Light unto the Nations" through its incredible technological achievements across many fields: numerous inventions and discoveries in biotech, math, chemistry, physics, optics, robotics, economics, theoretical computer science, defense, energy, agriculture, media, and medicine. With thousands of start-ups, Israel was ranked as the second most innovative country in the world, according to the World Economic Forum's Global Competitiveness Report (2016-17).

Israel has been called the "Start-Up Nation,[1] with attributes of intelligence, curiosity, productivity, problem solving, and being willing to fail and learn from mistakes to overcome obstacles. Other "startup" factors are the proximity of great universities to companies, egalitarianism, individualism, nurturance, and teamwork, traits often learned and inculcated during Army service.

It would be impossible to list all of Israel's inventions, but just to mention a few: Nanowire, disk-on-key (USB flash drive), first Intel Processor, world's smallest DNA computer, PC and laser keyboard, and not to mention ... the cell phone in everyone's hand, along with What's App? In software there is Viber, Mobileye, WAZE, wix.com, Windows XP, Java, Quictionary. In the Defense industry: the Uzi submachine gun, Iron Dome, David's Sling, surface-to-air-heat-seeking missiles, metal detectors, and tazers. In medicine and health, the Pill Cam endoscopic camera, drugs for Parkinsons disease and Gaucher disease, Copaxone for multiple sclerosis, Interferon proteins, discoveries in ophthalmology to improve vision, and emergency field hospital bandages. Israel is known for revolutionary advances in drip irrigation, desalination, hybrid seeds, lawn mowing robots, Biobee, new plant species; in energy, rechargeable batteries. In consumer goods: Soda Stream, Baby Sense Monitor, popular TV shows such as Homeland. And who could forget Gal Gadot as Wonder Woman?

For several reasons I deliberately placed "Light unto the Nations" as the final value after saving a life, justice, inclusivity, loving your neighbor, and compassion for the poor, vulnerable, and the stranger. First, by fully practicing all those prior values, Israel will become a better society and a "Light unto the Nations." The second reason is that the above values are about moral behavior between people in society. While brilliant creative inventions are dazzling, and contribute to societal advancements, kindness, fairness, compassion, and justice are necessary for a society to survive and thrive over the long haul. I always return to Ben-Gurion's comment: "The state of Israel will prove itself not by military might or technological achievement, but by its moral character and human values." As the prophets were want to remind, these values are paramount, superseding wealth and power.

In this chapter, you will read not only about Israel's use of technology, but technology for humanitarian purposes and for the good of mankind. The first story is about Israel's ingenuity, water technology, and solar energy that are literally changing lives in African countries. It is breathtaking to watch Sivan Yaari of Innovation Africa flick a switch to turn on a light bulb in a classroom of African children. The children begin joyfully cheering, because for the first time they will be able to learn better. Another story tells of a brilliant Israeli inventor who became quadriplegic, and then created devices to help handicapped people stand and walk again. Finally, while Israel helps so many around the world, I believe that enlightenment should begin at home. Two important high-tech programs enable Ethiopian-Israelis and Arab-Israelis to acquire the training and jobs necessary to succeed in Israel's most important and advanced hi-tech sector.

*Chapter 12*

## *Here Comes the Sun:*
*Harnessing Israeli Technology to Bring Energy, Water, and Light to the World*
## Genna Brand for Sivan Yaari

Today, millions of people have never seen light at night except for moonlight. 1.2 billion people live in extreme poverty, and one in every nine individuals are hungry and live without clean water. Imagine this – in Africa alone, more than 620 million people lack access to electricity. It is hard to understand the power that energy and electricity have over individuals, communities, regions, countries, and even continents today.

For those growing up in developed countries, smart phones, video games, internet, and other modern trends consume daily life; often people in these countries take for granted life's most basic needs, such as food, water, energy, and modern healthcare. The lack of energy in the developing world oppresses its inhabitants. Amid their primitive life style, light and water can only be mentioned in their prayers.

During the creation of Israel, Israeli Prime Minister David Ben-Gurion had a vision and hope for Israel to be a "Light unto the Nations." For that reason he specially chose the menorah as the emblem of Israel. Today, Israel is a driving force behind many innovations, companies, and organizations that are pushing the earth towards a better tomorrow. One of these unique organizations is called Innovation: Africa (iA). This American non-profit now operates in eight countries (Uganda, Malawi, Tanzania, Ethiopia, South Africa, the Democratic Republic of Congo, Senegal, and recently, Cameroon). Spanning across three continents, iA has focused on sharing Israeli innovations and literally bringing "light unto [other] nations" across the African continent, more specifically, sub-Saharan Africa.

Innovation Africa (iA) found that a simple solution lies within a free source of energy: the sun. The same sun that is drying the land and parching the tongues of people living in rural African villages can also be the source of the solution, providing the energy needed to help them break the cycle of poverty. The United Nations award winning U.S. based non-profit, Innovation: Africa, was founded in 2008 by Sivan Yaari. Its mission was to bring Israeli solar, water, and agricultural technologies to rural African villages. Since its founding iA has completed over 170 solar installations bringing light, access to clean water, improved education, refrigeration for vaccines and medicines, proper nutrition and food security to over one million people in eight countries located in the most remote villages of Africa.

In February 2017, Yaari and her team reached a new area to extend their projects into the northeastern Uganda-Karamoja region. For the first time they came face-to-face with a level of poverty, famine, and drought existing there that was beyond the comprehension of Yaari and her team; a situation that they could have never prepared for. Famine and drought had stolen the lives of thousands because of a lack of clean water, although water exists in aquifers beneath the ground. With a little bit of energy to pump water up from the aquifers, many lives could have been saved. Simply put, innocent lives were lost because technology couldn't get to the right places quick enough. In the mere seven days that iA arrived in Karamoja, 37 people died.

Yaari and her team began working immediately, meeting with each village to learn about their needs and daily struggles. iA instantly began drilling, installing, and providing solar water pumping systems with over twelve taps of water distributed throughout each of the six villages, allowing water to travel up to 4 kilometers in every direction. Upon completion of construction, for the first time, iA organized food relief efforts and sent trucks of beans and maize to the communities in order to keep people alive. Now and forever, these solar and water projects are providing access to clean safe water to 27,000 people.

iA is now installing Israeli-developed drip irrigation technology to allow farmers to grow more using less water. Not only will this ensure proper nutrition, but families will have a sustainable model for food security, and the ability to generate an income by selling surplus vegetables and crops. iA's local team, in partnership with Members of Parliament, is continuing to find more villages in Karamoja region in which to drill, pump, and install more solar water pumping systems and Israeli technologies that will empower and impact thousands of lives.

Moreover, something even bigger and more profound was apparent, that connected iA, the Jewish people, Israel, and the Karamoja region, making the story come full circle – *"lisgor et HaMa'agal."* In 1903 there was a British mandate to offer Karamoja region to Theodor Herzl as the homeland for the poor and homeless Jewish people! The story is indeed ironic, but most impressive is that today an American NGO with an office in Israel is sharing life-saving Israeli technologies to break this region's cycle of poverty and provide a sense of independence and self-sufficiency for the first time.

Yaari believes that the mission of the State of Israel is to be a "Light unto the Nations": "Innovation: Africa is rooted in Biblical values, a mission of *Tikkun Olam,* principles of Zionism, and the DNA of Israelis. We feel privileged by our heritage, and with privilege comes

## Chapter 12

responsibility. Our responsibility is to share Israeli technology in water, agriculture, solar, and health with those in need." Yaari and her team have been grateful to see the true impact of these simple technologies on the ground. These innovations can empower individuals' lives for future generations, so that thirst, hunger, sickness, disease, and ultimately poverty, can become a reality of the past.

Whether or not we want to accept it – this was always our destiny. Today more than ever, our work is crucial for humanitarian reasons and political reasons, for the safety of Israel and the safety of the world. By empowering people to become stronger and self-sufficient, we give them the support to move forward so that the days of lack of water will become memories of the past. Innovation: Africa prides itself on working fast and arriving to the village first – being the face of Israel and a life-saving one. Our team of Israeli and local professionals is often greeted with songs and dances of appreciation.

In a few of the countries where iA operates, however, extremist groups prey on the weak, poverty stricken families by promising one meal a day, free education and access to clean water, unfortunately luring people to become involved in movements that are not always peaceful. This drives iA's team to work even faster so people don't have to convert out of desperation. By working quickly on technological advancements, iA hopes to spread a positive image of Israel's helpfulness.

They don't call Israel the "Start-Up Nation" for nothing. iA's office in Israel gives immediate access to the most creative and innovative minds, start-ups that design highly efficient water, solar, and green technologies for use in rural villages. iA is able to learn, test, and implement the most effective technologies for off-grid areas where they currently operate across Africa.

Due to the vast impact that iA has had, it has received many awards, including the highly regarded "Innovation Award" from the United Nations. Additionally, Yaari has been recognized as one of the "40 under 40 Most Promising Israelis" by Globes magazine, and one of the "50 Most Influential Women in Israel" by Forbes Israel. iA has reached an audience of more than 100 million worldwide, and a social media following of over half a million people that grows by the day.

Yaari believes her Israeli heritage has given her much insight and knowledge. Israel was born out of necessity as a safe haven for Jews, and large areas of the country were nothing but dust prior to 1948 when the country gained independence. In those beginning years, Israel faced similar challenges of desertification and developed technology to deal with it successfully. The ability to solve all kinds of problems is a strong cultural trait that Yaari draws upon when operating in Africa. She believes that one of the main reasons Israel is home to such a vast number of start-ups is due to a spirit of persistence: "If we as a nation continue to persist, push boundaries, be proactive, problem-solve and challenge the status quo, we will indeed find a solution for any challenge we face."

The lights continue to shine brightly within the 170 villages that

*Chapter 12*

Innovation: Africa projects have transformed and empowered. The water flows with purpose, and the crops meet nutritional needs for people of all ages. But there are hundreds and thousands of villages that are yet to be reached. One village at a time, Innovation Africa will continue, not only turning on the light and sharing the light, but being a "Light unto the Nations" on its mission of repairing and improving the world, one village at a time.

## ReWalk and UPnRIDE:
## Helping Severely Disabled People Stand Tall and Walk
### Dr. Amit Goffer

Have you ever wondered what it is like to be an adult who never sees the adult world at eye level, but instead, has to look up to everyone from the height of a child? Or not being able to reach counters and being viewed as less capable? Or have you ever questioned why at the end of the twentieth century, disabled people have no other solution for mobility than to be confined to a wheelchair? These questions led me to undertake what at first seemed like a "mission impossible," namely to enable millions of people with spinal cord injuries and other illnesses to walk again.

I was born in Israel in 1953, attended the Technion to become an engineer, and then served five years in the Israeli Air Force as a captain, during which time I got married and studied for an M.Sc. at Tel-Aviv University. Following military service, I worked for an Israeli R & D institute (Raphael), then studied for a Ph.D. in Electrical and Computer Engineering at Drexel University in the U.S., and eventually returned to Israel in 1991. As an inventor and entrepreneur I founded an MRI Brain imaging company in 1995, where we sought to design a smaller, less intimidating version of the MRI machine.

My life took an irrevocable change in January 1997, when I had a serious ATV accident that left me a quadriplegic, paralyzed from the chest down. I went through a long inpatient rehabilitative process during which the only ray of light was the love of my wife and children, who kept the family together. So now you can understand why I know very well how it feels to sit in a wheelchair, not just physically, but emotionally as well. I began observing the world from a disabled person's perspective and wondering why a wheelchair was the only solution.

My dream became finding a way to help people walk again. I began exploring through computer design the physics of an alternative path and studied the feasibility of my idea and the size of the potential market. A Tnufa Fund grant from the Office of the Chief Scientist in the Ministry of Industry (now "Israel Innovation Authority") in 2000 helped motivate me to develop the ReWalk, and in 2001, to found Argo Medical Technologies (later became ReWalk Robotics), where I pioneered the invention of the Rewalk Exoskeleton.

ReWalk enables people paralyzed from the waist down to stand upright and walk, and even to navigate stairs up and down. What is

## Chapter 12

unique is that ReWalk gives the user full control over the system. When a person begins to use ReWalk, he or she watches a series of tutorials prepared by experienced physiotherapists; think of it like taking driving lessons. This is how the system works: By pushing on crutches and tilting the body forward, a frame-mounted sensor (a tilt sensor) signals an on-board computer which gives instructions for one step at a time to the exoskeleton. ReWalk creates a natural intuitive walk. The user has a wrist-mounted controller to select the mode of operation: "stand," or "sit," "walk," "stop," "stairs," "up," or "down."

With a team of volunteers, we started to train paraplegics to walk at home, and by 2006 I entered the Technion Incubator (MATAM, Haifa). In 2010 we moved our headquarters to Yokneam, northern Israel. In the same year, the device was presented to the public in the world's biggest exhibition, "RehaCare," in Dusseldorf, Germany. After a series of clinical trials in Sheba Medical Center, Tel-Hashomer, and in the VA Center of Excellence in the Bronx, NY, we received FDA approval in 2014, and became public (NASDAQ). In the same year, President Barack Obama visited Israel and was impressed with a female United States Veteran who demonstrated the device and its benefits.

ReWalk Robotics (formerly Argo Medical Technologies) now has dozens of employees in Israel, the United States, and Germany. There are two ReWalk devices, one for rehabilitation training and the other for home use. The battery can last for a full day or for three hours of intensive walking. ReWalk can now be purchased in many European countries: Britain, Ireland, Spain, Italy, Germany, and Austria, and in the USA. The hope is that mass production will lower the cost.

As the CEO from 2001-2012, ReWalk has been my life's work and passion. ReWalk has made the dream of walking again a reality for over one thousand people with lower limb paralysis. There is no doubt that ReWalk contributes to the quality of living of its users because movement improves physical condition and decreases the need for medicine prescribed to counter effects of prolonged sitting.

Moreover, ReWalk certainly lifts spirits and self-confidence for its users. One woman, Claire Lomus, who had been paralyzed from the waist down from a horse-riding accident, was eventually able to do a Marathon using ReWalk. Radi Kaufee, a soldier who was severely wounded at age 21, lay unconscious for over two weeks and was told he would never walk again. Today he is a member of our company's R&D team as a chief experimenter and demonstrator of ReWalk. Moreover, he has done the Tel Aviv Marathon and his children now view him just like other dads.

*Dr. Amit Goffer*

Despite this wonderful invention, however, I myself and other quadriplegics can't use ReWalk because it requires full use of one's arms. My legs are paralyzed and I have no control over my torso. I can't use my fingers and only have limited use of my arms. So I was driven to keep inventing to help more severely handicapped people like myself, because I didn't want to be defined by my handicap.

My next invention, UPnRIDE, is designed to help a wheelchair-bound person move also while standing. Everything can be activated by using a joystick and suitable switches for selecting mode of operation. Essentially UPnRIDE is a convertible wheelchair that can sit or stand and is designed to look like a Segway, which these days, is a relatively normal, familiar sight on the streets. The wheelchair can roll uphill and even travel on slopes. It was designed to be elegant, slim and to function safely in any outdoor urban environment.

UPnRIDE's moving part is in the middle of the wheelchair, to keep the center of gravity in the same place for more stability, and to enable a person to stand up without falling. A folding seat on the back makes it easy to either sit or stand. The user is located on the platform that adjusts the angle of the user into a vertical position. The chair balances the user in a vertical position. Jointed braces and harnessing straps provide support while transferring between sitting and standing positions. Computer motion technology creates stability on ramps by providing constant adjustment. If a problem arises it can seat the rider back.

August 25, 2015 was a momentous and happy day in my life. For the first time in eighteen years I went outside standing up on UPnRIDE. At first it was an odd feeling to be moving upright without apparent support, but I was being supported by UPnRIDE. I was very pleased to see that my hard work had led to success. UPnRIDE has health benefits and quality of life benefits because standing improves circulation, prevents urinary infections and pressure sores, which reduce additional health costs due to detrimental effects of sedentary wheelchairs.

*Chapter 12*

From a psychological point of view, standing allows users to be at eye level with others and appear more capable, which can improve social interaction as well as mood. The UPnRIDE user's focus can shift from the disability to a new perspective on what they can do in the world, offering the user emotional and spiritual benefits.

UPnRIDE is moving into the marketing stage, seeking copyright in Europe, and then will participate in clinical trials at the VA in Bronx, NY, before seeking FDA approval. The wheelchair could certainly have appeal to over eight million scooter users, paraplegics, quadriplegics, and people with multiple sclerosis, cerebral palsy, and traumatic brain injury. To develop and market UPnRIDE, we have received a grant from the Israel Innovation Authority, as well as investment from Our Crowd and "angels." I am very pleased and grateful that my technological inventions as an Israeli have qualitatively improved so many people's lives.

# Enlightenment Begins at Home:
## Tech-Career and Tsofen
### Naphtali Avraham / Sami Saadi

In today's world it is clear that high-tech is a pathway for joining and progressing in Israeli society. Training for high-tech jobs requires higher educational levels and thus offers new opportunities to advance in Israeli society. While Israel is widely known for its high-tech achievements around the world, perhaps less known are two shining examples of high-tech "at home" that benefit Israelis of Ethiopian descent and Israeli-Arab citizens.

### Tech-Career – Naphtali Avraham

Tech-Career was established by Asher Elias, whose parents made *Aliyah* in the 1960s. Like Asher, I am among the many who made the perilous journey through the Sudan to reach Israel. Our immigrant parents worked in low-paying jobs, and the unemployment rate for Israelis of Ethiopian descent was twice the national rate. Having fewer economic resources, Ethiopian-Israelis were at a disadvantage in preparing for competitive exams in the army and university.

Asher pursued a degree in business administration, studied software engineering, and got a marketing job in high-tech. He was very dismayed to discover only four other Ethiopians working in the high-tech sector. This led Asher to envision a different path, realizing that it was up to him as well as other Israelis of Ethiopian descent to help change their situation.

In 2002, together with an American software engineer, Asher started Tech-Career, a nonprofit "boot camp" to help prepare the younger generation of Ethiopian-Israelis for higher level jobs, narrow the digital gap, and serve as a "ticket out of poverty." Tech-Career was established by and for Ethiopian-Israelis to create a fast-track for talented Ethiopian Israelis ages 22-30 post-army, to achieve more full and social integration into Israeli society.

Today, thanks to Tech-Career, over 550 Ethiopian-Israelis are now employed in Israel's high-tech industries, commercial enterprises, and the public sector. Tech-Career offers five courses per year over six to eight months, totaling between 600 to 800 hours. Students live in dorms with 24-hour access to computers, and get a financial stipend, along with individual guidance and tutoring. Courses offer technological training along five tracks: Windows-Web Software Development, JAVA

Language Software Development, Quality Assurance, Data Security and Administration, and Network Management.

Students also learn "soft" business skills such as writing a Curriculum Vitae, business English, professional networking, job interviewing, time management, and teamwork. In less than a year, our students earn international certification in market-relevant skills to gain entry to sustainable careers. Volunteers, executives, and former graduates offer one-on-one mentoring, including sharing insights into high-tech culture. Senior Executives at Israel's high tech firms collaborate in designing the courses and hiring graduates.

In the first course offered, four out of nineteen students graduated. Now 95% do so. Tech-Career trains 110 graduates per year. 93% of certified graduates over the past four years are working in their field of training.

Tech-Career is transforming lives. In the words of one graduate: "I was the first Ethiopian-Israeli to work in my company, and today there are six Tech-Career graduates there. I know we are making a difference." One by one new doors are opening to economic inclusion and social equality in Israeli society.

***

## Tsofen – Sami Saadi

I was born in 1965 in the Arrabe village in the Galilee, and attended school to become an independent CPA. Looking around me, it was disturbing to realize that of the 120,000 engineers in the Israeli high-tech, less than 0.5% were Arabs, although Arabs comprise 21% of Israel's population. Gross monthly income for Arab citizens is less than half that of the general population. Moreover, there are thousands of Arab university graduates who cannot find employment in Israel's high-tech sector, so they wind up working in other professions. As a result, a vast wealth of talent remains underutilized.

Our goal became to achieve structural, not just cosmetic change. We realized that we must take responsibility for our fate. Together with Smadar Nehab, a high-tech entrepreneur, and Yossi Coten, a high-tech executive, we founded Tsofen to correct the pervasive lack of Arab employment in the high-tech industry. From the only 0.5% of high-tech employees, today they are 5%, and our goal is to increase employment to 10% by 2025.

Tsofen is a nonprofit organization whose mission is to promote integration of Israeli Arabs into high-tech and other advanced industries. Creating high value jobs in Arab urban centers could become a catalyst to reduce poverty, promote economic development, and ultimately better integrate Arab citizens into Israel's economy, creating a more shared society.

We believed that bringing high-tech and software engineering industry into the Arab community would be a more direct route to foster economic development. Tsofen works with Arab communities and stakeholders from local, governmental, and private sectors to integrate Arabs into Israeli high-tech as well as to create high-tech employment centers as anchors in Arab towns. This is useful as Israel needs high quality engineers and related talent which could be found within Israel at lower operational costs instead of relocating to find engineers in Eastern Europe.

Tsofen has been addressing these challenges by establishing high-tech centers in Arab communities in the Galilee and the Triangle regions: in Nazareth and Kafr Qassim respectively, with the goal of integrating thousands of additional Israeli-Arab software engineers. Tsofen offers a range of professional related skills to enhance participants' competitiveness for high-tech jobs, including the entry of more Arab women into the high tech industry. This increase will improve not only the economic situation of their families and communities, but positively impact Israeli society as a whole. Moreover, Arab-Jewish cooperation in these centers can serve as a model of diversity and inclusion, contributing to advancement of greater equality in Israeli society.

The word *"Tsofen"* means "code" or "cipher" in Hebrew and has two meanings. The first is coding and computer programming, which connects us to the world of high-tech; the second is cracking the *code* to a shared society between Jews and Arabs in Israel.

In 2016, Tsofen was awarded the Speaker of the Israeli Parliament's Prize for Promoting Mutual Understanding between Jews and Arabs, and helping make enlightened dreams come true.

# PART III

*Healing The Spirit And Seeking Peace*

*Chapter 13*

# HEALING THE SPIRIT IN CREATIVE WAYS

"The world breaks everyone, and afterward, some are strong at the broken places."

Ernest Hemingway

"For I will restore health to you and heal you of your wounds."

Jeremiah 30:17

"The wound is the place from where the light enters you."

Rumi

"There is a crack in everything. That's how the light gets in."

Leonard Cohen

Throughout the Bible there are stories about healing and healers. Abraham, Miriam, and Elisha the prophet are a few examples in which the process of healing, or attaining greater wholeness, involved some divine intervention. Abraham was visited by three angels, Moses prayed to God asking for Miriam's healing, and Elisha was inspired with divine breath to revive a dead child. Healing is as much about the spirit as the physical body, as Judaism has an integrated view of body and spirit. When illness or trauma occur, whether physical or emotional, the whole person is impacted.

It has been said that Israel is a healing for the Jewish people who found a home after the ravages of Jewish history. Yet Holocaust survivors who came to Israel encountered a country preoccupied with trying desperately to survive as a nation and rebuild lives. Eventually survivors were helped by organizations such as *Elah* (for Dutch survivors) and *Amcha*, organizations which recognized the need to create a community where survivors could gather, receive support, and strengthen one another.

Deaths and severe injuries of young Jewish soldiers in war and of civilians from terrorism have added new layers of continuing trauma in Israel for individuals, families, and communities. This reality has led Israel to develop new approaches to trauma and restoring functioning.

## Healing the Spirit in Creative Ways

Finding pathways to repair one's spirit after trauma, loss, or illness is as important as physical recovery. *Livui Ruchani,* or spiritual care, is a relatively new field in Israel that recognizes the emotional and spiritual dimensions, not just religious ones, of suffering and healing. In illness situations, when the body aches, so does the spirit. Healing necessarily involves addressing both dimensions.

One story in this chapter describes how spiritual care can lead to significant personal growth and greater wholeness when a person shares her life story with a supportive professional. Another story is of a little girl who struggled with a devastating and ultimately fatal illness, but together with her mother's loving guidance, courageously found spiritual tools such as poetry and art to sustain her spirits. Her illness journey inspired her mother to build a program using the creative arts in medical treatment, an approach that has helped many people.

People afflicted by loss of physical capabilities and trauma have been helped in through various creative approaches, such as therapeutic riding and adapted sports accommodations, methods which help them regain a sense of ability, personal agency, and control. Lastly, our rich tradition can be a source of healing. Jewish customs and rituals such as *mikveh* can be used in healing ceremonies to make a cleansing new start after physical or sexual trauma, or to celebrate a transition, such as conversion, marriage, birth, and parenthood. In this way, Jewish traditions can be creatively redefined and extended to serve a wider circle of people seeking healing and greater wholeness.

*Chapter 13*

## *Livui Ruchani: Spiritual Care*
## Rabbi Judith Edelman-Green

If *Livui Ruchani,* Pastoral Care, is healing the spirit, then Israel is a healing for so many lost and torn souls who found peace and home in Israel after the ravages of Jewish history.

My Rabbinical work in Israel involves doing Pastoral Care with the elderly. I help people who still have memories to write their life stories. This involves deep listening and seeing into their soul, transferring their words to paper, and then sharing the story with the person and their family. This process is a way of respecting and honoring a person who feels discarded by society and helps them to feel "seen" and understood.

A very beautiful gift that can be given to anyone is to sit quietly and to listen with all your heart, or to look into a person's eyes, hear their pain and story; to see who they really are. In the Biblical story of Hagar and Sarah, God creates a well called, *"Be'er L'Hai Roi."* This could be interpreted as The Well of Seeing and Life, or the Well which gives me life because I am seen.

What do I mean by deep listening and seeing? We say, "Shema Yisrael!" every day. Do we mean to listen with our ears, or perhaps, with our hearts? Some people feel extremely unimportant and as if they are invisible to their friends, family, and community. On a certain level, I could relate to feeling unappreciated and even singled out for being different, having experienced anti-Semitism before coming to Israel. Here in Israel my soul has found a home, a place which resonates; a place I belong. As a result, these past three decades I have made an effort to welcome newcomers, both Jews and non-Jews, new immigrants and refugees from Africa to my country, which is my home. My children and now a grandchild have been born here, and they love Israel as much as I do, and work to contribute to a kinder, more peaceful society.

I would like to share the story of Zohar (pseudonym), a woman who lives in a retirement home at a hospital, in a wheelchair, with a scarred face and never a smile. I visit her regularly to listen to her story, one of heartbreak and lack of opportunity. Zohar began by sharing: "I was born in Egypt into a Jewish family of extreme poverty. My mother was an invalid and my father was unemployed. My chief and only joy was school and learning, but at age fourteen my parents told me that as the eldest, I would have to leave school in order to take care of four younger siblings. I remember crying bitterly and feeling alone as I cooked, cleaned, and changed diapers.

When the state of Israel proclaimed its independence, most of the

Jews were expelled from Egypt. Our family was taken in by the Joint Distribution Committee, fed and cared for, and ended up in France. On the journey to France all of our meager belongings were stolen. Once in France, I was offered the chance to be taken on *Aliyah* to Israel together with my small siblings. My mother could not go along due to illness, and my father would not leave his wife. Therefore, I found myself on my own, in charge of four little children in a tent camp for refugees in Israel. There was no running water or electricity, and I had to both work and take care of my siblings."

Zohar explained that she got married in order to escape from her impoverished predicament, but soon found herself stuck in old patterns. Her husband didn't get out of bed or go to work, so all the responsibilities of life were on Zohar. When her parents finally came to Israel her mother fell and needed to be in a body cast and in Zohar's care. Zohar gave birth to two daughters, one of whom was born with a heart condition. Zohar spent much of her time taking her younger daughter to doctors. As a result, she missed many workdays and was unable to earn enough money for the family.

Zohar's daughters grew up, married, and had children. They called upon Zohar to care for her grandchildren. However, despite Zohar's caregiving efforts, the daughters treated their mother with disdain. In fact, when Zohar had a stroke, they told her she had never been any good, and had not given them enough as children. "And now," Zohar sighed: "I am all alone in an old age home."

I invited Zohar to write her life story with me. Each time I visited to listen to her, she lit up and smiled upon seeing me, her scarred face even looking happy. Finally, one day the story was complete and I prepared to read it to her for additions and corrections. I was not sure how she would react to such a tragic life story, her own. To my surprise, Zohar was overjoyed. She loved it and asked for copies to give to her daughters.

When we invited the daughters for Zohar to read the story to them, they said: "This is all made up; it never happened." I assured them that it did occur, saying: "No one could make up such a story of heartbreak and lack of opportunity." As a result of this encounter, however, the daughters began to view their mother in a different light. More importantly, Zohar started to see herself differently. When I asked her why she was so happy with her story, she said: "Because I was able to survive all of the traumas of my own life."

What happened next could not have been predicted. Not only did Zohar survive, but she started working hard with her physiotherapist and soon learned to walk again. She lost weight and convinced the staff and her daughters that she was able to live in her own apartment with a caregiver. She did, in fact, manage to leave the retirement home and begin a new life in her eighties. Before she left, Zohar expressed thanks and love for an improved relationship with her daughters, and mainly herself.

This is a very unusual and striking ending to a story with an elderly person because of the physical, emotional, and spiritual changes that ensued. It shows the potential power of deep listening, writing, and sharing a life story. Perhaps Zohar's response to acknowledging and sharing her suffering and surviving helped her discover her inner resilience that gave her life new meaning and purpose. More than a life story or history, this was HERstory.

# *Haverut:*
## *Healing the Spirit through Creative Arts and Community*
### Rachel Fox-Ettun

Haverut, meaning "friendship community," uses the creative arts to lift patients' spirits, provide support and companionship, elicit patients' strengths and resilience, and restore a sense of greater wholeness. Haverut began as a tribute to my beautiful daughter, Ruth. Her inspiring behavior and the creative tools she found to elevate her spirit during her progressive incurable illness taught me how the soul can be healed even when the body shuts down.

Born in 1985, the second of my five children, Ruth experienced a series of what seemed like colds, but then she deteriorated and was hospitalized. The doctors diagnosed Cystic Fibrosis, which causes constant accumulation of thick, sticky mucus in the lungs and airways, creating difficulties breathing, frequent infections, and inadequate absorption of nutrients in the small intestine.

By age six, Ruth was hooked up to oxygen for the first time in her life and was coughing up blood, certainly a scary thing for a little six-year-old and her worried mother. To manage her fears and my own, I asked Ruth: "What gives you strength? What things do you love? Let's make a list...." We took some scratch paper and wrote a list. Slowly and delicately, we realized that we could turn this list into verses and reorganize it as a poem.

### *"Strength"*

Sometimes when I feel sad and am in pain
I get the feeling that "it's" coming,
I call all of my angels.

Some are visible, some invisible.
Some come from within me, some from the outside....

The doctors who I love
The nurses who lovingly follow up on my weight
The family who hugs me....

Games, also, I have found, make me so happy;
Dolls and colors.
Now, I am finding out that my thoughts also have power

## Chapter 13

And I can control them and decide on them with my brain.
In this way, I can decide that actually now, it is good and pleasant
And the painful place doesn't even hurt.
Then suddenly, the world is less threatening and cold,
It is even sort of embracing and full of light.

Heavy burdens become bearable
Real pain is less felt.
Through this learnt wonder
I connect strongly to God in heaven
Who sits there and really and truly
Looks after me
And loves and loves....

We were surprised and delighted to discover that at such an upsetting, terrifying moment – being hospitalized after a drastic change for the worse, we were able to leave the scary straits of illness and move into the wide spaciousness of the infinite, where we could feel the love and embrace of the creator.

Throughout her illness, Ruth showed wisdom far beyond her years. She used creativity as a resource during her bedridden, limiting state, and terminal condition. At age seven Ruth said: "Feeling sorry for yourself just makes you sad. I try to think happy thoughts." Ruth kept a diary, painted constantly, wrote in a journal, did weaving, and requested music to lift her spirits. In her journal Ruth wrote that "each person has a difficult thing they face and need to deal with in life." Ruth learned to fight her war, express emotions, cry to let out stress, as well as to do things that made her happy, such as appreciating nature.

By age eight Ruth required a lung transplant in order to survive. We travelled to the United States for the surgery. Unfortunately, her body rejected the transplant and Ruth returned home. Even when receiving oxygen and morphine, Ruth continued to draw. Towards the end, she used art as a means of saying goodbye to loved ones, making each a small painting.

One year before her death at age 11½ Ruth wrote: "The physical power in my body may be small, but the power in my heart is renewed." Eleven days before her death, Ruth wrote: "God doesn't tell us when we will die, so that we do as much as we can every day and live in the present and not so much in the future." As her mom, it was remarkable to me that her soul seemed so healthy even as her little body was sick and died.

\*\*\*

Through Ruth's short life, illness, and death, I came to realize how important it is for patients who are coping with illness to access their inner creativity in order to better connect with their healing resources. The arts empower patients to fulfill the basic human drive to create. The creative arts, such as music, dance, movement, song, drawing, painting, poetry, writing, journaling, storytelling, drama, sculpture, and fabrics can have a major impact on strengthening a patient's sense of coping, wellbeing, and resilience. For example, music can reduce pain and distress and improve mood. The arts can occupy a patient's attention, distract them, lift spirits, and bring joy, making a difficult situation more bearable.

Through the arts patients can also connect with one another, access joy, a sense of wonder, wholeness, possibility, and playfulness. Relaxation techniques such as breathing exercises, guided imagery, art activities, and music can provide support and lower stress. Each particular art should be selected to fit the individual's preferences. The arts can provide alternative ways of communicating deeper meaning when words are difficult, and can restore a patient's sense of wholeness, confidence, identity, and dignity. Because the arts involve the senses, they directly reach the patient's inner spirit. Through accessing their inner creativity, patients can find new flexibility and possibilities, all of which can elevate their spirits.

\*\*\*

After Ruth's death I went back to school to study psychotherapy, and earned a Master's degree in Family Therapy and Counseling, in addition to my degrees in Special Ed, Theatre, and Jewish Thought. Ten years later I was ready to open a spiritual care program. Haverut was launched in 2007. Its name echoes Ruth's Hebrew name, Rut, and the program was intended to bring a new spirit into the healing process in medical centers.

Haverut opened as a nonprofit at Hadassah Mount Scopus in Jerusalem, and quickly involved Bezalel art students, musicians, and volunteers. We began using the arts as a pillar of spiritual care to help patients and families cope by channeling the creative and spiritual strength that resides in us all. Haverut brings community, creativity, and spirituality into the healing process, inspiring patients, families, and the medical team by the unique atmosphere it creates.

While beginning at Mount Scopus, soon other hospitals became involved: Hadassah Ein Kerem, Kfar Shaul, Ziv Hospital, Zefat, and

Sheba medical centers. Spiritual caregivers meet with patients in multiple hospital departments – Hematology, Dialysis, Rehabilitation, Oncology, Cystic Fibrosis, High Risk Pregnancy. Now it is also an elective at Hebrew University in a program for health care professionals.

One example of Haverut in action is Project Aynat, which operates as a kind of social club for patients in the Rehabilitation department at Hadassah Mount Scopus. Haverut trains volunteers to engage patients through playing games, chatting, and helping them remember their strengths. Involving a patient to move from sitting alone passively to interacting with others can help them feel more like a person. It may distract them from their illness for a while, lift their spirits, and create a new and more hopeful mindset. Patients learn that while their body is sick, their soul can still be whole and alive.

Spiritual caregivers who visit patients may offer a blessing, a prayer, or some encouraging words, construct a mantra or ritual with a patient, co-construct a personal prayer with the patient, read a text that may apply to the patient's life, or read a comforting psalm. They offer an opportunity to discuss life issues and one's relationship to God if the patient is open to talking about spirituality.

Through a caregiver's belief in each patient's worth and divinity and by showing interest in the patient as a whole person, not just a disease, patients feel supported and less alone during illness. As Ruth and I discovered during the many times of sitting together during her illness, bringing forth a patient's strengths and connecting with them around something that brings them pleasure can lift their spirits, help them appreciate their own resources, and feel more whole.

*Haverut – Founded in memory of*
*Ruth Ettun, z"l*
*October 16, 1985 – January 28, 1997*

## Horses that Heal: My Passion for Therapeutic Riding
### Dr. Anita Shkedi

At age three I had my first horse ride on a farm in the Lake District of the United Kingdom (UK), where my parents took me on holiday. By age seven, I moved with my parents and brother from London to the Lake District, where I had the glorious opportunity of growing up with horses. A local farmer allowed me to bring one of his ponies home and tie it to the back door of the house while I went inside for a drink. When I rode in the woods, I often pretended that the pony was mine. I always remember choosing storybooks about horses with special bonding relationships to human beings. I would imagine that I was the human in the book, and try to recapture every moment of their adventures.

Growing up, I was lucky to experience the way my parents opened our home to care for others, such as by having fun parties for disabled children from a local institution in our very large garden. Their example motivated me to decide to spend my life taking care of people as I discovered that I felt great satisfaction when helping others. I trained for a nursing career in London, UK where I worked as a registered nurse specializing in helping sick children at Great Ormond Street's Hospital for Sick Children in London.

After marriage and having children I became a keen horsewoman, competing and winning with my favorite horse, Sara, at the East Cheshire Riding Club, even becoming horse and rider of the year. Moving with my husband and our daughter to Cheshire in the northern UK, I managed my life as mother, *Rebbitzin,* (wife of a Rabbi) and district nursing sister. Day and night, I helped people with social, emotional, and physical problems. Wanting to learn more, I returned to college and studied to become a Health Visitor.

At this point in time, I knew little about therapeutic riding, or as it was known in the UK, "Riding for the Disabled". I volunteered once a week at a horseback riding center in Cheshire. Each week I went to an indoor arena to help a group of intellectually challenged people learn to ride. Without fully understanding "therapeutic riding," I noticed that people felt better and smiled a lot after a ride. Something was beginning to brew inside of me. I knew that my nursing jobs and health visiting fit well with my values, and I wondered if my passion for horses might also possibly merge with them.

In 1982, Israeli friends of ours came to the UK for a holiday. During the family's visit, they were involved in a car accident and

## Chapter 13

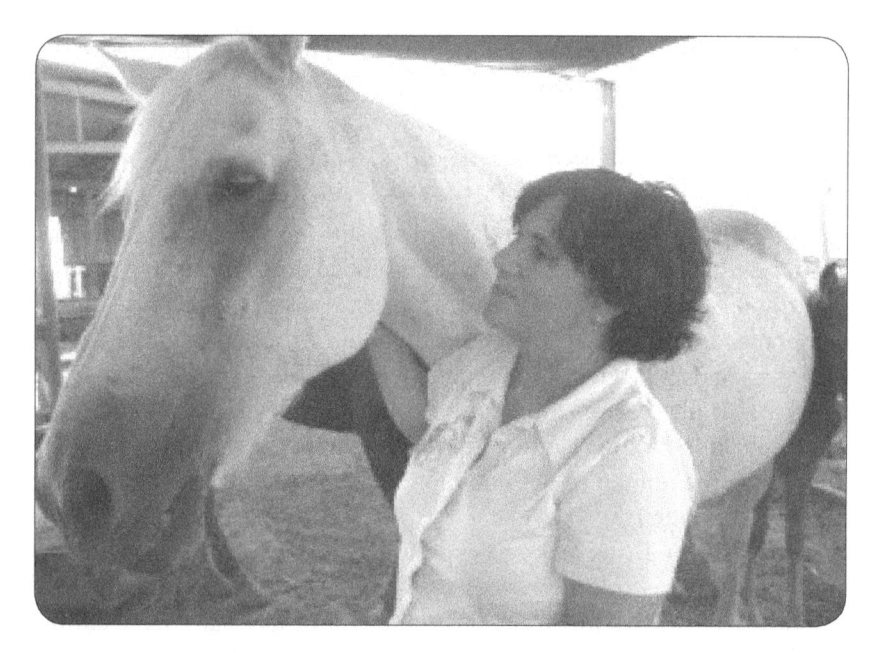

the parents were hospitalized. Their two sons came to live with us for three weeks. Several years later, their elder son enlisted in the Israeli army, and served in the war in Lebanon, but during his service, he was shot and severely wounded, leaving him paralyzed and wheelchair bound. When I found out about his injuries, I suggested that he come to the UK to stay with us to regain his strength and self-esteem. It was during his recuperation, when I took him to ride horses, that I realized the therapeutic and healing power of the horse and horseback riding.

I will never forget how dramatically the young man changed through riding horses. At first he looked like someone you would see in cowboy movies who was severely injured, riding slumped over his horse. After I spoke in a soft voice to the young man, reminding him how he used to sit up, he slowly found a way to sit up. And now he needed to find some power to get the horse to move. Using some arm strength and looking straight forward, the horse began to move. Over time, my young friend sat tall, looking elegant and magnificent on a horse. On the horse he saw the world from a height instead of looking up from a meter high in a wheelchair. He felt empowered, motivated, and wanted to do more.

After the death of our son Jonathan in the Lebanon War, in 1985 my husband and I made *Aliyah* to Israel. My young friend that I helped in England suggested that I do therapeutic riding with others, reminding me how it had helped him. He was now a regular rider with his own horse and training to be a psychologist. One of the first people who came to me was a mother who brought her severely brain-injured son. She mentioned that this was her second son; her first son had been killed in one of Israel's earlier wars. This stirred me to help the young soldier ride and find some healing.

In 1985 I founded Israeli National Therapeutic Riding Association. INTRA is a national charity that has provided over 200,000 subsidized sessions for challenged and disabled children and adults, ages two to seventy five. I work with a wide range of physical and emotional challenges, such as autism, cerebral palsy, scoliosis, stroke, and other disabilities. I have studied the subject from many different perspectives and tried different ideas, which has resulted in helping probably thousands of children and adults achieve a better quality of life.

A thirty-week scientific study evaluating physiological effects and outcomes of equine therapy found that little by little, sufferers discover the horse's ability to provide unconditional love and affection. As the person begins communicating with the horse, you can see tension reduced in the person. Eventually their emotional numbness goes away and they start to feel alive again.

On one occasion I remember going to a special needs school with a small pony. I found that children assessed with a low intelligence quota could be motivated to do mathematics easily through learning about a horse and its feeding routine. I requested the children bring a specified number of apple portions for the pony. The children were relaxed and focused as they performed the task correctly. This simple, yet powerful experiment led the school to include therapeutic riding in its curriculum.

On another occasion, I remember a very quiet little girl who was suffering from depression. When she first met a pony named Pilgrim at our center, she did not want to ride, but was willing to brush and clean the pony, and walk around the center with him. After a few weeks of visits, I asked her what she was thinking about when she was with the pony. She told me about a dream she had had that night: She was drowning in the sea, and Pilgrim the pony came into the water and saved her by lifting her up out of the water. From that day on, she began to recover. From this I saw how the horses could positively affect body and spirit, and could be particularly helpful in recovering from physical and psychological trauma.

In 1988, I founded the first Therapeutic Riding Diploma curriculum at the Wingate Institute of Physical Education. I wanted therapeutic riding to be available to all challenged children and adults throughout Israel. Currently there are eleven courses in Israel, all following my basic method. I have qualified more than one thousand four hundred instructors, who have gone on to work with thousands of children using therapeutic riding and contact with horses as tools for recovery. Hundreds of young instructors have jobs and careers and are continuing to spread the benefits of this wonderful treatment modality.

I have worked passionately for the past thirty-four years, observing first-hand the application and benefits of therapeutic riding to rehabilitate traumatized war victims, remediate challenged learners, and help severely disabled children. I have given lectures, workshops and clinics to therapeutic riding instructors around the world. I have built and managed three major therapeutic riding centers, establishing therapeutic riding as one of the most popular treatments for challenged children and adults in Israel. I was part of a group of people who convinced medical insurance to help pay for children's riding sessions.

In recent years, I have created a more advanced academic course for prospective practitioners to enable them to make a career in therapeutic riding. For my doctorate I examined therapeutic riding programs globally and made recommendations for improvements. I wrote a book on Traumatic Brain Injury and Therapeutic Riding with adults to help instructors learn from my experience. I have also worked with veteran soldiers worldwide.

In 2015, I received an Award for Excellence from the International Sports Hall of Fame for my contribution to helping challenged and disabled people find better health through horseback riding therapy. My commitment has always been to help the challenged and the disabled. I want their voices to be heard and I want people to realize the power of the horse. My husband and I continue to work full time running our horse farm and directing programs at Moshav Bnei Zion near Netanya. This is my passion and I remain entirely dedicated to its continued success.

## TIKVOT: Restoring Hope and Lifting Spirits after Trauma
### Simone Farbstein

When there is a terror attack, an army operation or war, the news informs us about how many people were killed and how many wounded. The country mourns the dead, but what about those thousands who were seriously injured and traumatized? With the passage of time, people tend to forget about the injured or bereaved, whose lives have changed forever in that one instant.

This is where TIKVOT comes into the picture. Amazingly, through modifications in equipment and sports, TIKVOT gets them back into society as they were before they were wounded. Moreover, it builds their confidence and their feeling of still being able to enjoy life. In doing so, TIKVOT heals not only the body, but perhaps more importantly, the spirit as well.

During the second intifada people were being hurt constantly. Bombs were going off and lives were destroyed and changed. Rocky Muravitz, a former South African, decided to form TIKVOT together with Victor Essakow and Ehud Edelman. Their clear message was: Through sports we can enable people to rehabilitate themselves and regain their self-confidence once again. TIKVOT, meaning "hopes," shows that sports can help overcome the pain of trauma and disability and rebuild productive lives. TIKVOT offers every single sport that 700 participants per year can choose, including go-karting, riding, swimming, triathlon, surfing, skiing, and marathon. Their mantra is: "Focus on the positive to feel more empowered."

Imagine to yourself what it might be like to be able to ski after sacrificing your legs for your country? Or what it means to conquer a mountain after losing your eyesight in battle. We can only imagine how daunting a challenge it must seem to our disabled heroes, but through TIKVOT they can conquer many mountains. The experience of doing a winter sport like skiing changes everything. It builds confidence, creates new opportunities, and gives them the ability to give back to other disabled veterans, showing them that barriers can be overcome.

An amazing example is the story of Noam Gershony, a helicopter pilot who miraculously survived a helicopter crash but was severely wounded during the Second Lebanon War. We met him when he was hospitalized in the neurology ward at Tel Hashomer Hospital. A formerly athletic man, Noam believed that his sports days were over, an understandably depressing thought. However, TIKVOT had a waterski activity that we invited him to join. Noam thought that we were joking,

## Chapter 13

and that it wasn't possible.

We explained that we have adaptive equipment and special instructors. Noam decided to come, skied successfully, and saw that everything is possible. Imagine the impact on his spirit! The next year, with the assistance of TIKVOT, Noam went skiing on Mount Blanc, the highest mountain in Western Europe. There he experienced that even he can still do sports, despite his injury. In 2012, Noam won the only gold medal for Israel at the London Paralympics in Tennis.

Eitan Hermon began running at age ten, as part of the Kfar Blum athletic program, where he grew up. He ran about 7 km a day as a teenager and was a competitive athlete. As a reservist in the Second Lebanon War, he was wounded in 2006 when a roadside bomb detonated under his armored personnel carrier. Lying on a stretcher while being evacuated, he kept saying over and over again: "I will still run a marathon." For one year doctors tried to save his leg, but after a long hospital stay and many months of rehabilitation, he still required a leg amputation below the knee.

Although Eitan's world was knocked upside down, he never gave up the hope of someday running again competitively and winning. He was fitted with a prosthetic leg organized and paid for by TIKVOT, and after a year, began training for competitions. His amazing determination led him to complete a full marathon (42 km) in Israel. In 2017, after running 17 marathons, Eitan broke the world record for amputees at the Vienna marathon, which he ran in 2:56:53.

Ofer Verpel had been confined to a wheelchair due to a bullet that went through his back while serving in the elite Navy Seals brigade. Despite his injury he continued to fight and was later awarded a "commendation" from the head of the Central Command. As a tribute in memory of his commander who was killed in battle, Ofer decided that after rehabilitation, he wanted to return to participate in different sports activities despite his physical disability, and to do so in memory of his commander who loved sports.

TIKVOT is proud that it has the biggest triathlon team for disabled people in Israel. The "TIKVOT Tigers" participate in every triathlon in Israel with pride as they amaze the people who watch them. Another beautiful project of TIKVOT is "Surfing with Sisters." When a brother is killed while defending the State of Israel, it leaves a void in the family, and also for the remaining sibling(s). Surfing is an activity that boosts adrenaline and energy and has a way of empowering the surfer. It can give the sibling an experience of enjoying the beauty and therapeutic wonder of the sea while being with others who face a similar pain. Weekly group activities offer opportunities for informal sharing, lending mutual support and building new bonds.

Through "TIKVOT" the hopes and spirits of many people who survive trauma are lifted and healed as they go forward in life.

## Chapter 13

## *Fulfilling An Israeli Mikveh Dream*
## Rabbi Dr. Haviva Ner-David

Growing up in Modern Orthodox Jewish Suburban New York in the 1970s, I remember my mother coming home one evening a month with her hair wet, but not from swimming. Once a year, on *Erev* Yom Kippur, my father would go to a place called the *mikveh*, although I had no idea what that meant. It was only in junior high school that I learned in my "How to be a Jewish Woman" classes, that the *mikveh* is a pool of water, about the size of a small Jacuzzi, used for ritual purposes.

We were taught that married women and brides immerse in a *mikveh* after they menstruate (and all uterine bleeding stops) so that they can have sex with their husbands (because sex while bleeding from the uterus is forbidden according to religious Jewish Law). Men may immerse in the *mikveh* whenever they wish to. We learned that *mikveh* immersion is also part of the conversion ceremony.

In ancient Jewish history, *mikveh* immersion was practiced by men and women equally in order to transition from the status of ritually impure (*tameh*) to ritually pure (*tahor*), because without becoming ritually pure, one could not worship in the Temple. Once the Temples were destroyed and Judaism was no longer a Temple-based religion, all ritual impurity practices fell out of use, except those related to uterine bleeding. In Rabbinic times a change allowed men to continue using the *mikveh* for spiritual (unrequired) immersions, but only married women could use it for post-uterine bleeding immersion.

I myself didn't actually immerse in a *mikveh* until the night before my wedding. I went with my mother, and she and the *"mikveh* lady" watched me immerse three times, saying the traditional blessing on immersion.

I love water and meaningful ritual. *Mikveh* has stayed with me through all of my varied phases of religious observance and belief. When I was living in Washington, D.C. I ran a *mikveh* myself. Located in a Conservative synagogue called Adas Israel, the *mikveh* was used for conversions and brides. When I took the job of running the *mikveh*, I encouraged people to use it for other types of rituals as well: transitions, life cycle events, spiritual centering, and healing.

We immersed our oldest daughter before her *"brit habat"* (what we named the celebration we held to welcome her into the Covenant), I created a "letting go" immersion ceremony for my friend after she received her "get" (writ of divorce) from her ex-husband, and I accompanied a woman in a post-mastectomy healing ceremony at the *mikveh* – to name a few examples. In other words, I expanded the use of *mikveh* for women to include purely spiritual uses. I did not know it then, but in the liberal Jewish world, there was a growing movement of "Reframing and Reclaiming" *mikveh*.

We left D.C. and eventually moved to Israel, where *mikveh* remained a love and fascination for me. I wrote my doctoral dissertation on *mikveh*, and in my rabbinical studies I learned the laws of *mikveh* for an entire year, from 9 a.m. to 5 p.m. five days a week! I dreamt of opening a *mikveh* in Israel that would be open to all. I wanted to provide educational programming as well, to spread the beauty and power of the immersion ritual.

In Israel, the only way to marry legally is through the official religious institutions of the State. This means that Jews can only marry legally through the Orthodox Jewish Israeli Rabbinate, which requires every bride to study the laws of *mikveh* immersion before she can marry legally. When I heard horrific stories of how these laws were being taught, I decided to offer an alternative option. I taught the laws and practices of *mikveh* in a uniquely open way to individuals and couples, and this teaching later became seminars for engaged couples preparing for marriage.[1]

One unique approach I suggested to couples was to go to the *mikveh* together every month as a couple ritual. Many of the couples who studied with me liked this idea. However, the Orthodox Rabbinate controls all state-funded *mikvaot*, with strict laws about who can use the *mikveh*, as well as when and how they use it. Only married women are allowed to immerse, and before doing so they are subject to physical and verbal checks, and only Rabbinate conversions are allowed to take place at these *mikvaot*.

Moreover, there are separate *mikvaot* for men and for women, or at the very least separate hours for men and women in the Rabbinate-run-and-funded *mikvaot*. This meant I had nowhere to send these couples, except to natural *mikvaot* like the one my husband and I immersed in monthly (a spring in the Jerusalem Hills, where we lived at the time). This solution was not practical for most, mainly because of the cold water in winter, difficult access, and lack of privacy.

It was just around that time that Jacob and I heard about the project to revive Kibbutz Hannaton in the Galilee. Hannaton had been founded in the 1980s as a Conservative Movement kibbutz, but like most classic kibbutzim in Israel, it was not surviving, so it was being revived as a pluralistic liberal Jewish cooperative community. When we visited there, I discovered an old *mikveh*, built by the State due to a law that any religious community in Israel who wants a *mikveh* is entitled to one. Terribly run-down, the *mikveh* had been used only for conversions and brides, and only for Conservative movement Jews. It was then I knew that this would be where I could fulfill my Israel *mikveh* dream. This would be how I could bring the "Reclaiming and Reframing *Mikveh*" movement to Israel!

First, I raised money to renovate the *mikveh*, and made it a lovely, warm, inviting sacred space. I learned that community *mikvaot* in the U.S. offered *mikveh* education, art shows, and community gatherings. The first and most famous *mikveh* was *Mayyim Hayyim* in Newton, Massachusetts. Founded by author Anita Diament and her remarkable assistant, Aliza Kline, it led the way to revive the *mikveh* movement in the liberal Jewish world.

Our *Shmaya mikveh* [2] in Kibbutz Hannaton is open not only to all Jews, but we are also open to all human beings; even people who do not identify as Jewish. We have interfaith groups, Christian groups, and Muslim groups who come to *Shmaya* to study and immerse. We also have groups of all ages, from pre-school, to pre-Bar and Bat Mitzvah, to pre-army, to post-army, to rabbinical school, to retired.

The *Shmaya mikveh* is open to conversions for all streams of Judaism, not just Conservative. When I founded *Shmaya*, one of the first calls I made was to rabbis in the Israeli Reform movement, inviting them to use the indoor *mikveh* for their conversion students as an alternative to the ocean immersions they had been doing until then.

Some of my personal favorite conversion-assistance experiences are couples (different- and same-sex) who bring surrogate babies (born to other-than-Jewish surrogate mothers outside of Israel) for conversion. These ceremonies are full of such joy and gratitude! Because Israel only legalized bringing these babies into the country in the past ten years, and because many of these couples hoped for a child for a long time, the *mikveh* experience often feels like a personal miracle in their lives.

People come to the *Shmaya mikveh* to mark every life cycle event or transition one can imagine: birth, Bar and Bat Mitzvah, menarche, marriage, menopause, divorce, graduation, ordination, post-illness, healing during illness, post-trauma, mourning, sex-change, coming out of the closet, etc. People also come to immerse to simply re-center themselves spiritually or renew their spirit. Pre-High Holiday immersions are also popular with even whole families coming together to immerse.

I believe I have seen it all: A bride and her mother spontaneously getting into the *mikveh* together (often because the mother's own pre-marriage *mikveh* experience was unpleasant or even traumatic); a woman who had never put her head under water in her life out of a fear of water, managing to do so before her wedding; a bride receiving the loving blessing of both her mother and her mother-in-law-to-be (her father's current wife); a couple who had been trying for 17 years to have a child, finally immersing their surrogate baby in the Living Waters, a gay couple of 20 years, who never thought they could have a child, came to convert their surrogate baby accompanied by loving and supportive grandparents, and a man who came to the *mikveh* to heal and renew his spirit after a major trauma in his life, emerging from the *mikveh* building (where I was waiting outside) to be greeted by a huge downpour accompanied by a beautiful rainbow. The stories are endless.

As a post-denominational, inter-spiritual rabbi, I feel blessed to be doing the work that I do. I am able to bring this powerful ancient ritual to all who want to experience it. Moreover, I try to help them fashion a ceremony and make their immersion experience as meaningful as possible.

Today we have the amazing gift of being able to immerse our bodies fully in those same waters that existed before Creation as water has constantly been recycling itself since the beginning of time. When we immerse fully and surround ourselves by those waters that contained the All that we call God, we re-connect with that Divine Spirit inside us and everyone around us. So if the first *mikveh* was the Primordial Waters, and the second was the Seas, let those be our model for what a *mikveh* today should be as well: open to all who want the experience of being fully enveloped in the amniotic fluid of God's womb!

## Chapter 14
# SEEKING PEACEFUL COEXISTENCE

"The entire Torah is for the sake of peace."

Babylonian Talmud, Gitten 59b

"We should be lovers of peace and pursuers of peace."

Hillel the Elder

"Peace is the true security. If there will be peace, there will be security ... The most careful thing to do is to dare."

Shimon Peres

"The first and hardest step toward peace is recognizing the humanity of your enemy ... The art of family living is to remember that there are two partners."

Shimon Peres

"There's no choice but to divide the home into two apartments and turn it into a two family house."

Amos Oz

In his last interview before his death in 1973, Ben-Gurion was asked if he thought Israel had reached its visionary mission in the world. He replied, "Not yet," suggesting there was and is work to be done. Ben-Gurion was one of the lone voices after the Six Day war victory who expressed concern that a continued occupation could become a burden to Israel's security, freedom, and democracy. In order to truly be a model for the world, he emphasized the importance of Israel's moral character and humanistic values of equality, justice, democracy, and human rights for all within its society. In my opinion this involves saying no to extremism, and seeking moderation and freedom of expression in religion and other societal matters.

Shimon Peres (1923-2016) perhaps best symbolized Israel's spirit of optimism and "applied hope." Serving Israel in many capacities over six decades, including President, Peres went from being a hawk who built up Israel's strength, to a dove advocating a two state solution until his last day. He believed that the first and hardest step toward peace is recognizing the humanity of your enemy. His only regret was that the vision of peace didn't materialize in his lifetime; instead he focused his energy on Israeli-Arab civil society projects through the Peres Center for Peace.

While demographics argue for separation into two states, as of now, a separation fence is all that was constructed, in lieu of a peace agreement. Despite several attempts at peace negotiations between the parties themselves, which were interrupted by intervening conflicts, peace remains elusive. Even though the majority of Israelis and Palestinians still favor a two state solution, there is deep mistrust of the other's intentions. Errors have been made by both sides, and the continuing standoff only creates more resentment and harm to both societies the longer it continues. A colleague expressed a wishful dream: "Coexistence should be the goal of Israel, with Arabs and Jews, the children of Ishmael and the children of Jacob, finding a way to live together in peace, and even friendship, on this land, where we can get to know one another as human beings and understand that we are all connected." [1]

The stories in this final chapter inspire me with hope for Israel's future. In one, a talented musician devotes his career to using music for healing and love between people. He tells the story of a beautiful village in Israel that for decades has been a model of peaceful co-existence between Arabs and Jews. I first learned of this village at a conference I attended in Israel in the 1990s. Village staff members shared their co-existence work, both the accomplishments as well as the challenges. That was the first time I learned that Israel's Independence Day, was experienced by some as the "Nakhba," meaning "catastrophe," a day of mourning, not celebration.

I recall feeling really saddened as I listened to an Israeli psychologist, a conference attendee and IDF reservist, as he shared his inner torment caused by the complex shifting emotional adjustment process from a position of fighting the Arabs as enemies in war, then trying to work towards peace as neighbors, only to have it shattered again in war. It made me realize how complicated people's inner emotions are about the "other," and how difficult it is when there are conflicting narratives and trauma on both sides.

Especially moving stories are from members of an extraordinary organization that is composed of Israeli and Palestinian families who have each lost a family member to the conflict and terrorism. Instead of succumbing to hatred and vengeance, they have found a way to listen to each other's pain, stay connected, and offer empathy and support on a human level. I am awed by these courageous people who come together to work on stopping the cycle of violence.

## Chapter 14

Another story is a personal journey of a next generation activist seeking a nuanced "richer Zionism" than the one he inherited from the older generation. His solution was to create an umbrella organization that now supports over 110 coexistence groups doing collaborative work on the ground between Israelis and Palestinians.

Another story imagines a green model for implementing peace, and lastly, is a story about using art to overcome trauma and send a message of peace across barriers.

As a parent and grandparent I am naturally concerned about the next generation and their relationship to Israel. So many young Jews have checked out, been turned off, and are uninvolved. Many others, however, do care deeply about Jewish and humanistic values, but may not see a pathway to stay engaged. I feel very blessed that each of my sons feels the importance of Hillel's words: "What is hateful to you do not do it to your neighbor," and they are teaching their children a values-based love for Israel.

Like many other young people, they very much want to see Israel remain a Jewish and democratic state with values of justice and fairness shining through, as envisioned by Israel's founders. However, they and others of their generation are not complacent, passive, nor silent, when they see these values being eroded. Fortunately, organizations such as ALLMEP (Alliance for Middle East Peace), the New Israel Fund, *Tzedakah* organizations, and other groups that support and strengthen civil society work in Israel provide a pathway for young American Jews to connect and remain positively engaged with Israel.

## Building an Oasis of Peace; Can a Song Heal?
### Yuval Ron

> Excerpts from *Divine Attunement: Music as a Path to Wisdom,* Chapters XV and XVII, written by master musician Yuval Ron (www.YuvalRonMusic.com). *Divine Attunement* has garnered book awards in two categories: Spirituality and Performing Arts. Reprinted with permission from the publisher, copyright © *2014 Oracle Institute Press (*www.TheOracleInstitute.org).

Up in the ancient hills leading to Jerusalem, there is a beautiful village called "Oasis of Peace" (*Neve Shalom* in Hebrew, *Wahat al-Salam* in Arabic). In this blossoming village, Jewish, Christian, and Muslim families have worked together to carry on a sacred mission: Remaining faithful to their religious traditions while respecting those of others, and dedicating their lives to advancing peace.

While their brothers and sisters all around them have suffered continuous bloodshed, hate and war, *these people,* in one village, have successfully resisted all hostilities. They have fruitfully kept their youth out of trouble, and they have accomplished this using conflict resolution councils, dialogue, mediation, meditation, and prayer practices. In this small village, all the children learn both Hebrew and Arabic, and all the children study the history-traditions of three Abrahamic faiths: Judaism, Christianity, and Islam. Their school is dedicated to the *Art of Peace*, because "peace is not spontaneous, it has to be learned." [2]

The story of this village sounds like a fairytale, but it is real. It began as a dream of one monk named Father Bruno. Bruno, who was born in Cairo, Egypt, where the great Nile River drains into the Mediterranean Sea. Even when very young, little Bruno believed that everything in life has some meaning. Each creature has a specific task and every living being has an important role to play; only he did not know what the role of little Bruno was to be. So he kept on searching and wondering.

When his family moved to France, Bruno kept looking for his answer. One day when he was eighteen or nineteen years old, Bruno met a group of Dominican Monks who fascinated him with their gentleness and kindness. Bruno was overjoyed, feeling he had finally discovered a meaningful framework, a path, and a calling. He decided to take the vows to become a Christian monk.

That evening Bruno came home and said, "Mama, I vowed to become a monk today. I finally found my life purpose!" His mother began to cry.

## Chapter 14

"Mama, why are you crying? This is the happiest day of my life!"

His mother mournfully replied, "Oh Bruno, you are Jewish. We are all Jewish. We had to keep it a secret…because of the times."

Suddenly Bruno's world collapsed in front of his eyes. Everything that seemed clear and certain shattered into pieces. He didn't know who he was: *Am I an Arab from Egypt? A Jew from France? Or a Catholic Dominican monk?*

And then he saw an opening, a light out of the darkness. He sensed that the answer *must* be found in the Holy Land, where all these identities and three religions have mingled together for over a thousand years. Bruno hoped he would find his answer there, so he embarked by ship on a sacred pilgrimage to Israel, landed, and headed straight to visit Jerusalem. On the way, an old monastery, set in heavy stone, lying halfway between the Mediterranean Sea and the mountains, caught his eye. This was the old "Silent Monastery," where monks vow to never, ever speak again. This is their path, their sacred journey. Bruno was moved and inspired to join. He was pleased to be silent and to be of service. He worked in the vegetable garden and took joy in feeding his brothers, the monks, feeling that he had found the meaning of his life.

Late one night Bruno had a terrible nightmare in his sleep. An unearthly, loud voice came into his head and said, "Bruno, you *must* find a way to help Jews, Christians, and Muslims live in peace in this Holy Land!" Bruno woke up in a cold sweat. *How can I, a simple monk, accomplish such an impossible decree?*

Then a vision magically unfolded in his mind: *I can start a village! A village where the sons and daughters of Abraham may live together on this sacred land and be an example of peace for the whole world!* With this grand vision and an incredible rush of energy, Bruno ran down the hallway of the monastery, where he saw the headmaster standing in deep contemplation. Bruno reached over, grabbed the headmaster by the shoulders, and cried, "Father, I *must speak* to you!" That moment ended Bruno's career in the silent monastery.

The kind headmaster knew Bruno had important work to do with larger meaning, so the headmaster assigned Bruno to a whole side of the hill belonging to the monastery. The land was barren, lacking water, trees, and roads. Undaunted, Bruno took a large crate, cut a door into it, and set it on top of the bare hill … to be his first cabin. For several years no one came, but eventually five families agreed to join him, and they began to turn the dream into a reality.

Today the village is thriving and many people want to move there. Families from neighboring villages send their children to study at the school in the village, because they too want their children to be educated in an Oasis of Peace. People from all over the world who work for non-governmental organizations and the United Nations go to study at the School of Peace in Bruno's village. They come to be trained in the methods and practices used by the residents of the village to learn how to bring peace to other troubled regions around the globe. Associations called "Friends of Oasis of Peace" now exist in eleven different countries so that many people can take inspiration from the courage, endurance, and methodologies of the village.

When Father Bruno died, his friends discovered an envelope on his desk which contained his last words. The entire village gathered around to read his final teachings:

*Friends, you thought this project of ours was about tolerance. You thought it was about mediation and non-violent conflict resolution. These were merely tools, my friends. In truth, this project of ours was about Love.*

## Can A Song Heal?

Fast forward to 2007, when a "Peace Mission" tour, consisting of the Yuval Ron Ensemble, along with thirty musicians from around the world, came to give a concert at the Oasis of Peace, nestled in the pastoral, quiet ancient hills of Jerusalem's biblical past. Yuval Ron formed this unique musical group not just for musical or artistic purposes, but with the intent that it be an educational tool to promote and inspire social action: namely to foster better understanding about and between Middle East cultures and religions. This step-by-step effort to forge positive change in the world through *Tikkun Olam* (repairing the brokenness in the world), gives his life meaning. Yuval believes that music, the language of the soul, is a vibration that stirs the human heart, evokes emotion, calms, inspires, and heals. It can be more powerful than words to bring down barriers between people.

The human brain tends to slice reality into separate parts so that we can react to danger, which makes it difficult for us to see humanity as one, instead of the usual separations by nationality, race, financial status, or level of education. By contrast, creativity with others, can activate our brain to recognize the interconnectedness and interdependence of all creatures. This recognition of our common humanity can lead us to care for our neighbors with more compassion and love, with peace as an outcome.

That evening the "Peace Mission" Ensemble offered a musical presentation for the Oasis of Peace village families as a way of showing

## Chapter 14

support to them. The families, couples, and individuals of the village filled the large stone house Spiritual Center. When the ensemble started playing, all the children began to dance. *What a beautiful moment*, Yuval thought to himself, to realize that one couldn't tell which of the children were Jewish, Christian, or Muslim. They were simply kids, dancing joyfully together and celebrating a place beyond borders and separations. There was great happiness in the room. It was *everything* they had hoped for.

But then, Yuval noticed a man and a woman sitting in the last row, staring at him with a bleak gaze as though he were doing something wrong. Although Yuval was in the middle of a song, he put down his oud and approached the couple. He asked them if they would like the ensemble to stop the music. Neither the man nor his wife looked at Yuval; they just kept staring straight ahead. Then the man solemnly said, "Keep playing." Somewhat bewildered, Yuval picked up his oud and the ensemble resumed playing.

A few minutes after this bizarre event, another unexpected twist unfolded: a female member of the group insisted, "You simply *must* play that old Israeli song about love, the chant for peace using the Hebrew word *shalom* and the Arabic word *salaam,* both meaning peace. You must play it right now!"

"Look," Yuval said. "I know this song from having grown up in Israel, but the ensemble doesn't know it and it is not part of our repertoire. I'm sorry; we can't."

"You must play it right now!"

Sensing a powerful energy confronting him, Yuval quickly decided to go along. He told his musicians to do their best following along. Amazingly the musicians picked up the tune in a few seconds, as if they knew the song by heart.

People started singing along with the ensemble – "*Shalom, Salaam*"[3] – as they began playing the song faster and faster. The villagers formed two circles and danced and danced, singing and chanting the word "peace" in their native tongues of Hebrew and Arabic, a word that reflected the essence of their life's long undertaking. Yuval looked up toward the back row, at the gloomy couple, who were still sitting, frozen as ice.

Suddenly the woman – the one who had been glaring at Yuval for so long – jumped up with a fire-colored scarf in her hand and ran into the circle. She held the scarf fiercely, as she started to dance in the middle of the circle. She moved in an ecstatic fiery rhythm and was an incredible dancer! She appeared as a flame in the middle of that circle, dancing for her life.

At the end of the concert, her husband walked slowly toward Yuval. He came close and whispered in a low and exhausted voice, "This was very difficult for us. It was hard for my wife to sit and not dance. But it was also painful for her to dance...." He paused and then uttered with finality, "My wife hasn't danced for three years. She hasn't danced since we lost our daughter."

Yuval looked at this bereaved father and it dawned on him that the visit to this oasis was not just to encourage coexistence, dialogue, and tolerance. Yes, they had come to inspire and support the village residents in their work, people who put the past in the past, to build a future of peace and prosperity for their children. On a much deeper level, however, there was a more profound purpose for being in the village that night, an unanticipated one: It was to free an imprisoned, grieving soul and to open a healing window for the life force to enter. They were there to mend one broken heart with a song.

*Chapter 14*

## The Parents Circle – Families Forum: Connecting through Grief, Listening, and Shared Humanity
### Rami Elhanan, Robi Damelin

### *Rami*

I am a 7th generation Jerusalemite, an Israeli Jew, son of an Auschwitz survivor, and before anything else, a human being. My personal story begins and ends on Yom Kippur, the Day of Atonement. In October 1973, I was a young reserve soldier caught in a terrible war in which I lost some of my very best friends. I came out of the war battered, bitter, and cynical. After the army I built a personal life: studies, family, and career as a graphic designer. On Yom Kippur evening, 1983, our youngest daughter Smadar was born. A vivid, smiling, active, and full of life girl joined our happy family, consisting of myself, my wife, my three sons, and we all lived in a bubble that we built around ourselves.

That is, until September 1997, a few days before Yom Kippur, when our bubble was smashed to smithereens. Smadar and her friends went to Ben Yehuda Street in Jerusalem to buy books for the new school year. There, they were killed by two Palestinian suicide bombers who murdered five people that day, among them three young girls aged 14, including Smadar. Thus began our long, dark night.

Smadar's funeral was held in Kibbutz Nachshon. She was buried next to her late grandfather General (ret.) and MK (ret.) Matti Peled, who was a Peace Fighter. Many mourners, representing the wonderful mosaic of this unbelievable country – Jews and Arabs, left-wingers and right-wingers, religious and secular people, from the representatives of the settlers in the Occupied Territories to the personal representatives of Chairman Yassar Arafat, came to visit and console us during the traditional seven day *Shiva* period.

On the eighth day I was faced with what to do when everything seems changed in your life. How to direct this new intolerable pain? When someone murders your 14-year-old little girl, it is natural that you have unlimited anger and an urge for revenge stronger than death. However, after the first madness of anger, you begin to ask yourself: If I kill someone in revenge, will that bring my baby back to me or ease my own pain? And the answer is absolutely "No." Then, during a long, slow, difficult, and painful process you wonder what can drive someone to such anger, hopelessness, and suicide? And most importantly: Is there something you can do to prevent such intolerable suffering from happening to others?

It took me almost a year, during which a change started so deep within me that I wasn't even aware of it. One day I met a big, impressive man named Yitzchak Frankenthal whose son Arik, was kidnapped and murdered by Hamas in 1994. As a result, in 1995 Frankenthal established a grassroots organization of people who had lost family members in the conflict but nevertheless wanted peace. In 1998 the group began to meet with Palestinian families from Gaza as well. Although the Intifada temporarily severed the connection, it resumed in 2000 with families on the West Bank and East Jerusalem.

Frankenthal invited me to attend a meeting of the Parents Circle to see for myself. I entered feeling cynical, but there I saw something completely new to me: Bereaved Palestinian families getting off the buses: men, women, and children, coming towards me, greeting me in peace, hugging me, and crying with me. Although I was 47 years old, I'm ashamed to admit this was the first time in my life that I met Palestinians as human beings.

I am not religious, so I am at a loss to explain the change I underwent at that moment. From that day on, I had a reason to get out of bed in the morning. I have dedicated my life to going from person to person, insisting: "This does not have to be our destiny!" Nowhere is it written that we must continue sacrificing our children in the Holy Land. We must stop this crazy violence, murder and retaliation, revenge and punishment, a purposeless cycle with no winners, and only losers.

So today I've found myself as the Israeli Co-Director of this amazing group which puts cracks of hope in these walls of hatred and fear. The PCFF has concluded that the process of reconciliation between nations is a prerequisite to achieving a sustainable peace. The organization thus utilizes all resources available in education, public meetings and the media, to spread these ideas in the Dialogue Encounters, Narrative groups, summer camps, and many other activities. You will not find many examples in history where bereaved people from both sides of the conflict hold out hands to one another. Intolerable pain can be directed for good or destruction.

## Chapter 14

## Robi

There is no pain like the pain of losing a child, especially in a cruel way. How can I reconcile with the Palestinian sniper who killed my beautiful son David, a student of philosophy of education at Tel Aviv university, a student leader, and part of the peace movement? My whole life was totally changed. I tried to flee but everywhere I went the pain came along with me. This terrible pain was the beginning of a pilgrimage that took many years in which I started to look for a way to prevent other families from experiencing this hole in the heart that can never be healed.

Eventually I went to a seminar where I met Palestinian mothers who also had lost children. Suddenly I realized that our shared pain can be a powerful energy and make us effective catalysts for change. My priorities evolved and I started travelling all over the world to spread a message of reconciliation. We go around telling our stories to inform, inspire, disturb, and motivate. I spoke at Israeli and Palestinian schools, encouraging students to believe in dialogue, even respectful arguments. I thought that if I stood on stage with a Palestinian mother, perhaps our example could make a difference, and people would realize that for us, who have the most difficulty of reconciling, we are talking together. Few Israelis and Palestinians know each other as people, and as a result, they construct negative images of the other out of fear. Yet, it is in our hands to look beyond our fear, listen to each other, and recognize each other's pain. Our goal is to end the violence with dialogue.

One day in October 2004 the Army came to my door to announce that they caught the man who killed David. That was a huge step and new test for me. Do I actually mean what I am saying about reconciliation? After many sleepless nights, I wrote a letter to the family of the sniper, and two Palestinians from my Bereaved Families group delivered the letter to the family. I waited two years until I got a letter back, and it wasn't a gentle letter. It was then I realized that my life doesn't depend on what this man does, and suddenly this freed me to go on.

I went to South Africa to study the Truth and Reconciliation process there. Then I returned to Israel. I eventually decided to visit the killer in prison. What mattered to me is that I was in integrity with my message of seeking reconciliation. Despite his lack of response, my work continues to be about shattering the terrible myth that there is no one to talk to on the other side and nothing to talk about; a myth that only maintains the status quo.

The problems of our two peoples begin at young ages. To break down walls of fear and hatred and engage students to believe in dialogue, we sponsor activities such as a summer camp for about fifty bereaved Palestinian and Israeli youth. The Parents Circle and Combatants for Peace organize Remembrance Day, an Israeli and Palestinian Memorial Day to pay respect to families who have lost loved ones on both sides of the conflict and share a common denominator of pain. This year over 7,000 people attended the ceremony in Israel and another 700 in the West Bank, and it was broadcast live all over the world.

If we want our children and grandchildren to live in a world without violence, there is no other alternative but to begin to take steps to build trust with one another, which only comes from getting to know each other as human beings. Of course, any future solution must be based on free negotiations between both sides, reconciliation as part of peace, two states for two peoples, and with recognition of basic human rights. Too many rivers of blood have made one thing clear: Palestinians will not be able to throw the Jews, who have no other homeland, into the sea, and Israelis will not succeed in suppressing the Palestinians' desire for freedom. It has been decreed that we must all live on this land and the sooner we understand that in war there are only losers, it will be better for all of us.

We must remember that war is not an act of fate, but one of human doing. We must put an end to the killing and look for a way through mutual understanding and empathy. The words on my David's grave are a quotation from Khalil Gibran that says:" The whole earth is my birthplace and all humans are my brothers."

*Chapter 14*

## On The Road To A Richer Zionism:
## *Israel Through Fresh Eyes*
## Avi Meyerstein

July 21, 2016. As Air Canada flight 84 climbs to cruising altitude, finally, we are on our way to Israel. My three daughters – ages 9 and younger – have learned about Israel in school, in camp, and at home. They've long yearned to go. They seem to know that it's not just a random trip but rather a homecoming to a home they've never seen. Since they were born, I'd hoped they would have that very feeling. But, I also worried that everything was now so much more complicated and textured. Could I give my kids a Zionism as rich as the one I had reached as an adult?

When I grew up, Israel was as straightforward as a 1950s propaganda reel. Its fairy-tale past and present were about good vs. evil, right or wrong, David and Goliath. On my first trip to Israel, I devoured Leon Uris' book, *Exodus*, on the plane. When we landed, the P.A. system played "Heveinu Shalom Aleichem" while the video projector played images of the Land of Milk and Honey. As the plane's rubber wheels touched down on Promised Land pavement, everyone cheered, as if a Jewish airplane landing safely was another small Zionist miracle.

My early Israel experiences were shaped especially by my parents. They were rightly in awe of what Israel had become – indeed the very fact that it had become at all. My mom was named after the State. Her close relatives escaped to there before and after the Holocaust. My dad spent his career as a rabbi defending Israel. They raised me on stories of their visits and time living there. It was only natural for my parents' generation to relate to Israel so deeply. They saw Israel fight for its very existence. Born just as she was born, they watched over her like protective older siblings. Naturally, they wanted to foster in the next generation the same deep homeland connection.

And so their generation told mine a simple story: The remnants of the Jewish people rose from the ashes to build a modern state in their ancient homeland. They were a people without a land that came to a land without a people. They just wanted to make the desert bloom in peace. But, their neighbors rose up to drive them into the sea. The Jews would be victims no longer. They boldly declared and defended a new state – the only democracy in the Middle East, a shining Light unto the Nations, where everyone is equal and free. The Middle East is a tough neighborhood, where others only understand force. But, Israel has sought peace at every turn.

To my parents and their friends, these were articles of faith. They believed that Israel remained in existential danger. It is thus no surprise that the Israel education their generation gave mine was rose-colored at best. There were only two sides, they reasoned – for or against. Israel is our homeland and needs our support. We cannot afford to show weakness by second-guessing. We don't hang our dirty laundry in public. Unfortunately, the tale was a little too good to be true. It set me up for disappointment. By the time I left for college, my support for Israel *sounded* strong. But, I soon discovered that it was relatively fragile. In trying to make me a zealous advocate and unabashed partisan, my community failed to prepare me for the texture and nuance of the real world. Raised on a mythical, almost heavenly Israel, I was caught by surprise by the human, earthly Israel.

My journey to a richer, more resilient Zionism started during a high school trip to Poland and Israel, when I saw the country for the first time with a critical young adult's mind. I saw things I had never seen before; reality came crashing in. One night, we ventured to a dance club. The teens inside were smoking and high on drugs. I almost became ill and ran outside. I completely broke down on the street. After all the destruction we had witnessed in Poland, how could the redemption in the Promised Land look like this? Was this the "hope of 2,000 years?"

We also witnessed first-hand political upheaval, which challenged some of the old talking points. We watched TV as Prime Minister Rabin signed the Oslo Accords, affirming for us that Israel was, as we had learned, a nation that would do anything for peace. But, on our trip in 1995, we saw Rabin, a founding father, loudly booed at an event. Angered by terrorism, the crowd rejected his peace process. I was stunned. Weren't Israelis on board with his pursuit of peace?

The next year, in college, when I rushed to defend Israel from every criticism, I encountered intelligent and thoughtful people whose families also felt victimhood, injustice, and dispossession. Yet, in their stories, the heroes and villains were reversed. I learned from them and from my studies facts I had never heard before. As my perspective grew, I never questioned that Israel had often been a victim, but I no longer saw it as having a monopoly on victimhood. As time when on, everywhere I looked, I saw inconsistencies in the party line. Were we to celebrate Israel as the powerhouse "Start-up Nation" or withhold criticism because Israel was an underdog, on the verge of destruction? If America and the world were not perfect and needed our *Tikkun Olam*, why would Israel be any different? How could Israel ever overcome her challenges if those who loved her most refused to discuss them?

## Chapter 14

All of this questioning was highly emotional, personal, and painful. I feared it could create distance from those I loved. I felt resentment that I had not be taught a more complete history. In hindsight, the way my generation was raised was dangerous. Too many became disillusioned and disaffected. Israel had been painted as some other-worldly place, where human problems simply didn't exist. Many young people came crashing down when they came to understand Israel in all of its struggle, triumph, and complexity. For too many, their Zionism was brittle, ready to shatter at first contact with a more complete view. I wanted something richer and stronger for my kids.

Fortunately, unlike many, I found a way to expand my Zionism. I managed to keep Israel in my heart even as I came to understand that Israel – like all human endeavors – is not perfect. On a good day, Israel faces the same kinds of social, economic, political, and security challenges as other nations. But, on most days, its democracy faces these challenges inside a pressure cooker. And yet, Israel's creation was miraculous. How often does a downtrodden people return to their ancestral homeland after millennia of exile? How often is a new state born and so quickly become a fertile home of culture and arts, technology and innovation?

Does Israel, like most countries, have plenty of work to do to realize the vision of its founders? Absolutely. It faces serious political, security, economic, social, and racial challenges. Significant segments of society, including Arab-Israelis, face widespread inequality and discrimination. Palestinians in the West Bank and Gaza deserve a state of their own. Israel's democracy is a messy and noisy one. Is someone who recognizes these realities a self-hating Jew or anti-Israel, as some suggest? Hardly. On the contrary, how can someone deny these realities – either to himself or to others – and still play a constructive role in solving these problems?

When it comes to the Israeli-Palestinian conflict, in particular, the current status quo is proof that the zero-sum Middle East I was taught simply does not work. A situation in which only one party can be the winner is a recipe for unending instability and violence. I long ago replaced an "or" Zionism of us-versus-them with an "and" Zionism. I support the equal rights of both Israelis and Palestinians to live in peace and security. Just as I feel a duty to support Israel's peace and security, I owe no less to other people of good will. We are all made in God's image. As my Zionism grew, I noticed that the one constant in the ups-and-downs of the peace process was majorities on both sides who wanted peace and were willing to compromise but did not believe they had partners on the other side. I could see from the sidelines that there were plenty of partners to go around. But, war, fear, and physical barriers kept Israelis and Palestinians from seeing this in each other or even seeing each other at all.

My expanded Zionism led me to devote a substantial part of my life to advancing peace. While working as a young lawyer at a big law firm, I established the Alliance for Middle East Peace (ALLMEP) so there would be a voice and a champion for those majorities, who seek peace and reconciliation through joint projects – schools, environmental clean-up, medical clinics, and basketball leagues. Today, ALLMEP is a coalition of more than 110 people-to-people organizations and tens of thousands of people. One day, it will be millions.

When I started these efforts by talking with three organizations, it quickly became clear that they were fragmented, disconnected, and feeling lonely. We soon discovered dozens of programs with thousands of people. By connecting them to each other, bringing more than $100 million so far in foreign aid to expand their activities, and amplifying their voices, we can join thousands of disparate voices into a critical mass of cooperation and good will. For me, this work was the ultimate escape from the mistaken zero-sum approach. By investing my energies in forward-looking solutions, I didn't have to keep debating the endless questions of who started it. By working with the good people on both sides who want better lives through cooperation, I didn't have to choose sides any longer.

When I became a parent, I worried that since it took me so long to reach a richer Zionism, how could I pass it on to my kids? Could they grasp the complexity and nuance? Could they develop and nurture a love for Israel and also embrace human rights and justice, even for the "other side?" As our family traveled around Israel for several weeks that summer, my worries melted away. We crisscrossed the country from corner to corner, border to border. From the surf of Herzliya in the West to the peace park inside the Jordanian border in the East, from Eilat's tropical fish in the South to a view of the Syrian civil war seen from the North.

My kids saw an Israel that doesn't fit on a postcard or bumper sticker. They met real people of all different backgrounds, especially kids their ages. We spent time in Arab communities, meeting the owner of a local dairy farm and enjoying home hospitality. We visited the Jerusalem Hand in Hand school, where we met bilingual Arab and Jewish kids in summer camp together. We shared hikes and meals with a variety of Israeli families. It was amazing to see how naturally the kids clicked

## Chapter 14

with each other – even when they had no language in common. My kids got an introduction to the conflict, too. An Israeli friend showed them a safe room in his house and told stories about rockets falling. A Palestinian friend shared an experience of discrimination on a public bus. We helped our kids understand how all these stories fit together. But, the kids could also see for themselves the complicated mix of separation, fear, cooperation, and coexistence.

In the end, my kids may not understand every twist and turn of a century-old political conflict (who really does, anyway?). But, on their own level, I think they got it. They know that Israel is special – and particularly special to us. They get that Israel faces threats and is also rich in opportunities. They saw that Israel has challenges and also people working hard on solutions. They see that good and evil is not about where you come from but rather about where you're trying to go. Their Israel education and journey are far from over. But, with a broader and more open viewpoint than I had, they've got a firm foundation for a durable, lifelong connection.

## *Imagining An Idea Whose Time Has Come*
## Nick Dahan

In 2005 my wife and I were vacationing in Italy, sitting in a quaint little restaurant on the banks of Lake Como, with majestic white-capped mountains on one side, and a collection of villages surrounding the lake. In this quiet, reflective place, without really knowing why, I suddenly felt as if an idea grabbed hold of me and wouldn't let go. I began to write three simple words on the paper placemat on the table: *Ideology + Investment = Hope*. Hope is the theme of Israel's national anthem because with hope, all things are possible, even a seemingly impossible dream of peace.

You don't have to look far today to realize that the Middle East is in a mess. Tempting as it might be to walk away from the troubles, what happens in the Middle East has a direct impact on our security. Certainly, it affects the security and viability of Israel, which has a special place in our hearts. Therefore, to the extent possible, it is incumbent on people of good will to explore ways to bring peace to the region.

Although it may seem like an impossible dream, these words: *Ideology+Investment = Hope*, can be the answer for the Middle East, and other places around the world. A new model is needed, one that inspires hope by delivering on the promise with jobs that can grow our economies, protect the environment, and help to weaken the hold of extremist thinking. Such a new model for the Middle East could become a reality on the ground.

What would such a model look like? The model I propose is a Green Industrial Zone, which will contain seven key elements, as represented by the acronym DESTINY. The key elements are:

> **D** is for Diversity: Have Jews, Christians and Muslims living and working together with common purpose. As a result, they will see the humanity in one another's eyes.
>
> **E** is for Education, Employment and Empowerment: Teach vocational skills, confer academic degrees, partner with employers to hire skilled workers, and finance young start-up entrepreneurs.
>
> **S** is for Sustainability: Use state-of-the-art green construction techniques to build a zone that produces cutting edge green goods and services which can improve the world in such fields as clean water, food production, healthcare, and green energy.

**T** is for Tolerance and Trust: Working together in common purpose, using a colony of artists to create a culture of diversity, tolerance, and trust in an effort to humanize one another, through producing movies, theater, concerts, and other aspects of cultural life.

**I** is for Ideology: *An ideology of common sense* would include the Golden Rule ("Treat others as you would have them treat you"), the Golden Mean ("The truth is usually somewhere in the middle of two extremes"), and the Greatest Good ("An action is just when it produces the greatest good for the greatest number."). Such an approach will inspire our thoughts, inform our speech, and respect our sense of personal dignity.

**N** is for New Models: Instead of doing or not doing the same old thing, why not try something new and give it a chance?

**Y** is for Young People: Give young people a place at the table and a stake in their future, by providing jobs as a reason to keep the peace.

Some may look at this project and say this is simply wishful thinking. However, there are hints that such a model is exactly what is called for in our time. Perhaps a strange alignment of the stars is happening, whereby the self-interest of some key players in the Middle East is coming into alignment with the best interest of the region.

Could it be that the Middle East is ready for a new model that inspires a sense of hope and delivers on that promise with jobs? The Arab Spring did not succeed, but it did put on alert some of the leaders, that the ground they're walking on is not quite as solid as they once thought; that it's more like the shifting sands of the desert. The leaders of such countries as Saudi Arabia, UAE, Jordan and Egypt, etc. are worried about strategic threats they face from ISIS and al Qaeda, and most of all from Iran. But they also worry about the threat from the man on the street, who is demanding a place at the table, a stake in his future, a reason to keep the peace ... in short, a job.

What if the common threats they face would cause the leaders to believe that they actually need one another? Perhaps a strategic/economic alliance between some of the Arab states, Israel and the U.S. could have two purposes in mind: To provide for a common defense and to create millions of jobs. Perhaps it could even lead to Arab leaders brokering a lasting peace between Israel and Palestine?

If you think this is just a dream, would you be surprised to learn that the first green city in the world has already been built? Its name is Masdar, and it is located in the desert of Abu Dhabi, part of the United Arab Emirates, the eighth largest oil producer in the world. Masdar has not yet realized her potential, but imagine sending a delegation of prominent Israeli and American start-up entrepreneurs to Masdar to cut business deals and helping the first green city in the world blossom.

Imagine such a city where Jews, Christians and Muslims show up to work on a daily basis; where young people, men and women alike, are taught the skills they need for good paying jobs, and for starting their own companies. Here in Masdar companies could produce green goods and services to change the world. Partnering with Dubai movie studios to produce movies, theater and concerts could inculcate a culture of tolerance and trust. A new *Ideology of Common Sense* can infuse how we to speak to one another. Where implemented, it can prove that peaceful coexistence on the ground is possible, giving young people hope for their futures.

My wife and I are taking steps to convince government officials, business people, and philanthropists alike, to jointly put in place a model of this sort for the Middle East and beyond. Masdar does actually exist and could easily accommodate the seven elements of the *DESTINY MODEL*.

Recently, we obtained, in writing, a commitment from some of the most successful start-up entrepreneurs in Israel, to travel to Masdar, if invited, to help introduce the model. Subsequently, we met with Ambassador Otaiba of the United Arab Emirates and discussed with him the possibility of using Masdar as an Arab initiative to move the entire region in a new direction. This would include an Arab initiative to broker a lasting peace between Israel and Palestine. After a two hour discussion, his reaction was very positive, and he said he would reach out to the Royal Family to see if they were interested. They responded that they would need more time to think it over.

Obviously, when you're talking about Middle East peace, there are no guarantees. However, considering the stakes as well the opportunity that may now exist for "regional peace," it's worth a try. This model answers the three greatest questions of our time: How do we grow our economies? How do we protect the environment? And how do we weaken the hold of extremist thinking? A well-configured Green Industrial Zone could be a beacon of hope, at a time when the world is looking for answers. It could easily blossom into a larger movement for change.

Remember Rosa Parks, the African American woman who refused to

## Chapter 14

give up her seat on a bus. Ordinarily, this might have remained a non-event, but Martin Luther King was a visionary who expanded on Rosa Parks' courageous action for justice by showing us the way forward. It must begin with a big vision of hope, and requires some reality on the ground to expand the vision and make it real. This is a time for a prescription for change in the Middle East. This is the time, before time runs out, to dream the impossible, and make the impossible come true.

## *Netiv L'Shalom: Mosaic Path to Peace*
## Tsameret Zamir

I have been a ceramic artist for many years, living and working in my studio at Moshav Netiv HaAsara. The *moshav* was formed in 1973, named after ten soldiers who were killed in a helicopter accident in 1971 in the northwest Negev. After the 1979 Peace Agreement with Egypt, and Yamit was evacuated (1982), the *moshav* moved and established a new home along the Gaza border. During peacetime Palestinians worked in our *moshav,* and villagers shopped and dined in Gaza. Today, sadly, no such contact exists between the two peoples.

I came here in 1998 with my husband and four children because I love the land and wanted to give my family a quiet country life and create a happy childhood for my children. At the *moshav* we have hothouses with beautiful flowers, cucumbers, and tomatoes. Just two years after we moved here, our village's tranquil atmosphere was violated by missile attacks. With the forced unilateral evacuation of Gush Katif ordered by Prime Minister Ariel Sharon, and the Hamas takeover of Gaza, suddenly Netiv HaAsara became the closest settlement inside Israel to the Gaza border, less than one kilometer away.

Our village stands on a hill over a valley, and there are hills on the other side as well. The border fence in the valley below does not really create a secure barrier between us and Gaza. Beyond that border fence is densely populated Gaza City. When the electrified fence is breached, information is transferred to the Israeli army. However, this alone did not create enough security, as we could see Hamas men perched on the opposite hills, waving green flags and shouting. Not only could we see them, but they could also see us, as well as look inside our homes, which was scary.

A border wall was built in front of Netiv HaAsara to create more security for us because we are literally on the border. However, this nine-meters-high wall is located in the valley and doesn't hide the *moshav* houses from view or prevent direct shooting. A year later Israel built a second nine-meters-high wall on higher ground, closer to our houses, and about 200 meters from the fence and border wall.

I watched them building our nine-meter high protective wall, putting it together section by section, like a huge grey jigsaw puzzle. It had the effect of closing the horizon for us, and shutting down the familiar landscape. The wall affects everyone here. On the one hand, it is very frightening and off putting; on the other, it affords us security. If you look right outside my studio, past the porch, you can see the barrier a few hundred yards away. The rocket shells on my porch were "delivered" from Gaza via missile. Since missiles remind me of bad memories, I tried to make them "softer" by gluing decorative ceramic flowers on them.

I must admit it isn't easy living with the missile threat. Actually, it is quite traumatic living on the border, especially during military operations. I have felt terror and witnessed terror in my children when the sirens go off and rockets fly as they wait at a bus stop for school. One night after our neighbor's house was hit by a rocket, I packed up our family and fled to my parents' house. For a week I was so traumatized that I couldn't speak at all. Many children and adults require professional help to deal with the trauma they experienced. I find it soothing to work with soft clay as a meditative coping tool.

Over the years many concrete shelters were built here. A public address system announces when a missile is launched in our direction, and we have five seconds to race for shelter. The reality is that my gut hurts and I am filled with sadness for all the little children who do not understand why an enemy tries to hurt them. We all somehow manage to stay strong for our children, and try to maintain ordinary life and be a mutually supportive community. I was always impressed by the special communal strength in the *moshav*, and how much power and optimism we can create when we work together.

I wanted to import this special model of working together into my creative art. While the border wall is the scariest place on our moshav, and in the past, people were even afraid to stand near it, this is precisely why I chose to go to the hardest place to try and change the atmosphere there into hope and even happiness. I personally wish there wouldn't be wars, hatred, and pain, and I want to promote listening and patience between people so that we can all live safely and peacefully.

I decided to use my art to make something to improve the situation here and I was grateful to receive positive encouragement for my plan. Peace became the theme of my project, and here is what I did: I painted a giant colorful mural on the border wall nearest us with the words: "Path to Peace" written in huge letters in English, Hebrew, and Arabic. Above the mural I made a huge dove with an olive branch. The mural is painted on both sides of the wall that protects us from direct shooting, and the other side is also painted and visible to our "neighbors."

I make pieces of mosaic tile by hand and work with people who have special needs as a way of supporting them to make a living. We use many colors that suggest hope and optimism. The pieces have different textures and shapes and each piece is important to me. The mosaics are shaped as images of flowers, butterflies, hearts, animals, houses, as well as the words "hope," "listening," and "peace" in multiple languages.

Visitors from all around the world come and glue the handmade tiles, decorate the mural, and write personal messages of hope. I also send tiles to schoolchildren for them to decorate and return to me so I can glue them on the wall. You are invited to come here and take an active part in creating the Peace Wall by gluing the mosaics onto the giant letters. When we act together we can affect more, spread our energy to others, and create wider meaning. You can tell people that a large border wall with a constant sense of danger is being turned into a symbol of hope and optimism.

I find a parallel between the mosaic and our lives here. The mosaic is a collection of individual broken pieces glued together to create a whole that is bigger and more beautiful than its parts. The collaborative creation brings forth strength, and the multitude of pieces on the wall reveal how many visitors chose to leave their mark and wishes for a better future. Those who come here hope that one day our dreams of a life of tranquility and peace will be fulfilled. I believe that other lessons can be learned here as well. Our villagers feel pride in the beautiful creation, and people from Israel and elsewhere are moved when they visit. Each person can identify difficulties, fears, and hurts that live inside them, and with courage, he or she can make them into something new, positive, and healing.

To further my objectives I formed Netiv L'Shalom, or Path to Peace, a joint creative project that fosters tolerance and kindness to others, optimism, and hope. I believe in the power of solving problems together. Path to Peace is a social project available to people of all ages, and participation is free for IDF soldiers. Our mission is to create hope for

## Chapter 14

peace among the citizens on both sides.

Obviously, in order to make peace with enemies, there has to be communication with them. I believe that just like us, the other side wants to make an honorable living and have a normal, positive family life. While I haven't yet heard from the Palestinians, I hope that the people living on the other side of the border will also see the messages and choose a peaceful future.

## *Postscript*

You have read many stories that hopefully express why I consider the nation of Israel to be an ongoing miracle. I hope the stories have inspired and motivated you to reflect and engage in your own *Tikkun Olam* work to improve our shared world. The words of our sages apply equally today: "It is not your obligation to complete the task of perfecting the world, but neither are you free to desist from doing all that you can." (Ethics of the Fathers).

In many ways, the book will now come full circle. If you remember the very first story you read was about a little boy, hidden during the *Shoah*, who found safety and healing in kibbutz life in Israel. His prayer was that the beloved *Sukkah* he built would be an emblem for Israel as a land of tolerance, diversity, fairness, and kindness to all, *"ufros aleynu sukkat shelomecha* – please spread over us Your sukkah of peace." The portable *sukkot* where *Bnai Yisrael* dwelled on their journey through the wilderness, suggest shelter and protection from the elements. However, the sukkah also had an opening on its side, so it would not be isolated, but rather open to other people and the community.

For me, the image of the *Sukkah* could be a metaphor for greater understanding between Jews of different persuasions, between Jews and their non-Jewish neighbors in Israel, as well as between all people. In Israel it would feel miraculous if both sides of the religious-secular divide could sit and talk in the same tent, as well as with their Arab and Christian neighbors. American Jews could also use a broader tent to encompass the younger generation's idealistic universalism and the older or more conservative generation's leaning towards tribalism and nationalism. And the world could certainly use more tolerance, dialogue, and peace.

The *Sukkah* could also be seen as metaphor for a *mifgash* – a meeting place, where conversation and food is shared, along with different views and perspectives. Recently, such a Sukkah of Hope was built in the Nazareth area by two Arab Muslims.[1] Realizing that their Jewish and Arab acquaintances rarely have an opportunity to meet one another and may be hesitant to do so, they decided to provide an opportunity during the holiday of *Sukkot*, a time when it is traditional to welcome guests for meals in the *Sukkah*. The large *Sukkah* was built on their deck in Upper Nazareth according to Jewish traditional regulations, with the help of Arab and Jewish neighbors, and the general public was invited. Over three days, 1200-1500 people from all over Israel visited.

The open *sukkah* had kosher and Arabic cuisine, and offered

*Postscript*

non-political discussions and dialogue sessions on issues of women, education, and health. The Jewish mayor of Upper Nazareth and two Arab deputy mayors attended, along with authors, actors, attorneys, physicians, journalist, and educators, and other neighbors. The gathering emphasized the common humanity shared, rather than separations based on religion or the color of one's skin. Such gatherings can help decrease Jewish-Muslim stereotypes through interaction and dialogue.

*Postscript*

## *Letter From Kids4peace To Kids*

Perhaps the most fitting ending to this book would be a letter from Kids4Peace to other young people, who represent the younger generation that will build the way forward in the future.

Dear Kids:
I am a 15-year-old Jewish Israeli who lives in Jerusalem. I used to love walking around the city while talking with my mom because Jerusalem is beautiful, but it is a very complicated city, not a simple or peaceful one. Jews and Arabs inhabit this city, but the two communities don't interact or engage with each other. There is a very clear separation for political and social reasons between East and West Jerusalem in public transportation, education, public spaces, and shopping centers.

When I was twelve years old I followed in the footsteps of my older brother and joined the youth movement Kids4Peace Jerusalem, whose mission is to build interfaith communities that embody a culture of peace and empower a *movement for change*. We bring together Muslim, Christian and Jewish, Israeli and Palestinian youth and their parents from East and West Jerusalem. Although these Israeli and Palestinian families live in the same city, they often have no other platform for getting to know each other outside of this community. Crazy, I know.

At my first K4P meeting I was scared because I had never met Palestinian kids and only heard about them on the media, or when my parents were talking about the situation in Jerusalem. I tried to figure out who was Israeli and who was Palestinian, but it was hard to tell because we all looked the same. We spent many weekly meetings together for two years, as well as summer camp programs. Through "get to know each other" games, sharing of each other's sacred religious objects, and cultural traditions, I got to know the Palestinians in my group and now consider them my friends. In Kids4Peace we believe that in order to stay friends during times of tension and violence we must create a foundation of understanding, friendship and trust and be able to have difficult conversations respectfully. Only then can we truly work together towards change and effectively advocate for peace in Jerusalem.

I was in eighth grade during the violence in the fall of 2015. We had only just begun a process of deep dialogue, so during this time, discussions were especially hard. Each one expressed their struggles and opinions, the daily challenges and fears they face living in a city filled with tension and violence. And even about the difficulties we face

## Postscript

from our own communities who may be critical of our involvement in Kids4Peace. But this is the beauty of Kids4Peace and its philosophy: Despite the hard times and challenging discussions, we care about each other as people and we want to support each other as part of a joint community.

Because of Kids4Peace, I am now more aware of what is happening around me. I keep up with politics, read the news, and have even spoken on a political panel at my school, sharing both political opinions and my personal story. I can speak from a place of knowledge about the other side instead of from a place of ignorance and fear. I feel more confident about who I am. At Kids4Peace we believe in sharing our story as part of creating change.

One day I was on my way to a Kids4Peace meeting at our center which is located on the seam between East and West Jerusalem in the entrance to Sheik-Jarrah, a place that took me a while to be comfortable visiting. Often I take the light rail to get to Kids4Peace, near the Ammunition-Hill station. On my way I witnessed a Palestinian man being asked to get off the train by the police, although he had not done anything wrong. The man was being treated this way due to the fact that he was Palestinian and there was tension, fear, and suspicion in the environment. The reality of violence in Jerusalem has led to countless similar tragedies of discrimination.

I am in Kids4Peace because I want to create change. So long as there is inequality, violence, occupation and fear, there is much work to be done. While it was not our generation that began the occupation, and it is not us who committed terror attacks, we are the ones who must live with this reality and we want a better future.

In Kids4Peace we create possibilities in what seems like an impossible situation. The Kids4Peace high school program called YAP (Youth Action Program) hosts Monthly Town Hall meetings, to which we invite exceptional Israeli and Palestinian leaders, artists and activists to come and speak to us and our friends. This is an opportunity to invite new members to be part of Kids4Peace. Our hope is that if more people grow up like we do, we will create more leaders who believe in change and advocate for peace in Jerusalem.

A large institution isn't needed to create change. It can happen through one relationship at a time. Each side of the relationship can influence its own community to see alternative perspectives. For example, I speak about this often with one of my really good Palestinian friends. He lives in a different community than I do, practices a different religion and speaks a different language. We are worlds apart – yet live in the same city.

*Postscript*

We are friends because of Kids4Peace. We share what we have learned about each other's communities with our friends and family, creating small ripple effects of change. We are two out of over 400 families working towards change in Kids4Peace. Imagine what Jerusalem would look like if we were part of 40,000 families! At Kids4Peace, in spite of the challenges and fears we face, I truly believe that we can create a better future, and it all starts with one friendship. I invite you to join with us in our hopes and dreams.

From Your Israeli And Palestinian Friends At Kids4peace

## *Song For Peace*

Music and English Lyrics by Rita Glassman, adapted from the prayer, *Oseh Shalom.* From the CD "*A World of Peace in Song and Prayer*" www.RitaGlassman.com All Rights Reserved (c) 2015

The say to everything there is a season
and miracles they happen every day
They say that we are more alike than different
and in the eyes of God we are the same

I dream one day we'll sing this prayer together
and war will be a distant memory
and we will learn to care for one another
and live to see a world of lasting peace

*O-seh sha-lom bim-ro-mav*
*Hu ya-a-she sha-lom a-ley-nu (2x)*
*Sha-lom al Yis-ra-el, Sha-lom-al Yish-ma-el*
*V'al kol yosh-vei, yosh-vei tey-vel, v'im-ru A-men.*

Let the one who makes peace in the heavens
bring peace to us on this earth (2x)
To all the children of Israel and the children of Ishmael
Peace in every heart, and in every land
and we sing Amen.

*Postscript*

## *Eli, Eli,*

O God, my God
On this sacred moment, give us
Hope for Israel
and her future.
Renew our wonder at
the miracle of the
Jewish state.

In the name of our
Fallen soldiers-give
us courage to stand
up to the words and
Ways of the zealots.
Those in our own
midst and those
Among our neighbors.

In the name of Israeli
inventors who have
amazed the world
with their innovations-help
us apply the same
ingenuity to finding a
path to peace.

In the name of all
these women and
men-grant us the
Strength to conquer
doubt and despair in
Israel.

Replacing doubt with
action.
replacing despair
with hope.
And let us say
Amen.

Anat Hoffman,<br>
Israel Religious Action Committee

*Postscript*

## *Prayer for Peace* [2]

Sovereign of the universe, accept in lovingkindness and with favor our prayers for the State of Israel, her government, and all who dwell within her boundaries and under her authority. Open our eyes and our hearts to the wonder of Israel, and strengthen our faith in Your power to work redemption in every human soul. Grant us also the fortitude to keep ever before us those ideals upon which the State of Israel was founded. Grant courage, wisdom, and strength to those entrusted with guiding Israel's destiny to do Your will. Be with those on whose shoulders Israel's safety depends and defend them from all harm. Spread over Israel and all the world Your shelter of peace, and may the vision of Your prophet soon be fulfilled:

> *Nation shall not lift up sword against nation, neither shall they learn war anymore. (Isaiah 2:4)*

# REFLECTIONS

The following section includes ideas to think about after reading the stories in each chapter. The questions lend themselves to personal reflection, group discussion, or possible educational projects emanating from the questions.

## *Introduction*

1. What is the story of your relationship to Israel? Do you have any relatives who live in Israel?
2. Is your knowledge of Israel from the news or from direct experience, such as a family trip, camp, or Birthright?
3. What were your first impressions of Israel? Describe or draw.
4. What do you see as Israel's biggest challenges?
5. Have your attitudes toward Israel changed over time? How?

## *Chapter 1: The Chosen; Chosen for What?*

1. How do you feel about the term "Chosen People?"
2. What responsibilities do you believe go along with being Jewish?
3. If you accept the idea of "chosen-ness," what do you see as your purpose in the world?
4. Do you think Israel lives up to its mission as a "Chosen People"? In what ways do you think it falls short?
5. Is it fair that Israel is held to higher standards than other nations of the world?

## *Chapter 2: Wandering Jews: Secrets of Survival*

1. What effects do you think persecution and expulsions have had on the Jewish people over the centuries?
2. Why do you think Jews are still here after thousands of years?
3. Is it important to remain a "nation that stands alone" as Jews, rather than blending in with others?
4. Do you agree that observances, such as Shabbat, have kept the Jewish people together? Which observances do you find meaningful?
5. What survival tools do you want to hand down to the next generation?

*Reflections*

*Chapter 3: Out of the Ashes of the Shoah: Finding a Safe Haven*
1. At what age did you first learn about the *Shoah* (the Holocaust)? From who? What feelings did learning about the *Shoah* evoke in you?
2. Does your family have a story relating to the *Shoah*? Who could you ask?
3. What feelings do you imagine a survivor had? Child of survivors? (second generation) Grandchild? Which are you?
4. We say "never again," but do you think a Holocaust could ever happen again? Why or why not?
5. What conditions led to the *Shoah*? What could be done to prevent it?

*Chapter 4: Israel's Birth: Miracles Do Happen*
1. Do you agree with Herzl's words: "If you will it, it is no dream"? What, besides will, led to Herzl's dream coming true?
2. Do you view Israel's birth as a miracle? Do humans play a role in miracles?
3. When you hear *Hatikvah* ("The Hope") being sung, what effect does it have on you?
4. Do you have any family members who were involved in the foundation of the State? How did Israel's birth affected survivors of the *Shoah*?
5. What do you know about Israel's Declaration of Independence?

*Chapter 5: Ingathering of the Exiles: A Nation of Immigrants*
1. Do you have relatives who immigrated to Israel? From where did they come? What are their stories?
2. What are some reasons why Jews make *Aliyah* to Israel?
3. What contributions have immigrants made to Israel?
4. Have you ever imagined what it feels like to be an immigrant?
5. What does Jewish tradition have to say about welcoming immigrants?

*Part II: Tikkun Olam Values*
1. What do you think motivates people to perform *Tikkun Olam?*
2. Can you think of a time when someone did a good deed for you? How did it feel?
3. How do you decide which cause is most important to support? What acts of *Tikkun Olam* do you currently perform, or might you do in the future?
4. Make a list of people who do good works that you admire (family

*Reflections*

        member, friends, strangers, public figures alive or dead). What qualities in them do you most admire?
5.     What do you think inspires the huge level of voluntarism in Israeli society? Do you think it is related to the Torah?

*Chapter 6: The Earth is the Lord's: Protecting Our Environment*
1.     Why did God have to specially remind Adam and Eve not to spoil the earth? Do you think that taking care of a gift has to be taught?
2.     Do you personally feel responsible for protecting the environment?
3.     What practices do you engage in towards that goal?
4.     How would you convince and motivate a Jewish climate change denier of the importance of protecting the environment?
5.     How could protecting the environment be related to peace efforts?

*Chapter 7: Saving a Life Above All: Pikuach Nefesh*
1.     Why do you think saving a life is the most important value in Judaism?
2.     What does our Torah have to say about saving a life? Should a person put him or herself in harm's way to save a life?
3.     What qualities enable a person to be able to save lives?
4.     What ethical dilemmas might be involved in saving a life?
5.     Have you ever experienced saving a life or being saved? What feelings did this experience evoke in you?

*Chapter 8:*
*Justice: Creating a More Equitable and Compassionate Society*
1.     On the High Holidays, why are justice and compassion described as God's two main characteristics?
2.     Why do you think justice is considered such an important value in the Torah? What *mitzvot* illustrate seeking justice?
3.     Have you ever participated in seeking justice for a cause? What was that like for you?
4.     What issues in Israeli society need greater attention to justice and compassion?
5.     Do you consider religious pluralism a form of justice?

*Chapter 9: God Loves All of His Creations: On Being Inclusive*
1.     Have you had a personal or family experience with disabilities? What have you learned from this situation?

*Reflections*

2. With what feelings do you imagine a person with disabilities struggles?
3. What obstacles in people and society to do you see that prevent greater inclusivity?
4. What qualities does a person need to have to foster a more inclusive attitude towards people with disabilities?
5. Do you have any ideas for better inclusion of people with differences?

*Chapter 10:*
*Loving Thy Neighbor: Building Friendship and Cooperation*

1. Do you think you act as a good neighbor? In what ways?
2. Have you had positive or negative experiences with neighbors?
3. Is it possible to love a neighbor who seems very different and even unfriendly?
4. What role can dialogue and shared experiences play in bridging gaps between people and creating greater respect and tolerance?
5. What special efforts are necessary to reconcile very different political and religious viewpoints in society?

*Chapter 11:*
*Compassion for the Poor, the Vulnerable, and the Stranger*

1. Why do Jews recite "Remember that you were strangers in the land of Egypt" at the Passover Seder? Why does that phrase appear 37 times in the Torah?
2. If one never experienced poverty, hunger, discrimination, what would motivate a person to work on these issues?
3. What are the greatest needs of people who are poor, vulnerable, and strangers?
4. If you have had experiences helping disadvantaged people, how did it make you feel? What did you learn from them?
5. What long term benefits are produced in a society by caring for the underserved and less fortunate?

*Chapter 12:*
*Light unto the Nations: Technology for the Good of Mankind*

1. Does a technologically advanced society bear responsibility for other countries in the world that are less developed?
2. What technological advances has Israel introduced that you are most proud of?
3. How can technology change people economically? Emotionally?

4. Do you think that sharing advanced technology is a modern day example of "being a Light unto the Nations?" In what way?
5. How can technological advancements within Israeli society help those less fortunate?

### Chapter 13: Healing the Spirit in Creative Ways

1. Have you ever experienced a trauma and then healing? Through what pathways did healing occur?
2. How can the arts and community heal the spirit?
3. What are ways in which "spiritual care" can be healing?
4. How can physical activity or work with animals lift one's spirits?
5. What Jewish rituals are you aware of that provide healing experiences to help people overcome trauma?

### Chapter 14: Seeking Peaceful Coexistence

1. What do you think enabled Jacob and Esau to eventually reconcile?
2. How can shared experiences between strangers affect attitudes about the other's culture? How can hearing the other's narrative and pain lead to greater connections between enemies?
3. What can Israel and the Palestinians do to facilitate more peaceful co-existence? Are both sides culpable if peace doesn't happen?
4. Short of actual peace talks, what actions can be taken to foster a climate moving towards peace?
5. Do you think co-existence efforts on the ground can someday "bubble up" to the top?

# NOTES

*Chapter 1: The Chosen People; Chosen For What?*

1  Greenberg, I. (1982). *The Voluntary Covenant* (New York: National Jewish Resource Center). Cited in Kamenetz, R. (1994), *The Jew in the Lotus: A Poet's Rediscovery of Jewish Identity in Buddhist India*. New York: Harper One.
2  Cahill, T. (1998). *The Gifts of the Jews: How a Tribe of Desert Nomads Changed the Way Everyone Thinks and Feels*. New York: Anchor Books.

*Chapter 2: Those Wandering Jews: Secrets of Survival*

1  Kamenetz, R. (1994). *The Jew in the Lotus: A Poet's Rediscovery of Jewish Identity in Buddhist India*. New York: Harper One.
2  Oz, A. & Oz-Salzberger, F. (2012) *jewsandwords*. New Haven: Yale University Press.
3  Heschel, A.J. (1988, originally published in 1967). *Israel: An Echo of Eternity*. New York: Farrar Straus Giroux.
4  Greenberg, I. (1988). *The Jewish Way: Living the Holidays*. New York: Touchstone.
5  Cahill, T. (1998). *The Gifts of the Jews: How a Tribe of Desert Nomads Changed the Way Everyone Thinks and Feels*. New York: Anchor Books.
6  Oz, A. & Oz-Salzberger, F. (2012). *jewsandwords,* New Haven: Yale University Press.
7  Greenberg, I. (1988). *The Jewish Way: Living the Holidays*. New York: Touchstone.

*Chapter 3: Out of the Ashes of the Shoah: Finding a Safe Haven*

1  Excerpted from Whispers in Hiding by Kathy Kacer and Sharon McKay. Copyright (c) Sharon E. McKay and Kathy Kacer. Reprinted by permission of Puffin Canada, a division of Penguin Random House Canada Limited.
2  Adam Furstenburg (Adash) survived with his family and moved to Canada in 1951. He received a Bachelor's degree in English and History, and a Master's degree in English. He became known in Canada as an authority in English and Yiddish literature and served, for many years, as the Director of the Holocaust Centre of Toronto. Adam passed away in 2016.
3  Bearing Witness: A Tribute to Elie Wiesel, Baltimore Jewish Council Yom HaShoah Holocaust Memorial Booklet 4/23/17.

## Notes

### Chapter 4: Israel's Birth: Miracles Do Happen
1. Tom Segev, *1949: The First Israelis*. New York: Henry Holt & Co. p.513.
2. Glassman, R. (2018) Personal Communication. *"It's a Miracle"* is an expression of gratitude for life, for healing, and the human capacity to continue to love, hope, and carry on after terrible events. When I (Israela Meyerstein) first heard Rita Glassman's inspirational song, I immediately thought of Jewish survival after the Holocaust and the miraculous birth of the State of Israel.
3. Heschel, A.J. (1988). *Israel: An Echo of Eternity.* New York: Farrar Straus Giroux.

### Part II: Tikkun Olam Values
1. *Eretz Acheret*, Summer 2015, p.27.
2. Gurevich, Michal. Personal Communication about Good Deeds Day Initiative.

### Chapter 6: The Earth is the Lord's: Protecting Our Environment
1. B'Yachad: Together, The Newsletter of the Jewish National Fund. Winter 2018.
2. The author is indebted to Seth M. Siegel, whose wonderful book, *Let There Be Water; Israel's Solution for a Water-Starved World* (2015), New York: Thomas Dunne Books, was a chief source of information about Israel's water story.

### Chapter 7: Saving a Life Above All: Pikuach Nefesh
1. Permission granted by Naama Cifrony to use excerpts from interview with Yair Golan in *Eretz Acheret*, Summer 2015.
2. Based on the one-woman show, *Heroic Measures: The Henrietta Szold Story*, written by Dale Jones of Making History Connections, and commissioned by the Jewish Museum of Maryland. Premiered on 9/22/16 at the Jewish Museum of Maryland.

### Chapter 8: Justice: Creating a More Equitable and Compassionate Society
1. An earlier version of this story appeared in "More than Managing - The Pursuit of Effective Jewish Leadership," edited by Rabbi Lawrence A. Hoffman, Jewish Lights Publishing (2016).

### Chapter 9: God loves all of His Creations: On Being Inclusive
1. Permission to use prayer granted by Harold S. Kushner
2. Eisner, J. (2016). A Good Week. Forward. (6/18/16)
3. Excerpts taken from previous story, *Rays of Light*, by Zimra Vigoda, published in Yediyot Achronot.

*Notes*

*Chapter 12:*
*Light unto the Nations: Technology for the Good of Mankind*

1. Senor, D. & Singer. S. (2009). *Start-up Nation: The Story of Israel's Economic Miracle.* New York.

*Chapter 13: Healing the Spirit in Creative Ways*

1. Ner-David, H. (2017). *Getting (and Staying) Married Jewishly: A Guide for Couples.* Ben Yehuda Press.
2. *Shmaya is* Aramaic for sky, and like its Hebrew counterpart, *shamayim,* it contains the word for water (*maya* or *mayim*) within it. The choice of this name for the *mikveh* was to evoke the idea of the Primordial "upper waters" and the interconnectedness of all water, all beings, and all of creation. According to the biblical narrative, at the beginning of time only water and Divine Spirit existed … God's womb, until the Divine Spirit brought separation into that peaceful, unified reality, separating water from dry land. God said: "And the waters will gather – yikavu hamayim", (the root of the word *mikveh* in Hebrew) into one place. And God called that gathering of water *"mikveh"* or "the seas."

*Chapter 14: Seeking Peaceful Coexistence*

1. Personal communication – Rabbi Haviva Ner-David (11/20/16).
2. Father Bruno Hussar (1911-1996) from his autobiography, *When the Cloud Lifted.* This rendering of Father Bruno's story is based on personal interviews, various publications, and news stories about Oasis of Peace and Father Bruno's life. It is an artistic retelling and not an historical account. Bruno's autobiography is the best source for an historical narrative of his amazing life.
3. The song is *"Erev Shel Shoshanim/Shalom-Salaam,"* as recorded for the first time in Hebrew and Arabic by the Yuval Ron Ensemble of the CD *Seeker of Truth.* You may hear the song at: www.cdbaby.com/cd/yuval9.

*Postscript*

1. www.israel21c.org/israeli-arab-couple-welcomes-all-in-sukkah-of-hope/
2. Adapted from Siddur Lev Shalem for Shabbat and Festivals. New York: The Rabbinical Assembly, 2016, p.178.

# CONTRIBUTORS

*Chapter 3: Out of the Ashes of the Shoah: Finding a Safe Haven*

**Dr. George Gorin** (1909-1988) attended the Hebrew Gymnasium in Bialystok, Poland, and studied medicine in Geneva, Switzerland. He came to the United States in 1937, and served in the United States Army in Europe during World War II. An ophthalmologist who specialized in glaucoma, he was on the Faculty of the Albert Einstein College of Medicine, and published several medical books. He was an avid Zionist who loved Hebrew, and after age 72, he wrote seven poetry books (in English and Hebrew).

**Joseph Gosler** – A former finance director in schools, Joe and his wife founded the Beginning Nursery School. Today he travels, gardens, is writing a memoir, and most importantly, walks his dog, Milton. Married to Sheila Wolper, they have one son, Jacob, and a grandchild.

**Kathy Kacer** is the author of more than twenty books since 1999. A winner of the Jewish Book Award in Canada and the U.S., as well as the Yad Vashem Award for Children's Holocaust Literature in Israel. Previously worked as Psychologist with troubled teens, and now teaches writing at the University of Toronto, Canada (Continuing Studies), as well as lectures on teaching sensitive material to young children.

*Chapter 4: Israel's Birth: Miracles Do Happen*

**Nick Dahan** – Born in Israel, where his extended family lived for over 200 years. Maternal Grandparents were one of 66 families who founded city of Tel Aviv. He grew up in the US since age 7 and worked as a builder and developer with his father, Haron Dahan. For past ten years, Nick has been working together with his wife, Mira, to put in place a new model for the Middle East that inspires a sense of hope by delivering on the promise of jobs.

**David Gamliel** – Born in Jerusalem in 1936, David explored and translated early Semitic writings in graduate studies, mastered Hebrew and ancient Jewish texts, and studied the modern poetry and prose of great Jewish thinkers. As a Jewish educator, he developed curriculum in Israel and North America during his adult professional life. Truly a son of the State of Israel, he continues to impart his knowledge to inspire the younger generation,

**Rita Glassman** – Cantor, Singer-Songwriter, Board-Certified Chaplain, and Recording Artist based in the San Francisco Bay area. Her original "Song for Peace" was performed at the White House for President Barak and Michelle Obama in 2015. Rita is a child of Holocaust survivors and deeply proud of her Jewish heritage.

*Chapter 5: Ingathering of the Exiles: A Nation of Immigrants*
**Shlomo Alima** – Born in Jerusalem in 1945. Has one sister and two half-siblings. He married his lovely American wife and moved to Baltimore, Maryland in 1970. Together they have two children and five grandchildren.

**Dr. Janette Lazarovits** – Deputy Head in Life Science at the Israeli Innovation Authority (IIA), promoting innovation in Israel. She received a Ph.D. in Molecular and Cell Biology at University of Texas at Dallas, and a Post-Doc Fellowship at Weizmann Institute. She worked in the biotech industry for a decade, and was CSO of a company developing biologics to treat Leukemia. Married to Danny, a computer engineer, she has four children: two doctors, one engineer, and an officer in the Israeli army.

**Nicole Rosenberg** – Born in South Africa, Nicole now lives on a moshav near Ashkelon with her husband, David. They have two grown sons. Nicole is currently working for the Baltimore-Ashkelon Partnership in charge of various projects, among them is the HaZamir Choir.

**Cantor Robbie Solomon** – Cantor Emeritus of Baltimore Hebrew Congregation. He came of age in the 1960s, a time of student activism. That experience led him to identify with the struggle for the freedom of Soviet Jewry in the 1980s and to the creation of his song, Leaving Mother Russia.

*Chapter 6: The Earth is the Lord's: Protecting Our Environment*
**Rabbi Michael M. Cohen** – Director of Community Relations, Friends of the Arava Institute (www.arava.org). Rabbi Emeritus of Israel Congregation in Manchester Center, Vermont, and on the faculty of the Arava Institute for Environmental Studies as well as Bennington College.

**Rabbi Micha Odenheimer** is an Orthodox trained rabbi, journalist, and writer, and the Founding Director of Tevel B'Tzedek, an Israel-based organization working with the extreme poor in the developing world. He lives in Jerusalem with his wife, artist Sosie Vanek, and three grown children, Natan, Tamar, and Ayala. www.tevelbtzedek.org

**Sophie Clarke** – Intern for Eco-Peace Middle East, January-April 2017. info@ecopeaceme.org

*Chapter 7: Saving a Life Above All: Pikuach Nefesh*
**Major-General Yair Golan** – Former Deputy Chief of Staff Major, Former Commander of the Northern Command, head of the IDF Operations Directorate, commander of the Judea and Samaria

Division, and commander of the Home Front Command, he has a B.A. degree in political science from Tel Aviv University, a Master of Public Administration from Harvard University, and is a graduate of the IDF's Command and Staff College and the U.S. Army College. Currently he is a visiting military fellow at the Washington Institute for Near East Policy.

**Dr. Shaanan Meyerstein,** MD, MPH, FAAP, is a General Pediatrician with a particular interest in medical diplomacy and working with migrant populations with complex medical needs.

*Chapter 8:*
*Justice: Creating a More Equitable and Compassionate Society*
**Sharon Abraham-Weiss**, LL.B., B.Sc., LL.M., is the Executive Director of the Association for Civil Rights in Israel (ACRI), and has represented ACRI in landmark cases. She is a founding member of Itach-Maaki (Women Lawyers for Social Justice), and Co-Founder of the Hebrew University of Jerusalem's Breira Center. In addition to Law degrees, she has an M.A. in public administration from Harvard Kennedy School, where she was a Wexner Fellow.

**Professor Julie Cwikel** is the Chilewich Family Chair in Studies in Social Integration. She is a social epidemiologist and Founder and Director of the Center for Women's Health Studies and Promotion at the Spitzer Department of Social Work of Ben Gurion University of the Negev (BGU).

**Nechama Namal** – Resource Development Director of Women of the Wall. After a ten-year career in Jewish Communal Service, she made *Aliyah* in 2009. She has a B.A. from Temple University, an MBA in International Business from University of New Haven, and a Fellow in Temple Administration certification from the National Association of Temple Administrators of the Union for Reform Judaism. She is active in Reform congregations in Israel

*Chapter 9: God loves all of His Creations: On Being Inclusive*
**Lieutenant Colonel Tiran Attia** – As Director of Special in Uniform, he is a compassionate advocate for people with special needs and disabilities. A decorated Israel Defense Forces Lieutenant Colonel for 28 years, he commanded a tank and training program for the IDF's Technology and Logistics Forces, and spent ten years as Commander of Sar-El volunteers. He is married and the proud father of three boys.

**Rabbi Judith Edelman-Green** – Founding Director of the program, "Bar/Bat Mitzvah for the Special Child" for the Masorti Movement (1995-2005), she works in Pastoral Care in Israel. She is involved in social justice work, such as peace, welcoming refugees, and serving as a Rabbi in India and Africa.

**Adele Goldberg** is Executive Director of Friends of Yad Sarah in the US, and internationally, at the United Nations. She coordinates fundraising efforts to provide resources for Yad Sarah's volunteers. Her co-authored manual "How to Start and Manage a Respite Program: A Guide for Community Based Organization," a model of social adult day care, has helped over 200 organizations. She has a Master's degree in Social Work from Yeshiva University.

**Elie Klein** – A Jerusalem-based public relations veteran, Elie Klein manages a robust Jewish World and non-profit practice, representing cause organizations and educational institutions in Israel and across North America.

*Chapter 10:*
*Loving Thy Neighbor: Building Friendship and Cooperation*

**Lydia Aisenberg** – A freelance journalist, writer, special study tour guide, and Informal Educator, CoLab, Givat Haviva International Center, Lydia made *Aliyah* from South Wales, Britain in the 1960s, and became a member of Kibbutz Mishmar HaEmek. She has been involved with Givat Haviva Center for Shared Society in Wadi Ara for 30 years, and helps build educational programs that emphasize people-to-people aspect of conflict resolution. She is a mother of five and grandmother of twelve (so far). www.givathaviva.org

**Rabbi Yoav Ende** – An influential leader in Israel in promoting pluralism and Jewish religious freedom, he is the Executive Director of the Hannaton Midrasha at Kibbutz Hannaton. Ordained by the Schechter Rabbinical Seminary in Jerusalem in 2008, he has a B.A. in Jewish Philosophy and an M.A. in Conflict Resolution and Management. Married to Shira, and father to four children, Yoav and his family were among the original families to renew the kibbutz in 2008. Yoav is currently a blogger for the Times of Israel.

**Zimra Vigoda** – Immigrated to Israel in 1994 and serves as a resource development expert on the Civics and Education Team at the Center for Educational Technology (CET) in Tel Aviv. She previously worked as Director of Resource Development at AJEEC-NISPED, an Israeli non-profit. Zimra has four children, ages 10-19. Her 15-year-old son Amit, a lower limb amputee, inspired her to become passionate about competitive wheelchair basketball.

*Contributors*

*Chapter 11:*
*Compassion for the Poor, the Vulnerable, and the Stranger*
**Ruti Glasner** – Born in Tel Aviv in 1944. After studies she served in the Army and went to Kibbutz Erez, where she met and married husband Gabi. They have three children, and for 35 years they travelled on Shelichut to Camp Ramah Nyack, NY. She lives in Bat Yam, where she and Gabi volunteer together at Fat Meir's Kitchen.

**Dr. Bernie Green** – Made *Aliyah* from England in 1984 and is a Family Physician, working for Maccabi Health Services, Kfar Saba, Group Practice. Works with the Refugee Clinic in Tel Aviv, Israel. He is married, with three children, and one grandchild.

**Yotam Polizer** is the Co-Chief Executive Officer of IsraAID: The Israel Forum for International Humanitarian Aid, Israel's biggest humanitarian NGO, operating in 18 countries. He has built and led psycho-education programs after disasters in Japan, the Phillipines, and South Korea, and has led missions in Lesbos, Greece, Nepal, and Sierra Leone. He has more than ten years' experience in education, humanitarian aid, and international development. www.israaid.org

*Chapter 12:*
*Light unto the Nations: Technology for the Good of Mankind*
**Naphtali Avraham** – Executive Director of Tech-Career since 2014, he came to Israel in 1984. Naphtali earned a B.Sc. in Engineering at the Technion's School of Agricultural Engineering, and a M.Sc. in Environmental Engineering. An IDF Major, he advocated for Ethiopian Israeli soldiers within the Air Force's technical divisions, and provided guidance regarding the Ethiopian Israeli community. A graduate of the Mandel Institute for Leadership, Naphtali is a founding member of "Olim Beyahad," a non-profit that helps Ethiopian Israeli academics and students find suitable employment.

**Dr. Amit Goffer** – B.Sc., M.Sc., Ph.D., is the inventor of ReWalk and founder of Argo Medical Technologies in 2001, serving as its CEO until 2012 and President until 2015. He founded UPnRIDE Robotics, Ltd. in 2014 and serves as its President and CTO. Amit is the recipient of Rafael Award (1989), a PhD in Electrical and Computer Engineering from Drexel University, and is an Honorary Fellow of the Technion Israel Institute of Technology. He lives in Tivon, Israel with his wife Lili, and has three children and four grandchildren.

**Sami Saadi** studied accounting and economics at the Hebrew University of Jerusalem from 1984-89, and for a CPA accounting license as an auditor in 1989-91. He is self-employed, with an office in Arraba that offers accounting services and financial advice to companies, self-employed individuals, and non-profit organizations. In 2007 Saami established Tsofen in Nazareth, together with Smadar Nehab and Yosi Coten. He has four sons and is active in Arab and Jewish organizations in the Galilee.

**Sivan Ya'ari** is the Founder and CEO of Innovation: Africa. Born in Israel, raised in France, and educated in the United States, she has degrees in Finance from Pace University and a Masters in International Energy Management and Policy from Columbia University. Having worked in Africa since age 20, she has vast knowledge, experience, understanding, and love for the African continent. Through iA she has impacted over one million lives through Israeli technology. A prominent business woman in Israel, Sivan lives with her husband and three children in Tel Aviv.

## Chapter 13: Healing the Spirit in Creative Ways

**Simone Farbstein** believes that sports can elevate one's ability, no matter what disability one has. She has dedicated much time and care in rehabilitating injured brave heroes through sports activities that direct their energy and skills toward success. She has three beautiful daughters, Nitzan, Shaked, and Ela, who follow the family motto of helping others.

**Rachel Fox-Ettun** is a family therapist specializing in work with families facing chronic illness and loss. One of the leaders in the field of spiritual care in Israel, Rachel is a Certified Spiritual Caregiver and a certified educator in spiritual care, who teaches senior healthcare professionals as well as medical students and interns. Rachel is the Founder and CEO of Haverut, a non-profit in memory of her daughter, Rut, that empowers medical centers through the use of spiritual care, the arts, and community.

**Rabbi Dr. Haviva Ner-David** is a writer and rabbi who does spiritual counseling and ritual guide work. She founded the Shmaya Mikveh at Kibbutz Hannaton, where she lives with her life partner, Jacob, and their seven children. She received private rabbinic ordination from an Orthodox rabbi in Jerusalem, was ordained as an interfaith minister at the One Spirit Interfaith Seminary in New York, and earned a Ph.D. from Bar Ilan University. Author of two spiritual journey memoirs, *Life on the Fringes* and *Chanah's Voice*, and a forthcoming book, *Getting and Staying Married Jewishly: A Guidebook for Couples.*

**Dr. Anita Shkedi** – A State Registered Nurse in London, Dr. Shkedi integrated her passion for horses as to work as an Equine Assisted Therapist practitioner. She made *Aliyah* from Britain in

1985, and founded Equine Assisted Activities/Therapy (EAAT) in Israel to rehabilitate traumatized war victims, challenged learners, and severely disabled children. She established the first Therapeutic Riding Instructors Certificate at the Nat Hofman School of Coaches the Wingate Institute for Physical Education, and has trained several thousand practitioners. Author of Traumatic Brain Injury and Therapeutic Riding (2012), in 2016 she was awarded a Doctorate in Education from Derby University, UK.

## Chapter 14: Seeking Peaceful Coexistence

**Robi Damelin** is the Israeli spokesperson and member of the Parents Circle-Families Forum (PCFF), who has spoken to hundreds and thousands of Israelis, Palestinians, and people around the world about the importance of reconciliation for a peace agreement. Named as 2015 Woman of Impact by Women in the World, and one of four Women PeaceMakers in 2014 by the Joan B. Kroc Institute for Peace and Justice, she is the protagonist featured in the documentary, One Day after Peace.

**Rami Elhanan** is a 68-year-old graphic designer who was born in Jerusalem. He fought in the Yom Kippur War as a young soldier. Today he is the Israeli Co-Director of the Parents Circle, the Israeli-Palestinian Bereaved Families Forum for Peace and Reconciliation.

**Avi Meyerstein** is the founder of the Alliance for Middle East Peace (ALLMEP), the coalition of 110 NGO's building people-to-people cooperation and coexistence between Israelis and Palestinian, Arabs and Jews in the Middle East. He is also a Washington D.C. lawyer and partner at law firm Husch Blackwell LLP.

**Yuval Ron** is an internationally known musician who travels around the world encouraging peaceful coexistence. He composed music for the Oscar winning film, West Bank Story, and was invited to perform for the Dalai Lama. A noted lecturer, he has spoken and performed for numerous universities, and was awarded grants from the National Endowment for the Arts. His book, *Divine Attunement: Music as a Path to Wisdom*, won the Gold Medal for Best Book in the Spirituality Category at the Indie Book Awards 2015.

**Tsameret Zamir** – Born on kibbutz, she studied art and became a ceramic artist. She is married and the mother of four children. For the past twenty years Tsameret has lived on a moshav on the border of the Gaza Strip. She is the initiator of the "Path to Peace" mosaic.

*Contributors*

*Postscript*

**Anat Hoffman** – Executive Director of the Israel Religious Action Center (IRAC), promoting Jewish pluralism, tolerance, equality, and combating racism, corruption, and religious coercion, she served as a Jerusalem City Councilperson for 14 years, advocating for adequate municipal services for Palestinian residents of Jerusalem, and preserving lifestyle choices of the secular population. Founding member and Chairperson of Women of the Wall since 1988.

# ALSO BY THE AUTHOR
*Bridge To Healing: Finding Strength To Cope With Illness*

English Edition ISBN: 978-1936778-485
Hebrew Edition ISBN: 978-1946124-050

"Bridge To Healing" is just what the title implies. Healing and curing are two distinct entities. I have learned that when you heal your life, your body gets a live message and does all it can to help you to survive.

Cancer is a unique experience for each individual. When you are willing to explore your experience and ask what you are to learn from your journey through Hell, the curse can become a blessing; just as hunger makes us seek nourishment, so can our disease.

Israela shares some of the universal themes one can find in many religions and philosophies which have proven to be effective. She shows us how to heal, find peace, and not wage a war against the cancer enemy and empower it. She shows us how to treat the experience and not just the result.

Israela removes the guilt, shame and blame issues, and like Maimonides, understands that disease is not God's punishment. What you need to do is seek help by looking for what you have lost: your health. I have seen self-induced healing occur when people had faith, left their troubles to God, and had their cancers disappear. I have learned from exceptional patients about survivor behavior.

God loves His children and our healing potential is amazing. So read on and learn from the wisdom of the sages and ages that you are not a diagnosis or a statistic. You are a survivor.

Bernie S. Siegel, M.D.

CPSIA information can be obtained
at www.ICGtesting.com
Printed in the USA
BVHW04s0518130818
524310BV00001B/1/P